Governance

KEY CONCEPTS

Published

Governance

Anne Mette Kjær

polity

First published in 2004 by Polity Press.
Reprinted 2005, 2006
Reprinted 2007
Polity Press
65 Bridge Street
Cambridge CB2 1UR, UK

Polity Press
350 Main Street
Malden, MA 02148, USA

A catalogue record for this book is available from the British Library.

Library of Congress Cataloging-in-Publication Data
Kjær, Anne Mette.
    Governance / Anne Mette Kjær.
        p.   cm. – (Key concepts in the social sciences)
Includes bibliographical references and index.
    ISBN 978-0-7456-2978-0 (hb : alk. paper) – ISBN 978-0-7456-2979-7 (pb : alk. paper)
    1. Legitimacy of governments.   2. Policy networks.   3. Corporate governance.   4. Democracy.   5. Globalization.   I. Title.   II. Series.
    JC497 .K52 2004
    320'.01'1 – dc22
                                                                2003016302

Typeset in 10.5 on 12 pt Sabon
by SNP Best-set Typesetter Ltd., Hong Kong
Printed and bound in United States by Odyssey Press Inc., Gonic, NH

For further information on Polity, visit our website: http://www.polity.co.uk

Contents

Figures and Tables

Figures

Tables

Acknowledgements

Although this book makes no claim to have covered all issues related to governance, its aim is nonetheless to give a broad overview of political science governance debates. To that end, being employed with a large institution like the Department of Political Science, University of Aarhus, where office doors are never closed, has been tremendously helpful. A number of colleagues were always ready to lend books or refer to debates and I am grateful for their help.

The Danish Social Science Research Council provided a grant for a project of which this book became a part. I wish to thank Palgrave Macmillan for the kind permission to reproduce three tables from a book by Gerry Stoker. I am grateful to Georg Sørensen for suggesting that I engage in the book project in the first place, and particular thanks to Louise Knight at Polity for entrusting me with the task and in general to staff at Polity for their professionalism. For reading parts of the manuscript, I would like to thank Jens Blom-Hansen, Jørgen Elklit, Karin Hilmer Pedersen, Goran Hyden, Lars Johannsen, Knud-Erik Jørgensen, Ole Nørgaard, Liselotte Odgaard and Linda Weiss. I would also like to thank students attending my graduate seminar on 'Governance' for their engagement, and participants at the 'Democratic Governance Network Conference, 2003', particularly Jacob Torfing and Peter Bogason, for helpful comments on a paper based on the book. Two anonymous readers also provided very useful and thoughtful comments. The author remains, of course, the only person responsible for the book's contents. I am grateful beyond words to Jesper Svennum, Ida and Frederik for being a constant source of joy.

Finally, I wish to dedicate this book to Birte and Mogens Kjær.

1
Introduction: The Meanings of Governance

In the mid-fourteenth century, an Italian artist named Lorenzetti painted his famous frescos illustrating the stark contrasts between good and bad governance. One part of the frescos pictures a beautiful city where justice reigns, where young women are dancing, children playing, and men working. Some are ploughing, others cultivating vine. In contrast, the part of the frescos illustrating bad governance shows a satanic tyrant on a throne and justice lying tied up on the ground. There are no cultivated fields, no one is working, and the only activity is the killing of men and raping of women.[1]

Like Lorenzetti, political scientists have long considered governance to be important for the well-being of a country's citizens. However, governance was traditionally associated with govern*ment*, with the exercise of power by political leaders. The concept was not widely used in the post-Second World War years, but during the 1980s it re-emerged with a new meaning, now referring to something broader than government. Reference to processes and actors outside the narrow realm of government was now included; yet no common definition of governance seemed to emerge. Governance is used in various fields, such as economics, cultural geography and politics. A simple search on 'governance' in the Social Sciences Index results in 1,774 articles in the twelve years from 1986 to 1998. In the three years from 1999 to the present, the Index comes up with 1,855 articles. In other words, more articles on governance have been written in the past three years than in the preceding twelve. Moreover, the articles appear in a wide range of journals, from, just to mention a few, *Far Eastern Economic Review*, to *Urban Studies* and *Environment and Planning*, to *Public Administration Review*, *American Political Science Review* and *Foreign Affairs*. The usage of the concept of governance, then, is applied in many different contexts and with as many different meanings. There is not one coherent body of governance theory, and it is difficult to get a clear picture of what governance theory is about.

The purpose of this book is to give sense to the concept of governance by introducing the many ways in which it is used and by sketching the many different theoretical debates lying behind these ways. This is, of course, a big task, considering the amount of material already in existence. The book makes no claim to cover the whole range of usages. It deliberately excludes, for example, works on corporate governance (which belong in the field of economics) and concentrates on governance as it is used in political science. But placing this literature out of the scope of the book still leaves us with a concept that has multiple meanings.

This introductory chapter has three sections. The first section asks what governance is about: it outlines different definitions of governance in political science, and categorizes them within three political science sub-fields of public administration and public policy, international relations, and comparative politics. The second section finds that identifying a common ground for the three sub-fields is indeed possible if the concept is grounded more explicitly than is presently the case in the new institutionalism. The new institutionalism has become central in all corners of the political science discipline and can be used to identify a broad core that is basic to most governance theory. The final section discusses some key concepts in the governance literature that are important in all usages of governance, and it thereafter outlines the plan of the book.

What is governance?

Etymologically, governance can be traced back to the Greek verb *kubernân* (to pilot or steer) and was used by Plato with regard to how to design a system of rule. The Greek term gave rise to the medieval Latin *gubernare*, which has the same connotation of piloting, rule-making or steering. The term has been used as synonymous with govern*ment*, as the definition in the *Concise Oxford Dictionary* implies. Here, governance is 'the act or manner of governing; the office or function of governing'. To govern is 'to rule or control with authority; to be in government'. During the 1980s, however, political scientists referred to the term as distinct from government and as including civil-society actors. The definitions below are illustrative:

> Governance refers to self-organizing, interorganizational networks characterized by interdependence, resource-exchange, rules of the game, and significant autonomy from the state. (Rhodes, 1997a: 15)

> Global governance is conceived to include systems of rule at all levels of human activity – from the family to the international organization – in which the pursuit of goals through the exercise of control has transnational repercussions. (Rosenau, 1995: 13)

> Governance is the stewardship of formal and informal political rules of the game. Governance refers to those measures that involve setting the rules for the exercise of power and settling conflicts over such rules. (Hyden, 1999: 185)

These definitions of governance are a small sample of many that can be encountered when assessing the literature. Is there any core to be identified in these definitions or do they refer to completely different phenomena? As noted above, all of them refer to something broader than government. The new use of governance does not point at *state* actors and institutions as the only relevant institutions and actors in the authoritative allocation of values (Easton, 1965). They all, to some extent, focus on the role of networks in the pursuit of common goals; these networks could be intergovernmental or inter-organizational (Rhodes); they could be transnational (Rosenau) or they could be networks of trust and reciprocity crossing the state–society divide (Hyden).

Despite the similarities, the definitions are used in different sub-fields of political science, and therefore they refer to different debates. For example, in a seminal article on governance, Rod Rhodes (Rhodes, 1996) refers to governance as a vogue word for *reforming the public sector*. Yet governance is also used in other contexts. When Rosenau talks about governance, he most certainly does not refer to public sector reform, but rather to the emergence of global political problems requiring global solutions. When Goran Hyden talks about governance, he relates it to theories of development and democratization in the Third World. Hence, the three definitions can be placed within the fields of public administration and policy, international relations, and comparative politics.

Rod Rhodes's definition of governance can be placed in the field of *public administration and public policy*. Scholars in this field study the tasks, organization, management and accountability structure of the public sector. Traditionally, this involved assuming that the public sector functioned best when it was apolitical, structured as a hierarchy, and based on a system of merit-recruitment and promotion. However, this traditional notion was increasingly challenged by scholars, who emphasized the essentially political nature of public bureaucracy (Peters and Wright, 1996: 628–9). They pointed at 'pathologies' of the public sector and found that it often did not work in an effective manner.

During the 1980s, a wave of public sector reforms characterized many western countries, entailing privatization, the transfer of private sector management principles to the public sector, and decentralization. Central government functions were decentralized to lower levels and in some regions political authority was increasingly transferred to supranational organizations. Additionally, in many countries, civil-society organizations have become more involved in the delivery of public services. The consequence has been an increasing fragmentation of political systems. Scholars have begun to take notice of the plurality of actors and organizations involved in the pursuit of common goals, and they are rejecting the sharp distinction between public and private that characterizes traditional public administration theory. The question of how to steer these self-organizing inter-organizational networks becomes crucial.

Rosenau's account of global governance belongs in the field of *international relations*. The study of international relations has long been dominated by the realist paradigm, which maintains that states are the most important units in the international system and that the study of international relations is mainly about the relations between states. Since there is no government reigning over all states, the international system is anarchic, and states are in constant preparation for war. However, the realist paradigm has been challenged by many significant developments. One is the internationalization, or globalization, of the world economy, which has raised the discussion of the extent to which states really are in control of their territories. If they do not have full sovereignty, they are no longer the only important units in international relations. Another development is the growth of non-governmental movements and organizations, and the creation of global organizations such as the WTO to respond to problems that have a global, or transnational, nature. In other words, increasing globalization has raised a need for global governance in many arenas such as trade regulation, the environment and conflict resolution.

Hyden's understanding of governance belongs in the *comparative politics* field. Comparative politics refers to the scholarship engaged in the systematic comparison of political systems (Almond et al., 2000; Mair, 1996: 309). Before the Second World War, this would most often involve the comparison of different countries' constitutions. During the 1950s and 1960s comparisons became increasingly based on *inputs* to the political system: political culture, parties and interest groups, and electoral behaviour. In the 1980s, the study of state institutions was brought back in. The comparison of the effects of different institutions on various *outputs*, for example studying the consequences of federal or unitary systems for tax policies, became commonplace. The focus on the state soon became supplemented with the comparison of state–society interactions. Hyden's governance work can be seen as a part of this focus on state–society interaction in comparative politics. His approach refers to the literature on democratization processes. The three fields of political science should not be seen as entirely separate. On the contrary, the frequent blurring of their boundaries means that sharp divisions can no longer exist. For example, European integration used to be a preoccupation of international relations theory, but multi-level governance and the impact of the EU on national policy-making have made the EU a concern for comparative public policy as well. In general, the globalization of the economy has rendered obsolete the clear boundaries between domestic and international politics. The notion of state sovereignty, i.e. that a state has full decision-making authority within its territory, has been challenged by social and economic developments where the state has been found to lose authority. For example, international finance flows make it difficult for national policy-makers to control the interest rate. And member states of the European Union find they have to comply with rulings of the European Court of Justice, while creditor governments find they have to comply with policy conditions of the International Monetary Fund in order to achieve funding.

Since national policy-making is affected by domestic as well as international events in the real world, the disciplinary boundaries in political science have also been questioned. The increasing use of the concept of governance can be seen as a reaction to a change in political practices, together with changing realities involving, among other things, increasing globalization, the rise of networks crossing the state–civil society divide and increasing fragmentation. Such developments call for a debate about how to steer in an increasingly complex world (Hirst, 2000). There is thus ground for arguing that sharp divisions among academic sub-fields should be abandoned. The reasons why they have not been abandoned here are twofold: first, surprisingly, the use of governance has developed quite separately in the different fields and the debates on governance in each field relate to distinct theoretical debates. James Rosenau (2000), for example, criticizes traditional IR theory for focusing on intergovernmental, rather than transnational, relations. And Goran Hyden criticizes traditional transition theory for presupposing that transitions will invariably end with democracy. Hence, although governance theories are often reactions to perceived inadequacies in earlier theoretical paradigms, they nonetheless have distinctive theoretical roots (Jessop, 1995). The second reason for upholding the distinction is analytical and practical. An overview of the usages of governance is presented in a clear way if related to different sub-fields. Upholding the distinction is thus a way to structure the overview.

In sum, at this point we can say that governance refers to something broader than government, and it is about steering and the rules of the game. The reference to rule-making and rules of the game provides a hint that there is an additional common feature of governance in the three sub-fields of political science. They all, to some extent, grow out of a focus on institutions and institutional change. Therefore, to search for a broad common definition of governance, a brief sketch of institutionalism is warranted.

Governance and institutionalism

Various versions of the new institutionalism have been called 'historical institutionalism', 'rational choice institutionalism', 'sociological institutionalism', 'normative institutionalism' or 'international institutionalism', to mention a few (Hall and Taylor, 1996; Peters, 1999). The differences between various institutionalisms boil down to two assumptions about human behaviour, one rational and one sociological. In the rational behavioural model, preferences are exogenous: the individual lists his or her alternatives for action, decides which alternative would best maximize utility and then acts accordingly. March and Olsen have called this the logic of consequentiality (March and Olsen, 1989: 22–3; 160–2).

In the sociological behavioural model, preferences are endogenous: the individual has been socialized into having certain values and norms that determine behaviour. For instance, if an individual has grown up in a working-class family, that person is most likely to identify with a political party that represents the working class and hence vote accordingly. The individual evaluates a situation and acts according to what is most appropriate in that situation, rather than considering the consequences. Hence, March and Olsen call this the logic of appropriateness. They argue that it is the latter logic which guides behaviour: 'Action is often based more on identifying the normatively appropriate behaviour than on calculating the return expected from alternative choices' (ibid.: 22). According to March and Olsen, we often act according to what is most appropriate and then, afterwards, justify our action with a consequential logic. For example, an individual votes for a social-democratic party because she has grown up in a working-class neighbourhood, but she justifies her behaviour by arguing that social-democratic policies benefit her economic situation more than right-wing policies.

Elinor Ostrom has argued that the two models can be conceptualized so as to make up a general approach to the study of institutions (Ostrom, 1991). Her point is that we are all constrained by cultural values and norms. In that sense, we all take into consideration what constitutes an appropriate action. However, the norms and values rarely give us specific guidelines as to which exact action to take. Within the rules in which we find ourselves, we can choose between various courses of action: 'Some actions are ruled in (permitted) and some are ruled out (forbidden)' (ibid.: 239). Individual choices are bounded by what is appropriate, but we choose among the permitted actions using a logic of consequentiality. In that sense, the two behavioural assumptions do not imply using different approaches for the study of institutions. They both share the assumption that behaviour is rule-bound, and the core task for institutional analysis becomes one of identifying the rules that are relevant for the political phenomenon one wishes to study.

The issue here is not whether Ostrom's argument can be supported. In governance theory, both sociological (cultural) and rational (calculus) approaches can be found. However, the important point to make here is that governance theory has a broad institutional grounding. A common definition of an institution may be: *formal and informal rules, behavioural codes and norms that constitute prescriptions ordering repeated, interdependent relations* (see, for example, North, 1990; or Hall and Taylor, 1996). Institutions may thus be informal requirements and norms about what is appropriate, but they also exist in the form of written documents, such as constitutions.

Two key questions in institutional analysis are:

• How do institutions affect political behaviour?
• How do institutions emerge and change?

Most institutional analyses have focused on the first question, and they have often studied the effects of *formal* institutions. For example, the consequences of type of, say, party system (two-party vs. multiparty system), electoral system (proportional vs. majoritarian) or government structure (unitarian vs. federalist) for political behaviour have been studied (Rothstein, 1996: 135–6). One example of an institutional approach is Sven Steinmo's study of tax policy. He shows that a country's tax system is greatly influenced by that country's constitutional structure. The United States has a federal structure. It is a fragmented political system with many checks and balances, and this, according to Steinmo, has led to an ineffective, complex tax system with a relatively low revenue yield (Steinmo, 1993: 8).

In spite of their virtues of illustrating the significance and autonomy of institutions, these approaches do share one problem. They all have a hard time explaining institutional change. Many of these approaches have a tendency to reify institutions and give them objective existence. For instance, if the (unwritten) constitution gives the British government a high degree of autonomy, then why are some British governments more autonomous than others? As Joel Wolfe has aptly argued, 'Mrs Thatcher's immediate predecessors, as concerned about and determined to reverse Britain's political deliberation and economic decline as she, failed to find that the British constitutional order gave them automatic autonomy' (Wolfe, 1991: 244). Wolfe goes on to argue that institutions cannot explain why some governments implement policy reforms effectively while others do not: ideology and the way strong individuals use ideology as a tool to carry out changes play a role at least as significant as institutional structures.

Governance theory is mainly occupied with institutional change and it involves human agency. Governance theory thus introduces an element of change which is often lacking in institutionalism. Ideally, governance thus combines rule-structures with agency. From an institutional perspective, governance is about affecting 'the frameworks within which citizens and officials act and politics occurs, and which shape the identities and institutions of civil society' (March and Olsen, 1995: 6). A broad institutional definition would thus refer to governance as *the setting of rules, the application of rules, and the enforcement of rules* (see also Feeny, 1993: 172). Although this is a broad and quite abstract definition, it nonetheless provides a common ground to all of the different perceptions of governance.

It goes without saying that such a broad definition only applies at a general level. The sub-disciplines in political science abound with definitions and usages of governance that refer to more substantial policies or features of social systems. For example, Gerry Stoker (1998: 17) has criticized the use of governance as the 'acceptable face of spending cuts'. By underlining the positive impact on efficiency when involving private sector actors, policy-makers have used governance as a reason to reduce public expenditure. However, as academics, we should not allow governance to be hijacked by proponents of neo-liberal policy.[2] Rather, governance analysts explore the processes by which rules about the pursuance of public goods are designed and enforced. Thus, rather than referring to a specific organizational set-up, such as the minimal state, or a specific policy, such as privatization, governance theory more openly explores changes in political practices and their implications for political rules of the game.

Second, some governance theorists identify governance more closely with government: 'Governance is the capacity of government to make and implement policy, in other words, to steer society' (Pierre and Peters, 2000: 1). This definition refers more to traditional steering capacities of states and it introduces an important distinction between 'old' and 'new' governance (Peters, 2000). Inherent in the old governance is a traditional notion of steering by national governments from the top down. It has to do with the degree of control the government is able to exert over social and economic activities. The new governance has more to do with how the centre interacts with society and asks whether there is more self-steering in networks. Self-organizing networks can block implementation and thus have a negative impact on the capacity to steer, or they can increase efficiency by co-operating in policy implementation. In new governance theory, networks may thus have both negative and positive impacts on steering capacity (Peters, 2000: 40–1). Thus, governance analysts often explore the nature of governance: is it old or new? Has the role of the state declined? Or if it has not declined, has it changed?

Finally, some use governance in both the old and the new sense: 'Governance is the institutional capacity of public organizations to provide the public and other goods demanded by a country's citizens or their representatives in an effective, transparent, impartial, and accountable manner, subject to resource constraints' (World Bank, 2000a: 48). This definition of governance is typical of an international organization in the development community, such as the World Bank, which, through 'good governance' programmes, wishes to support reforms that strengthen the recipient governments' capacity to steer, while, at the same time, aiming to promote and strengthen participation by civil society in governing. The aim is to have not only smaller but also better, and more efficient, government.

This leads to a broader concern in all governance theory: how to steer, but also how to improve accountability. In this sense, governance resurrects an old discussion about the relationship between legitimacy and efficiency (Peters, 2000). So, having identified governance as broadly referring to the setting and management of political rules of the game, and more substantially with a search for control, steering and accountability, some core concepts in governance theory should be clarified: these are legitimacy, efficiency, democracy and accountability.

Governance and core concepts

We have defined governance broadly as the setting, application and enforcement of the rules of the game. Such rules need to be legitimated if they are to be stable. If rules are upheld through the use of raw force or arbitrary power, individuals are likely to resist, either through exit or through violent action (Hirschman, 1970). But how is legitimacy generated? A useful distinction here is between 'input-oriented' and 'output-oriented' legitimacy (Scharpf, 1997b: 152–5). Input-oriented legitimacy derives from agreement of those who are asked to comply with the rules. Output-oriented legitimacy derives from the effectiveness of rules to produce tangible results. Hence, input-oriented arguments concern the establishment of democratic procedures, accepted by a majority, for taking collectively binding decisions; while output-oriented arguments refer to 'substantive criteria of *buon governo*, in the sense that effective policies can claim legitimacy if they serve the common good' (ibid.: 153).

Thus, legitimacy may derive from democracy as well as from efficiency. The issue is whether it is possible to have both or whether there is a trade-off between the two. It is sometimes argued that democracy can entail 'too much talk and too little action', and hence democratic procedures may weaken decision-making efficiency. Yet the argument can also be turned on its head: if democratic inclusion of citizens is not ensured, their cooperation in achieving social and economic outcomes will probably not be obtained. Hence, the argument goes, democratic legitimacy matters not only in a normative sense, i.e. that it is desirable in its own right; it matters also because democratic procedures are necessary in order to ensure active endorsement of citizens and therefore efficient policy outcomes. In the words of Gerry Stoker (2003: 9), 'to launch a waste recycling scheme or change driving habits requires an extensive dialogue and high levels of trust between the public and authorities'. Thus, democracy and efficiency can arguably be seen to have a mutually constitutive relation.

When is an institution or a process of governance democratic? Referring to the two models of action described above, the rational and the sociological, we can outline two different models of democracy, the aggregative model and the integrative model. The rational model of behaviour assumes that preferences are exogenous and fixed. Hence the model would fit with an aggregative notion of democracy, in which political actors convert individual wants and resources to collective action through bargaining, pay-offs and coalition formation (March and Olsen, 1995: 7–26). Such a democratic process requires some institutional guarantees, most notably a set of civil and political rights, as well as regular free and fair elections. The cultural (sociological) model of behaviour assumes that preferences are endogenous; they are continuously evaluated when individuals adapt to surrounding norms and expectations. Identities and roles are socially constructed. Preferences are not fixed, and citizens and office-holders are presumed to act according to norms associated with their roles, rather than in pursuit of personal advantage and interests. When ordinary people act in the role of citizen, they are capable of considering the common good. Democracy in this sense involves supporting and creating civic institutions and participatory processes that facilitate the construction, maintenance and development of democratic identities (March and Olsen, 1995: 27–45).

The two interpretations of democracy, the aggregative and the integrative, need not be mutually exclusive. Representative democracy can be supplemented with more participatory forms. In this text, deliberative democracy is suggested as one possible way to address the problem of democratic control posed by self-governing networks at sub-national as well as transnational levels. However, Paul Hirst suggests a more radical form of democratization, which he terms associative democracy (Hirst, 1994, 2000). The idea is to supplement representative democracy with constitutionally ordered self-governing associations. This would involve a continuous flow of information between governors and the governed, whereby the former seek the consent and cooperation of the latter. In an increasingly complex world, argues Hirst, associative democracy would be a way to increase the accountability of employees in all sorts of organizations to the wider public. It is not necessary here to settle on one distinct meaning of democracy, but rather to point out that most governance theory takes the view that representative democracy on its own is an increasingly inadequate institutional method to achieve democratic accountability in the modern world. Thus, although governance scholars by no means reject majority rule they nonetheless argue that it needs to be supplemented with other forms as well.

The argument that the traditional model of democratic accountability cannot stand on its own brings out the importance of the concept of accountability to governance theory. Accountability implies responsibility: To be accountable is to be held responsible. 'To talk about accountability is to define who can call for an account, and who owes a duty of explanation' (Day and Klein, 1987: 5). Governance has a lot to do with defining mechanisms of accountability. In Athenian democracy, the delegates of the people were directly responsible for their behaviour. Ten times a year they reported to the assembly of citizens in Athens. Accountability was direct and continuous. In representative democracy, the governors are accountable to the people and the civil servants are accountable to the governors. With the growth of the welfare state, these relatively simple accountability chains have become longer and more complicated. Professional bodies with monopoly on expertise in certain fields provide services and are held accountable mostly by members of their own peer group. The growth of local government complicates accountability further. Local governors are accountable to their local constituencies as well as to the centre. Service providers, or 'street-level bureaucrats', are accountable to users of the services, but they are also accountable to the public employer. In addition, corporatist structures involving trade unions and employers' organizations tend to privatize accountability (Day and Klein, 1987: 10–15; see also chapter 2).

Governance scholars see the growth of policy networks at local and transnational levels as further complicating accountability structures. How central government funding for health services is spent, for example, may be difficult to detect when a plurality of health authorities, private sector providers and voluntary organizations become involved in service provision. Accountability may simply disappear in such a web of institutions because defining who did what is no longer straightforward (Rhodes, 2000: 76–7; Day and

Klein, 1987: 13). This development infers a lack of control on the part of central government (Peters, 2000), because inability to make someone accountable implies a lack of power and control (Day and Klein, 1987: 21). To compensate for the mounting inefficiency of traditional accountability mechanisms, more participation by citizens has been called for, in order to reintroduce direct accountability and thereby short-circuit the increasingly complex structures of accountability. Participation in, for example, user committees helps to ensure that service providers are responsive to the users' needs. This, however, raises the paradox that participation in the networks may in itself be a part of the privatization of accountability. Members of the network may develop identical interests and initiate goals that will promote them. This, in turn, may not be in accordance with the aggregated interest of the electorate. Representative democracy is there to ensure that all interests are considered. Most governance scholars therefore seem to prefer both accountability mechanisms, so that accountability is ensured through traditional parliamentary routes, as well as through more participatory means.

To sum up, governance is about managing rules of the game in order to enhance the legitimacy of the public realm. Legitimacy may be derived from democracy as well as from efficiency. Regarding governance theory in general, the focus has been on efficiency, but there is a growing literature on democratic accountability which should not be ignored. This text sketches the debates as they have evolved, and the efficiency concerns therefore take up more space than the concerns with democracy. However, each chapter ends with a look at the literature on democracy within the particular sub-field. The concern with democracy may be more normative than the concern with efficiency. However, it is a concern that is of growing importance in the governance debate and it is therefore appropriate to give it due attention.

Outline of the book

In *public administration and public policy* (chapter 2), the object of governance studies is mainly to describe how policy networks come into existence, how they function and how they change. Networks can be defined as 'informal rules governing interactions between the state and organized interests' (Blom-Hansen, 1997: 676). The relevant actors are politicians, top officials in interest organizations or representatives of civil-society associations, as well as public sector employees. In many of these studies, the focus is on outputs, the argument being that networks are often more efficient at delivering services than hierarchies or markets. However, there is also an increasing concern with democracy: to whom or what are the networks accountable and who sets these rules? Hence, there is also an ongoing debate about how to establish procedures of democratic accountability within the context of policy networks.

In *international relations* (chapter 3), the main question is how to establish rules and procedures that can help solve problems arising from intensified globalization. Such problems may be threats to the global environment, the challenge of combating poverty through global redistribution, or global trade agreements. The relevant actors are states, as well as transnational or supra-national organizations. The main focus has long been, and still is, the efficiency of global decision-making, that is on outputs. Key to this are the challenges of establishing rules at the global level to regulate the environment, abolish landmines or combat drug-trafficking – all of primary concern to governance scholars. In particular, the debate focuses on how to ensure compliance on the part of nation-states. Yet, although establishing a parallel to national representative democracy at the global level is far from feasible, there is a growing concern among governance theorists about how to hold international organizations accountable. In addition, some international governance scholars have an explicit normative concern with global democracy.

In *studies of European governance* (chapter 4), multi-level governance implies a shift from a policy-making process which was primarily intergovernmental to a process that involves the supra-national level, i.e. the EU Commission, the Court of Justice and the Parliament; the national level, i.e. the Council of Ministers; and the sub-national level, i.e. the regions. Efficiency in regulation of the single market, the environment and labour-market policy, to mention just a few areas, has been the main concern. However, some governance theorists have raised the critique that the occupation with multi-level governance has been biased towards output legitimacy and therefore it has ignored the democratic deficit of the EU. Although the contributions combining governance theory and democracy in the EU still form a small part of the total literature on European governance, they nonetheless exist and deserve attention.[3]

In *comparative politics* (chapters 5 and 6), there are two main debates of importance to governance. The first (chapter 5) is what may be termed comparative political economy and concerns the role of state regulation in economic and social development. The task is to identify the rules guiding public policy-making and implementation; these rules could be institutions or networks securing public–private cooperation, or they could be rules of recruitment based on achievement rather than merit. The actors involved in setting and altering the rules are presidents, top officials, or representatives of a certain industrial sector, but they may also be local officials who engage in networking and capacity-building in the local community. The literature on economic governance and regulation is large and the focus here is on the state and economic growth in developing countries rather than in developed societies. There will, however, be references to the latter as well.

The other debate is about democratization (chapter 6). By its very nature, this concern is with input legitimacy and it is a normative concern. However, the debate has also been analytical; in particular, the discussion on the role of structures vis-à-vis that of actors in democratization has been important. The study here is thus of regime rules, the task being to identify the rules governing access to power, and how they change, as well as the individuals and groups who implement the changes. These may be civil-society groups, political elites, or representatives of international organizations or other governments.

Main themes in governance and comparative politics are thus democratization, state capacity and the nature of state–society relations (Peters, 2000). Studying governance processes in comparative politics implies asking questions about how best to establish rules that are stable, promote legitimacy and enhance efficiency. It is about identifying models of governance that work and discussing whether these models can be applied in other countries with other socio-cultural and economic structures. It implies investigating the capacity of the centre to govern, with variations of that capacity. Governance in comparative politics is thus an explorative concept, addressing issues of regulation, steering and democratic control.

Chapter 7 examines governance and the World Bank. The World Bank is an international organization that raises many governance concerns. The Bank is engaged in development programmes in poor countries and it is constantly searching for ways to promote 'good governance'. The Bank therefore calls for a debate on 'the optimal' model of economic governance, a call which has also been raised in comparative political economy. In addition, the Bank's call for responsive, accountable government touches upon issues of democratization, and the feasibility of simultaneous political and economic liberalization. But a preoccupation with World Bank practices also provokes a discussion on the accountability of the Bank itself and its role in global governance. Finally, chapter 8 sums up the debates and gives some consideration to common concerns and common problems in governance theory.

2
Governance in Public Administration and Public Policy: Steering Inter-Organizational Networks

> The transformation of the public sector involves 'less government' (or less rowing) but 'more governance' (or more steering). (Rhodes, 1996: 655)

In public administration, the governance debate is about changes that have taken place in the public sector since the 1980s. From a model based on Weberian principles of hierarchy, neutrality and career civil servants, public sector reforms introduced other models of governing: those of markets and networks. The (intended or unintended) outcomes of these reforms have been to reduce the direct 'hands-on' control of service delivery and instead to increase steering through policy networks.

This chapter looks at how governance emerged as a central concept in public administration and discusses the questions raised by governance theory. It starts by sketching the traditional model of public administration and its basic assumptions. It then goes on to discuss the deficiencies and the critique of this model, the wave of public sector reform of the 1980s and 1990s, the results and consequences of the reforms, and how governance emerged as a part of that debate. The final section will discuss questions of democratic governance raised in relation to the new steering challenges.

The traditional model of the public sector

Max Weber was one of the first scholars to systematically sketch the principles of a modern bureaucracy. Modern public servants, according to Weber, should be career bureaucrats, recruited on the basis of ability rather than ascription. In what Weber called a bureaucratic state, 'public moneys and equipment are divorced from the private property of the official' (Weber, 1978: 957). Modern bureaucracy is characterized by general rules, and it is decisive that the 'freely creative administration would not constitute a realm of free, arbitrary action and discretion of personally motivated favor and valuation' (ibid.: 979). Thus, in an ideal bureaucracy, public and private interests are completely separated.

These basic assumptions still roughly characterize the way we think about modern Western states and how they operate. We conceive of the bureaucracy as a neutral implementer of laws decided by parliament and policy decisions taken by the government. The normative assumption is predominantly one of a liberal democracy. The descriptions of the model vary according to country. For instance, the British Westminster model is characterized by a stronger executive than the Scandinavian parliamentarian systems. However, Johan P. Olsen's description of what he calls 'the parliamentary governance chain' basically holds for most Western democracies (figure 2.1).[1]

The basis for all political authority according to this model is the *sovereign people*, yet power is exercised by the people in an indirect way through elected representatives. The basic organizing principle for connecting the people, or the electorate, to its representatives is the principle of plurality: of free association and speech, with regular free and fair elections based on one person, one vote, and the secret ballot. The *legislative assembly* defines the common interest of the nation, and it oversees the government's implementation of its decisions. The organizing principle between the assembly

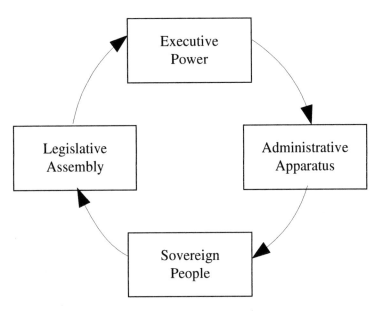

Figure 2.1 The parliamentary governance chain
Source: Based on Olsen (1978)

and the government is the principle of separation of powers and (in some systems) parliamentarianism. The *executive power* is the highest administrative authority. It prepares policies and introduces them to the parliament for decision. The organizing principle between the government (the executive) and the *administrative apparatus* is one of hierarchical authority and rules of competence as outlined above. There is a clear distinction between politics and administration. The politicians are supposed to set policy goals, and the administration is supposed to find the means by which these goals can be reached (Olsen, 1978: 22–8). The basic organizing principle between the administrative apparatus and the sovereign people is the acceptance of undeniable human rights, the principle of the rule of law, and the state's monopoly of the means of coercion. This description of the parliamentary chain of governance is very general, but it has, nonetheless, long been the dominant perception of the role of the public bureaucracy in a representative democracy.

Challenges to the traditional model

The traditional model was never a picture of how bureaucracy worked in real life, but rather an ideal-type model, describing how a representative democracy ideally would look. However, many of its assumptions were soon questioned in light of rapid socio-economic changes.

Already in the 1970s there was concern that the structure of the public sector was out of line with the many new tasks the state had begun to perform after the Second World War (Olsen, 1978). From a mainly regulatory state, preserving law and order and providing basic infrastructure, the state expanded to deliver more services in education, health, pension programmes, unemployment schemes, and other schemes leading to increased public budgets and increasing levels of public taxation. These expanding tasks were generally seen as legitimate, but the organization of the public sector came under increasing criticism. It was argued that the hierarchic structures functioned in a rigid manner because of standard operating procedures and bureaucratic rules, and therefore they were not appropriate for the type of service-tasks in which responsiveness and efficiency towards clients were important. For example, caring for children or the elderly requires a different behaviour from implementing tax legislation or regulating labour policy. 'Street-level bureaucrats' facing citizens daily often have to make hard choices that influence who gets what from government (Lipsky, 1980). Service workers are accountable not only to their superiors in the administrative hierarchy, but also to their clients, or to their own group of professional peers (Day and Klein, 1987). Therefore the central assumption in the traditional model that a hierarchy involves direct control, with the public employee being accountable only to their superior, is challenged.

Another challenge to the traditional model was the observation that, in many countries, interest aggregation did not follow the pluralist prescription entailed in the model. Instead of being vested in a plurality of individuals, interests were represented by powerful organizations that gained direct access to the state administration and permanent representation in various committees. Formal rules for bargaining with and consulting interest organizations were established in many countries (Olsen, 1978). These rules have been named as a certain form of governance: that of corporatism. Corporatism is an institutional arrangement for linking the organized interests of civil society with the decisional structures of the state. It is defined as:

> a system of interest representation in which constituent units are organized into a limited number of singular, compulsory, noncompetitive, hierarchically ordered and functionally differentiated categories, recognized or licensed by the state and granted a deliberate representational monopoly within their respective categories in exchange for observing certain controls on their selection of leaders and articulation of demands and supports. (Schmitter, 1974: 94)

A typical example is that of workers' unions and employers' organizations gaining access to the ministry of labour to represent their members in matters such as labour and social policy. Corporatism can thus be seen as an alternative form of interest representation that constitutes a rupture of the parliamentary governance chain (corporatism would have implied an arrow from the sovereign people directly to the administrative apparatus). In corporatist structures accountability is, in a sense, privatized, because it is directed at particular interest organizations (Day and Klein, 1987).

A third challenge to the model arose with increasing internationalization of the economy and with the integration process of the European Community, which meant that national governments could sometimes be bypassed and resources could be obtained elsewhere. For example, municipal or regional governments can apply to the European Union's regional funds for funding of agricultural projects and the like. Such access to funding, bypassing the central government, provides a rupture of the governance chain of the traditional model.

A fourth challenge to the traditional model came from economists, who used assumptions of the utility-maximizing individual to analyse the behaviour of public bureaucrats. These political economists criticized the assumption that the public bureaucracy should be a neutral instrument finding the best means to implement political goals. On the contrary, they claimed, such bureaucrats develop interests of their own; they will tend to maximize agency budgets because bigger budgets will offer better career opportunities (Niskanen, 1994, chapters 6 and 12). If budgets are cut or restricted, the bureaucrats will tend to maximize *slack,* i.e. they will try to reduce their workload. The result is not only a tendency of bureaucracy to grow, but also a decline of efficiency; that is, more resource inputs buy relatively less outputs in the form of services to the population. Hospitals were criticized for inefficient treatment of patients, for having long waiting lists, etc., and schools were accused of not educating the children well enough. The increasing criticism of the traditional organization of the bureaucracy led to a new wave of reforms sweeping across many Western democracies during the 1980s and 1990s.

The new public management (NPM) reforms

> Almost all essential truths that guided practising public administration and students of administration have now been challenged and often replaced. (Peters and Wright, 1996: 628)

Public sector reform can be defined in many ways, but common elements in definitions of public sector reform (or, as some prefer to call it, administrative reform) are:

(i)   Deliberate planned change to public bureaucracies.
(ii) It is synonymous with innovation.
(iii) Improvements in public service efficiency and effectiveness are the intended outcomes of the reform process.
(iv) The urgency of reform is justified by the need to cope with the uncertainties and rapid changes taking place in the organizational environment. (Turner and Hulme, 1997: 106)

The public sector reforms known under the rubric of NPM were deliberate changes set in motion by newly elected neoconservative governments that were determined to change the public bureaucracy and remove what they saw as obstacles to efficient service delivery. NPM was first introduced by the Thatcher government in Britain, but also in the United States under Reagan, and countries like Australia and New Zealand followed suit (Pierre and Peters, 2000). NPM principles were also applied in many Third World countries as a condition for loans set by the international financial institutions. What were these reforms about and what were their consequences? Many different types of reform measures have been grouped under the label of NPM, and there is no agreement as to which exact measures belong there, but a tentative offer is made in the following section.

The transfer of private sector management principles to the public sector

Introducing private sector management into the public sector has been referred to as managerialism. It stresses: hands-on, professional management; explicit standards and measures of performance; managing by results, and value for money. It is often referred to as the three Es of Economy, Efficiency and Effectiveness (Rhodes, 1997a: 93). The focus on results reflects the criticism above that there was too much 'slack' or waste in the public sector. Instead of allocating money to agencies without considering the actual services provided, budgets were to be created on the basis of output (for example, the more students that graduate, the more money to the school). This is also called output-budgeting. Another issue here is performance pay: public employees should be promoted and remunerated according to their performance rather than according to the number of years in office. Critical voices have argued that it is impossible to measure performance in the public sector, but, nonetheless, the principles of performance pay and output-budgeting have sneaked into many reform programmes. Even Sweden, with a tradition for pay solidarity, has adopted a more competitive reward scheme (Peters and Wright, 1996: 636).

Private sector management principles also found their way into the reform agendas of many Third World governments, mainly because these principles had been adopted by economists in international financial institutions, such as the World Bank and the International Monetary Fund (IMF). The Ugandan civil service reform programme, for example, had an agenda strongly resembling that of the British. In August 1993, in a speech to a Ministers' conference, the Ugandan president stressed that the service should adopt approaches that:

(i)   determine objectives and achievement targets for Ministries, Departments and subordinate units all the way down to individual officers;

(ii) that stress the importance of concrete results over expenditure of money and materials;

(iii) achieve speedy results by mobilising all the talents and expertise necessary for the execution of programmes and projects;

(iv) that regularly appraises performance in order to take timely remedial action when necessary. (Republic of Uganda, 1994: 43)

Whereas the emphasis on managerialism in the developed countries derived from a long-standing critique of how the public sector had worked, managerialism in the developing world reflected a transfer from the Western NPM principles with little consideration as to whether they could be adapted to another cultural, social and economic setting.

Privatization

Privatization simply means the selling or transferral of public sector enterprises to private ownership. Usually, this happens through a new share flotation on the stock market. Sometimes, the enterprise may just be closed down. The underlying philosophy is that the private sector can take care of many functions more efficiently than the state. So privatization aims at increasing efficiency, reducing costs to consumers and reducing public sector expenditure. Britain's Thatcher government was the forerunner, introducing far-reaching privatization programmes that resulted in the privatization of nationally owned coalmines, the postal services, the national railways and other large organizations. Since 1979, approximately 50 per cent of the British public sector, with some 650,000 employees, returned to the private sector (Rhodes, 1997a: 89).

Another milder version of privatization is the system of contracting out. This means that the state remains the buyer of the service, but the service itself is undertaken by a private agency; i.e. the state as purchaser, the private sector as provider. Examples of functions that could be leased or contracted out to the private sectors are garbage collection, cleaning in public schools, universities and hospitals, and water supply schemes. The more radical countries, such as the United Kingdom, have contracted out services that have traditionally been considered as the core of the state, such as prison services and security (Peters and Wright, 1996: 630).

From Britain, the privatization fashion swept through diverse countries, such as Pinochet's Chile and even, to some extent, Communist China (Peters and Wright, 1996: 630). Third World governments also undertook privatization, which was often posited as a condition for acquiring loans from the IMF and the World Bank. Public sector enterprises in developing countries had often served as ways to provide patronage. Persons whose political loyalty was important were appointed by the president as directors of the enterprise, rather than persons who were the best qualified. Through privatization, these means of patronage were removed. Between 1988 and 1993, for example, over 2,700 public enterprises in more than sixty developing countries were transferred to private ownership (Turner and Hulme, 1997: 190). The post-Communist countries also launched comprehensive privatization programmes. A characteristic of many of these programmes, in the South as well as in the East, was a high level of corruption due to the fact that important or influential people were often able to acquire shares in the privatized enterprises on favourable terms. Not everywhere did privatization result in increased efficiency.

Agencification

Agencification refers to the establishment of semi-autonomous agencies responsible for operational management. The key notion is distance from the central department, so there is freedom to manage. Paradoxically, this is a principle derived from the traditional model's idea of separating politics and administration. The logic is that by isolating the agency from political pressures it can be run more efficiently. The British government set up many such agencies during the 1980s and, by 1995, there were 109 agencies employing 67 per cent of the civil service. Each agency has a document setting out its objectives and performance targets. The chief executive of the agency is not a career civil servant but appointed in a competition open to all. The executive is accountable to the relevant minister, who is accountable to parliament (Rhodes, 1997a: 96). Agencification means that implementation becomes more distinct from policy-making, because the agency's explicit guidelines are to implement policy already decided by government.

Agencification policies have also found their way into many developing countries. Revenue authorities, for example, have become the fashion in Africa: all revenue-collecting functions are removed from their relevant ministries (usually, those of finance and the interior) and relocated to a semi-autonomous agency that is put in charge of all tax collection. The employees get higher wages than the rest of the service to try to avoid corruption, and the agency is equipped with new technology.

Competition

Another element in the new public management is to emphasize competition as an instrument to enhance efficiency. Introducing competition can be done though privatization where the state's monopoly is dismantled, but it can also be done through the introduction of quasi-markets into the public sector, as for example in health, where citizens (turned into customers) are allowed to shop for the best provider by choosing freely among hospitals and practitioners. This can be done by supplying people with vouchers that they can use wherever they please. For example, in the debate about racial integration of American schools, the introduction of school vouchers has been suggested, so that parents can choose where to spend education money. This would allow them much greater choice than in the current system, where forced 'busing' of children in the name of integration has been much criticized.[2]

Decentralization

An increasing number of governments has come to regard decentralized services as more efficient than centrally delivered services. When decision-making is concentrated at the level of central government, it is believed to be too remote from the ordinary citizen, and lacking knowledge of real problems and preferences at the lowest level. When the functions and powers are transferred to lower levels, decisions can be taken that are more responsive to the needs of the local community. The central government is the coordinator, setting overall priorities, but authority with respect to many services should be decentralized to the lowest level possible. For instance, the provision of child care or primary schooling more appropriately belongs at the level of local government.

It is common to distinguish between two types of decentralization: deconcentration and devolution. In deconcentration, policy-making authority remains at the central level and only policy implementation is decentralized. The local government is supposed to be accountable to the central government. In devolution, however, all authority is decentralized, and the local government is no longer accountable to the central level, but rather to the local population through local elections (Turner and Hulme, 1997: 154). New public management is mostly about devolution, the more radical form of decentralization. There are, however, varying views as to how far decentralization should be carried. Some reforms have stressed decentralization, while others have maintained a high degree of central control. This is the case in Britain, where there was extensive privatization and contracting out, to the extent that local government was bypassed and lost authority (Rhodes, 1997a). In Britain decentralization has thus been limited. However, other developed countries (some but not all of which are dedicated to

NPM) have decentralized more, for example, New Zealand, Denmark and Germany.

Many Third World countries have – often rightly – been accused of being overly centralized, dominated by authoritarian presidents and politicians, who are afraid of giving away too much power. But the decentralization wave has also reached the Third World, and many countries have set up special decentralization secretariats to coordinate the reforms. Perhaps the most comprehensive has been the Ugandan decentralization programme. From being merely instruments of the central government, the local governments have now been empowered with resources (block grants) and real decision-making authority, for which they are held accountable through local elections (Nsibambi, 1998).

Citizens' empowerment

The observation that lower-level bureaucrats often have great leeway in exercising political authority led to a recognition that it was no longer feasible to maintain the fiction of the traditional hierarchy. Consequently, it would be better to recognize that public officials could also be held accountable by their clients and users, and that this might even increase the quality of services. Thus, user committees in schools or daycare centres have been set up in many countries in an effort to increase parents' influence on the service. In addition, in some countries, such as England or France, Citizens' Charters were introduced, listing the kind of services that citizens should expect from government (Peters and Wright, 1996; Rhodes, 1997a).

This strategy has sometimes been used in developing countries, too. For example, Judith Tendler (1997) describes a health project in the Brazilian state Ceará, in which citizens were sensitized about what to expect from health workers (for example, a regular home visit), and the programme had enormous success reducing under-five mortality and the incidence of common diseases.

In all, these six headings roughly describe the new public management.[3] The new approach to management recognizes that the realities of governing do not look like the ideal, traditional model, and therefore it points out ways in which the organization of the public sector can be reformed. The reforms were implemented most eagerly by the conservative Reagan and Thatcher governments, but the reforms, or parts of them, were also carried out by governments of a more liberal or social-democratic orientation, and they were also adopted by many weak states. Paradoxically, the states which have undertaken the most comprehensive reform programmes have often been the ones with the least capacity to do so, because they have had very little power with which to resist donors' demands. In any case, this dominant 'minimize the state' paradigm has had enormous significance, and the changes it has been equated with have given rise to the debate on networks and governance. Thus, the governance literature has emerged from the attempts to analyse changes in the public sector, not least the intended and unintended consequences of the new public management.

Changes in the aftermath of public sector reforms

'Governance' means there is no one centre but multiple centres; there is no sovereign authority because networks have considerable autonomy. (Rhodes, 1997a: 109)

When discussing consequences of public sector reforms, it is difficult to identify which changes are intended outcomes of reform processes, which changes are unintended, or which changes are results of developments that would have taken place regardless of reforms. For example, it is difficult to conclude whether a change in trade union strength after 1979 is a consequence of the Thatcher government's industrial relations strategy or of changes in the economic structure (Marsh and Rhodes, 1992). Planned reforms were only one of the factors inducing change; others were service sector growth and the economic recession in the 1970s. In the following section, analyses of public sector changes will be sketched (whether changes are consequences of planned initiatives or not): first, the impact of the changes on central government's authority will be assessed; and, second, the impact on local government will be discussed.

The impact of changes on central government

'Your Majesty remains at the very epicentre of governance', Disraeli, Queen Victoria's prime minister, should allegedly have told his queen when she complained about her inability to control the Irish churches. If the queen was then at the epicentre of governance, this hardly remains the case in modern times! Rather, the notion of 'the hollow crown' has been introduced to suggest that the authority of the central government is being hollowed out (Weller et al., 1997; Rhodes, 1997a), or, in other words, the ability of central government to give direction to society has been weakened. The centre is becoming hollow because of three tendencies: (i) the core executive is losing or conceding capacities to societal actors, (ii) the core executive is losing or conceding its capacity to other state actors; and (iii) the core executive is losing or conceding capacities to supra-state entities (Saward, 1997: 20).

The first two points refer to the state's internal hollowing out, while the latter refers to the state's external hollowing out. External hollowing out refers to the loss of authority that occurs because of globalization, that is, the global market makes economic decision-making less autonomous, and European integration has a large impact on the policy-making autonomy of member states. In 1986, the British Conservative Party passed the Single European Act, which strengthened the power of the (then) European Community by increasing the scope for majority voting. In 1992, the Maastricht Treaty paved the way for greater cooperation in the European Union in such policy areas as justice and home affairs (Pierre and Stoker, 2000).

The tendencies in the core executive should be understood as hypotheses about the developments taking place rather than as facts. Some scholars think the tendencies have gone very far, while others maintain that the central government is still strong. Britain is a good case to discuss because it has carried out more radical reforms than most other countries. But even with regard to Britain there is no agreement about the effects of reform. Rod Rhodes argues that reforms have led to 'institutional differentiation and pluralization in British government which erodes the capacity of the core executive to steer' (Rhodes, 1997a: 89), while Michael Saward argues that reforms can be seen as a way for core actors to 'flex their political muscles' and actually strengthen rather than weaken the regulatory capacity of the state (Saward, 1997: 22).

The two arguments may both be of value: when examining the first and second theses – that the executive is losing capacities to societal actors and other state actors – one finds descriptions of centralization, as well as fragmentation, in Great Britain (Wolfe, 1991; Rhodes, 1997a: 15). On the one hand, privatization and agencification led to institutional fragmentation. Privatization was one of the government's success stories. Since 1979, 50 per cent of the public sector, with some 650,000 employees, returned to the private sector (Rhodes, 1997a: 89). In addition, high numbers of special purpose bodies were set up. These reforms apparently resulted in an institutional fragmentation that impeded policy implementation.

Many reforms were not carried out to the same extent as privatization, due to the existence of an 'implementation gap'. For example, although it was an explicit goal throughout the reform period to reduce public spending, government expenditure remained the same. In the health sector, the 'working for patients' reforms were only partly implemented and the most market-oriented reforms such as contracts and tender were hardly implemented at all (Pallesen, 1997). Thus, in spite of a strong executive dedicated to reform, many of the reforms were not implemented, which points at a deteriorating ability of central government to control implementation.[4]

On the other hand, there was a tendency on the part of the government to reassert top-down control. The situation described in the popular TV series *Yes, Minister*, in which civil servants can more or less dictate policies to the minister, thus no longer applies. During the Thatcher era, government cracked down hard on the civil servants, laying off some, abolished union membership for civil servants, and politi-

cized the service because the number of political appointments increased. Further, regulation and audits were
extended, with more management consultants hired in order
to control the accounts of all public agencies (Rhodes, 1997a:
90–100). Thus, Rhodes concludes that 'the minimal state
remained both large and hyperactive' (ibid.: 89). Paradoxically, although the Thatcher reforms were intended to result
in hands-off management, they often resulted in more centralization – more hands-*on*!

Policy networks

The paradox of simultaneous centralization and fragmentation has been explained by a focus on the rising importance
of policy networks in implementation.

> Interorganizational linkages are a defining characteristic of
> service delivery and I use the term network to describe the
> several interdependent actors involved in delivering services.
> These networks are made up of organizations which need to
> exchange resources (for example, money, information, exper-
> tise) to achieve their objectives ... As British government
> creates agencies, bypasses local government, uses special
> purpose bodies to deliver services, and encourages
> public–private partnerships, so networks become increasingly
> prominent among British governing structures. (Rhodes,
> 1996: 658)

The existence of inter-organizational networks can become
an obstacle to policy implementation. This is especially so
when implementation requires the cooperation of the networks. Rhodes argues that the Thatcher government often
'handbagged', or bypassed, the networks, particularly the
professions. Therefore, an authoritative policy decision at the
centre was often followed by a lack of implementation. An
example would be the failed attempt to reduce local government expenditures. Before Thatcher, the Labour government
had put in place a successful consultative mechanism through
which central and local governments negotiated about local
government finance. The local governments generally com-
plied with the agreements reached through consultation.

However, in efforts to put a downward pressure on local expenditures, the government introduced a new grant system that would punish over-spenders. When this system did not show immediate results, the government took unilateral action, and removed the power of local authorities to determine their own rate level, as well as abolishing the Greater London Council and six Metropolitan County Councils. However, none of these measures were successful in reducing the expenditure of the local authorities (Marsh and Rhodes, 1992: 50–64). An important explanation for such failure was that the government had ignored the existing intergovernmental network and the existing consultative mechanisms, and, by doing so, ensured that there would be no cooperation on the part of local authorities in implementing its decisions. More hands-on control meant erasing the previously established point of contacts with the networks. Consequently, policy networks may explain why a simultaneous move toward centralization and fragmentation was possible in Britain.

In continental Europe, the emergence of policy networks was also a significant development. In countries like Germany, or the Scandinavian countries, public sector reforms had been far less radical than in the United Kingdom. However, changes consisting of a shift in the balance between the public and private sector in favour of the private sector were observed in these countries too. This shift is only partly the result of reforms such as privatization and deregulation, according to Jan Kooiman (1993); it is also due to new ideas about public–private partnerships and task-sharing. Such new patterns of interaction can be observed in areas such as social welfare, environmental protection, education and physical planning (Kooiman, 1993: 1).

The continental literature on networks has a broad understanding of networks as 'stable patterns of social relations between interdependent actors which take shape around policy problems and/or policy programmes' (Kickert, Klijn and Koppenjan, 1999: 6). The broad consensus among public policy scholars in Holland is that networks set limits to the centre's ability to implement policy. If the government ignores networks, implementation may simply fail, as was the case in the Netherlands when the government tried to introduce a new EU passport in the 1980s, by setting up a new network under the Foreign Office while ignoring the interests of local governments. The result was complete failure because actors with different ideas about the passport were excluded, and the Foreign Office depended upon one new partner to produce the passport. When this partnership failed, the whole project collapsed (Klijn, Koppenjan and Termeer, 1995).

In Germany, Renate Mayntz took notice of a widespread understanding of 'governance failure', i.e. that the state, because of the inherent shortcomings of its traditional instruments, is no longer able to solve the economic and social problems it has identified to steer the society in the direction it wishes (Mayntz, 1993: 10). For example, German scholars have often noticed how target groups of particular state interventions often tried to resist such state regulation of their behaviour. These target groups are no longer perceived as particular persons or organizations, but as societal sub-systems (or networks). Mayntz quotes two scholars arguing that 'self-reference and internal dynamics of differentiated societal subsystems make centralized political control in the traditional juridical way more and more difficult'.[5] Such sub-systems are auto-poetic, i.e. they are self-steering and have a high degree of closure. Hence, they are difficult to control. Solutions to such governability problems would be to decentralize authority, because giving local authorities more autonomy would improve their ability to adapt to changing environments. In addition, experimenting with other solutions, such as markets or information networks, could be alternative solutions to the traditional hierarchical ones.

However, Mayntz argues that the governability problems are less a result of the basic auto-poetic character of social sub-systems, but more related to the special dynamics that characterize complex modern systems, together with the capacity of networks to build organized resistance towards government policy. This insight is indeed important because it points to the fact that the existence of networks may facilitate implementation of a policy if it is based on negotiation. Thus, Renate Mayntz reaches basically the same conclusion as Rhodes: that the emergence of networks requires coordinating and bargaining skills on the part of the government. The rise of policy networks thus poses a challenge to governance, and the key question concerns the best strategies for political actors to adopt. Before turning to this discussion, however, we will discuss the impact of public sector changes at the local level.

The impact of changes on local government: networks in service delivery

The increase of networks in policy implementation may be best observed at the local level, where most service delivery takes place. Benyon and Edwards (1999) describe the shift as a move from local government to community governance (table 2.1). The Local Governance Programme was a research programme about the changes in British local government, carried out during the mid-1990s and directed by Gerry Stoker. One of the aims was to document the transformation from local government into a system of local governance, involving complex sets of organizations drawn from the public and private sectors (Rhodes, 1999: xiv). The project's findings document such a transformation in an array of services, e.g. community care, education, housing and crime control. One case study describes how the provision of social housing depends increasingly on networks rather than the local authorities alone (Reid, 1999). The Thatcher government's policy was to reduce the role for public sector housing operators and to emphasize private sector solutions to housing problems, for example privatizing through the right to buy (ibid.: 129). The result was, according to Reid, that housing services became fragmented, and a need to reintegrate the service through joint projects arose. Thus,

> the reframing of housing policy at local level has partly been driven by central government policy on privatization and reducing the size of the state sector through the formation of partnerships with the private sector. However, the local response to this has led to the growth of more broadly focused inter-organizational networks which go beyond the public–private partnership model and incorporate a wider range of organizations, interests and competencies. (ibid.: 131)

Table 2.1 From local government to community governance

	Focus	Orientation	Technique
Local government	Delivery of services addressing social problems, regarded as separate and discrete	Unilateral interventions by single agencies	Rigid dependence on hierarchical/bureaucratic or (quasi-) market mechanisms
Community governance	Managing the problems of citizens' 'well-being', regarded as multifaceted and interdependent	Multi-lateral interventions by public–private partnerships	Flexible deployment of bureaucratic (quasi-) market and networking mechanisms

Source: Benyon and Edwards (1999: 146), in Gerry Stoker (ed.), *The New Management of British Local Level Governance*, Basingstoke: Palgrave Macmillan. Reproduced with permission of Palgrave Macmillan.

Reid observes that, although local authorities initially emphasized bilateral joint implementation arrangements, implementation has now become a multi-actor affair. An example is cooperation between groups of housing associations, working together to innovate and secure economies of scale across several small-scale developments. What was intended as market reform in effect resulted in the emergence of new networks. The advantage of these is that they are very flexible, as they are able to develop new products, services and solutions within a short time-span; but the disadvantage is that they are difficult to control, they are not very durable and they may impede overall coordination of housing policy.

This tension between flexibility and control is also found in some of the other case studies. For example, Benyon and Edwards (1999) examine the new policy on crime control. Government policy shifted from focusing on individual criminals and their crimes to problems of community safety, from being oriented towards independent police organization to being more oriented towards multi-agency partnerships that included police, local authorities, probation services and local populations. To illustrate the shift in policy, Benyon and Edwards (1999), use a table parallel to the one in table 2.2.

Benyon and Edwards see the advantages of multi-agency partnerships in crime control (they do increase the safety of local communities); but they argue that the government policy on crime prevention is undermined by the fact that there is no national strategy and all projects have to compete for funding, which means that the partnerships become short-term, and overall coordination is lacking. In all, the findings of case studies of local governance imply that there is fragmentation, but that networks are also contributing to efficient service delivery that is more responsive towards the needs of the users. This poses a challenge to public authorities: which strategies should be chosen in a context of profound change?

Table 2.2 Crime control from local government to community governance

	Focus	Orientation	Technique
Local (police) government of crime control	Individual criminals and their crimes	Police operations independent of other crime control and prevention agencies	Law enforcement, including uniformed patrolling, rapid response to calls for assistance and heavy investment in detection
Community governance of crime control	Problems of community safety, constituted by a range of crime events and forms of anti-social behaviour	Multi-agency partnerships, including the police, local authorities, probation services and local populations	Strategic crime prevention, including networking between, and coordination of, partners' preventive efforts

Source: Benyon and Edwards (1999: 149), in Gerry Stoker (ed.), *The New Management of British Local Level Governance*, Basingstoke: Palgrave Macmillan. Reproduced with permission of Palgrave Macmillan.

Governance in a modern complex setting

> Governance is about managing networks. (Rhodes, 1996: 658)[6]

While there is consensus that the emergence of policy networks poses a challenge for governance, the literature appears rather more diffuse in its definitions of governance and the strategies that political actors should adopt in modern complex systems. In Germany, the concept of Steuerung (steering) has often been used as synonymous with governance, but Steuerung covers both govern*ance* and govern*ing*, according to Mayntz (1993: 11). Kooiman (1993: 2) thus distinguishes the two by defining governing as 'all those activities of social, political and administrative actors that can be seen as purposeful efforts to guide, steer, control, or manage (sectors or facets of) societies', and governance as 'the patterns that emerge from governing activities of social, political and administrative actors'. Governing, then, presupposes a subject (an actor) while governance is the result of the actions taken, a mode of social coordination.

The Dutch school defines governance as 'directed influence of social processes. It covers all kinds of guidance mechanisms which are connected with public policy processes . . . these forms of guidance are not restricted to conscious or deliberate forms of guidance . . . Nor is governance restricted to public actors' (Kickert, Klijn and Koppenjan, 1999: 2). This latter definition is equal to Kooiman and Mayntz's concept of governing: it is a process that involves actors. And it is a process that takes place through different mechanisms. For example, rules of trust between networks can be established and thereby promote consensus around a particular policy. Or rules of authority and command may be adopted, in which case a policy is implemented through hierarchical steering mechanisms.

In table 2.3, Rhodes identifies the different rules characterizing three distinct types of guidance mechanism. The table illustrates how the three governing structures of market, hierarchy and network function through different mechanisms. Markets operate through competition and with prices as the

Table 2.3 Comparing markets, hierarchies and networks

	Markets	Hierarchies	Networks
Basis of relationships	Contract and property rights	Employment relationship	Resource exchange
Degree of dependence	Independent	Dependent	Interdependent
Medium of exchange	Prices	Authority	Trust
Means of conflict resolution and coordination	Haggling and the courts	Rules and commands	Diplomacy
Culture	Competition	Subordination	Reciprocity

Source: Rhodes (1999: xviii), in Gerry Stoker (ed.), *The New Management of British Local Level Governance*, Basingstoke: Palgrave Macmillan. Reproduced with permission of Palgrave Macmillan.

medium of exchange. Hierarchies use power as the medium and rely on chains of command and control. Networks are based on reciprocity and trust. The different characteristics make clear that the modes of governance can do different things.

As we have seen, those who believe in *market* solutions agree that government should be minimized. They build on the economic model that individuals are utility maximizers; public bureaucracies become ineffective and public bureaucrats become rent-seekers, acting for their own good rather than the collective good. Introducing competition in the provision of public goods makes for more efficient service delivery. On the contrary, those in favour of government intervention in coordination problems criticize markets for inefficiency in the allocation of values and focus on market failure to provide public goods.[7]

Others express the opinion that since the traditional hierarchical instruments have become out of line with modern society, and since markets also frequently fail, governments should rely on *networks* in order to deliver services. According to Rhodes:

> Governance as self-organizing networks is as distinct a governing structure as markets and hierarchies. A key challenge for government is to enable these networks and to seek out new forms of co-operation. . . . The challenge for British government is to recognize the constraints on central action imposed by the shift to self-organizing; and to search for new tools for managing such networks. Game-playing, joint action, mutual adjustment and networking are the new skills of the public manager. (Rhodes, 1996: 666)

So, according to this view, government has to accept its loss of steering capacity and learn how to manage networks in an indirect way to enable service delivery to become efficient. Rhodes in other words equals the governance concept with network management. Public managers should learn the art of networking and participate in the networks instead of maintaining their position as somehow standing above or outside them.

However, networks and hierarchies may coexist or even overlap. There are several reasons for maintaining the hierarchic model. One obvious reason is that hierarchy is still the formal model upon which representative democracy is built. It is true that governance increasingly involves non-governmental actors, but policies still have to be approved by elected bodies, and governments still have to put them in motion. Networks have not entirely superseded this basic policy-making model, but rather supplemented it. Horizontal network negotiations may benefit from being embedded in hierarchical structures because the state can sanction opportunists, and ratify and enact compromises reached within the networks (Scharpf, 1994: 41). Networks might need to be coordinated by hierarchy. Fritz Scharpf (1994: 37–8) has argued that horizontal networking may take place even within hierarchical organizations; a phenomenon which he terms 'self-coordination in the shadow of hierarchy'. When networks and hierarchies coexist, governance becomes a matter of confronting complex and varying institutional arrangements. In that sense, Rhodes's title 'The New Governance: governing without Government' is misleading. 'Governing with *more than* government' would be more to the point![8]

In a context of coexisting hierarchy, market and networks, which strategies should public managers adopt? There may be situations in which self-regulation in networks is possible because the public good is accessible only locally, and is of a 'common pool' nature. In this confined area (as for example a lake for fishing) individuals interact repeatedly face-to-face, they develop mutual trust and can therefore regulate the use of the common pool resource (limit the number of fishes each fisherman can catch) (Ostrom, 1990). When the public good is not of a common pool nature, self-regulation in networks may not be the optimal solution. In some situations actors may thus achieve cooperation, while in other situations a consensus may not emerge. In the latter circumstance, some outside impetus is needed. However, the alternatives to choose from may not be merely self-regulation, hierarchy or market. Elinor Ostrom (1990) mentions public sector backing of self-regulation as an option. Kickert and Koppenjan (1999) argue that network management is a form of such public sector backing of networks. When central steering is not possible, network management can be important, they argue. Such network management involves negotiation and coordination, and it is therefore very different from the new public management. The relationship between the public and private sector is businesslike in NPM, and the public sector relies on central administrative control. NPM upholds and sharpens even further the distinction between politics and administration, which characterizes the hierarchic model. On the contrary, governance in policy networks recognizes that politics take place in networks too; the relationship between public and private is blurred and government is not the single dominant actor that can unilaterally impose its will (ibid.: 39). 'Hierarchical, central top-down steering does not work in networks, which have no top' (ibid.). The sharp distinction between politics and administration is therefore not upheld in network management.

Network management can take different forms. The Dutch literature on network management distinguishes between two forms: game management and network structuring (Kickert et al., 1999; Klijn et al., 1995). Game management is about influencing the interaction processes between actors within the network, while network structuring is about changing the characteristics of the network. Game management does not change the network, but facilitates agreement within it. For example, prior to expansion of the Dutch Schiphol Airport, the relevant ministry invited important stakeholders, such as representatives from relevant ministries, the municipalities located around the airport, the airport authority and the national airline, to take part in negotiations. Some (particularly the municipalities) were afraid the expansion would mean too much noise and environmental damage, while others were keen to have the airport upgraded and to construct a fifth runway. These interests were difficult to reconcile and the first round of negotiations failed. But the introduction of setting interaction rules, such as making all parties sign a contract, committed them to reach an agreement. Second, when the first round of negotiations failed, the ministry in charge made a 'selective activation of actors' by limiting the number of participants in the second round. Thus, a final decision to expand the airport was reached, in which environmental damage was minimized while the airport still got the fifth runway (Klijn et al., 1995). A win–win situation had been created.

In network structuring the characteristics of the network are seen as an obstacle to joint decision-making. For example, when renovating housing in some areas of the Dutch city of Groningen, a local housing network of relevant ministerial departments, housing associations, tenant organizations, politicians, local estate agents, financial organizations, developers, architects and research associations existed. However, the renovation was blocked due to resistance from local tenants. Since the tenants' association was very broad and represented a wider circle than the particular neighbourhoods in question, the local council changed the long-term organizational arrangements by giving economic incentives for tenants to form associations at the neighbourhood level. By introducing new actors into the network, a compromise was finally reached with which everybody was happy.

These examples show that network management needs a coordinator, which is often a government agency. The increasing importance of networks in service provision does not in itself bring about less government. Rather, it poses new challenges to government actors, challenges that may not always be handled well. Successful governance of policy networks results in win–win situations, such as those described above. However, there is an inherent risk of governance failure, because the stakeholders may continue to disagree and the network may fail to redefine objectives or reach a compromise (Jessop, 1998, 2000). Some policy problems may be difficult to solve no matter what strategy is adopted. Thus, the object of governance may affect which strategy should be adopted. If the object of governance is a highly conflict-ridden policy area, it may be difficult to reach a consensus through dialogue.

The strategy to adopt may, then, depend on policy sector. Much of the literature on networks tends to focus on the service sector. However, what may be the most efficient mode of organization for delivery of health or education may not be appropriate for other sectors. The appropriate role of central government agencies may vary across policy areas. To distinguish the type of sectors best suited to network politics, it may help to examine the type of societal interests at stake in different policy areas. There are four types of political environments surrounding government agencies: (i) a dominant interest group that favours the agency's goals; (ii) a dominant interest group hostile to its goals; (iii) two or more rival interest groups in conflict over the agency's goals; (iv) no important interest group (Wilson, 1989: 75–9). The first political environment gives rise to what James Wilson calls *client politics*, where the benefits of a policy are highly concentrated with one interest (an industry, profession or locality), and the costs are borne by a large number of people (for example, all taxpayers). Because the recipient's benefits of a programme will be large, they have a strong incentive to pressure for such a law, while the costs are shared by such a large number of individuals that they are not likely to organize against the law. An example would be support for agricultural prices and export subsidies for agricultural produce. The agricultural industry employs only a small percentage of the population in developed countries, yet large sums of taxpayers' money are spent on agricultural support. If networks alone were to dominate such a policy sector, the industry could be allowed even more influence, and policies could become even more beneficial to agricultural interests. Another example of client politics would be care of children, or primary schooling, in which certain groups, parents and teachers, have a strong interest, but the costs are borne by all taxpayers. Although networks may deliver education more efficiently, networks alone will tend to be biased towards the groups who benefit from the service and decisions on resource allocations would probably not consider all interests equally.

The opposite type of political environment is where the benefits of a policy apply to a large number of people, but the costs are highly concentrated on an industry, profession or locality. Such policies are difficult to decide upon and therefore require a skilled political entrepreneur who can raise public awareness of the policy. Wilson calls it *entrepreneurial* politics. Policies to purify air and water would be an example because polluting industries bear the costs, while the benefits will be enjoyed by everyone (Daugbjerg, 1998). In such a case, hierarchy is needed to balance the interests at stake; networks alone would not be able to do so. Another example would be the central government's efforts to control local government expenditure: local governments receive a great deal of benefit from raising local government taxation, but the costs are borne by all taxpayers (Blom-Hansen, 1997). Hence, if there were no hierarchy to control local government behaviour, policies to raise local taxes could lead to higher taxes than desired by the majority of citizens. In the third type, political environment is characterized by *interest groups politics*, and the programme will be subject to conflicting pressures from rival interest groups. Both costs and benefits are concentrated and both the likely beneficiaries and the likely cost-payers have a strong incentive to organize and press their competing claims (Wilson, 1989: 78). This type of policy sector may be more suitable for tightly knit networks, where the number of members is stable and limited. Although Rhodes's main concern is with service delivery, a good example would be industrial relations, with the struggle between organized business and organized labour that is institutionalized in corporatism.

Finally, in some environments, no important interest group is continuously active. This occurs when a policy offers widely distributed benefits and widely distributed costs. In this kind of *majoritarian* politics, networks are not likely to arise: since benefits have low per capita value, no one organizes to seek them; and because costs have a low per capita value, no one organizes against them. An example is anti-trust regulation which, in America, was a result of a widespread popular sentiment that corporations had too much power, and, since the policy was aimed at no particular industry, no one organized against it.

In sum, governance through networks is more likely to make sense in interest group politics, where opposing interests exist. In other policy sectors interests may be highly skewed in favour of or against a certain policy, and steering through networks would have to be supplemented by other forms of coordination. In some cases, the government would be needed to do 'networks structuring', for example, to create new actors in networks by providing incentives to form associations, or to equalize different kinds of institutional arrangements. This is what has also been termed 'meta-governance' (Jessop, 2002a). Governance is thus used in two senses. One is the narrow sense of managing self-organizing networks. The other is the broader sense of managing rules and patterns of coordination, organizing the complex structures of hierarchies, networks and markets. Governments do play an important role in meta-governance: because they get involved in constitutional change, they can strengthen the weakest parties in situations where some are more resourceful than others. This brings us again to the important point that network governance should not stand alone. The fascination with networks tends to highlight their positive effects in win–win situations, while ignoring the distributions of power and interests in particular policy sectors. To conclude that governance now takes place without government, or should take place without government, is premature.

The search for efficient coordination of hierarchy, markets and networks has been dominant in the governance literature. However, the search for democratic accountability in an increasingly complex, self-organized and globalized world is occupying scholars interested in governance to an increasing extent (Hirst, 2000; Peters, 2000). To whom are the networks accountable and how is representative democracy working in a context of increasing influence of public–private partnerships, involvement of voluntary organizations, and intergovernmental relations? The final section discusses issues of democracy in relation to the new governance structures.

Democratic governance: holding networks accountable

Self-organizing, inter-organizational networks may be efficient when delivering services, but they typically have a high degree of closure. They are 'auto-poetic', not in the sense that they do not receive inputs from the environment, but rather that they are self-steering; they steer the inputs in directions they determine themselves. Steering signals may therefore not penetrate into the system (Kickert and Koppenjan, 1999), and the closedness of the system increases the difficulty of achieving democratic accountability.

To what extent are networks a problem for democracy? To answer this question it may be fruitful to return to the parliamentary governance chain introduced at the outset of this chapter. The basic assumption underlying the parliamentary governance chain is one of representative democracy. The people are sovereign and enjoy the basic political and civil freedoms. The people ultimately hold political authorities (parliament and government) to account. They are able to do this as long as political authorities are responsible for policy decisions and implementation. If the political authorities no longer have full control over policy, in other words, if the basic organizing principle is no longer a hierarchy, then the representatives of the people cannot be sure that their decisions are *effectuated*. The model assumes that it is possible to locate the exercise of power. Yet one of the characteristics of networks is that power is more diffuse and lies in relations among actors. Hence, responsibility for a particular policy or policy outcome may be difficult to place, and accountability difficult to ensure.

The following section begins by examining the version of power underlying the traditional model of public administration, and the versions of power relating to networks. Then we study a particular case of a policy decision to build a 'culture-house' in a Danish town, in which networks were strongly involved. We ask whether democratic governance was exercised in this particular case. Finally, we ask how democratic accountability in general can be strengthened.

Notions of power in models of public administration

The underlying notion of power in the traditional model is an actor-oriented understanding of power: power is exercised when A gets B to do something B would not otherwise have done. In this understanding of power, power is visible and identifiable; power, and therefore responsibility, can be placed with a specific actor. Therefore, the exercise of power can be studied by observing specific policy decisions, as Robert Dahl (1961) did in his famous New Haven study, where he found that power was not held by one group but by many different individuals and groupings in the community (see also Ricci, 1971). This version of power is pluralist; and Steven Lukes (1974) has called it the one-dimensional view of power. In this view, the exercise of power can be observed only when there is disagreement, i.e. actual and observable conflict. However, this was soon questioned by Bachrach and Baratz (1962), who argued that A also exercises power over B when B is prevented by A from bringing to the fore any issues that might be detrimental to A. Thus, Bachrach and Baratz argued that if actors are prevented from putting issues on the political agenda that they consider important, power is indeed exercised. It is not enough to identify powerful interests in a particular decision; in addition, decisions that might have been taken *in the absence* of the exercise of power, i.e. nondecisions, should be identified. Steven Lukes calls this version the two-dimensional view of power. Although it differs from the first, they have in common the view that an overt or covert conflict of interest has to be present in order for power to have been exercised. Lukes now adds a third dimension: he argues that conflict is not necessarily observable. Conflict, according to Lukes, may be latent, because some actors do not realize what is in their best interest: 'A may exercise power over B by getting him to do what he does not want to do, but he also exercises power over him by influencing, shaping or determining his very wants' (Lukes, 1974: 23). In other words, there would be a conflict, were B to become aware of his real interests.

The third version of power renders it more difficult to detect when power has been exercised and by whom. It is difficult to establish an individual's real interests. And it is difficult to establish how an individual's interests have been formed by various structures, institutions and other individuals. However, Steven Lukes (ibid.: 54–6) maintains that only actors, not structures, can exercise power. Within a given structure, A or B could have acted differently and, although conflict is latent, power may still be identified as belonging to an actor. Therefore, responsibility for the action or actions can be placed with a group or an individual. But if the exercise of power is more invisible, for example, if it is exercised through a powerful discourse developed in relations *between* actors within a network, then it has a more diffuse character, and it is more difficult to place responsibility, and hence to hold anybody to account for the exercise of power.

This 'Foucaldian' version of power focuses more on the interpersonal nature of power (Scott, 2001; Frølund

Thomsen, 2000). Power, according to this view, cannot be possessed but only exercised; it does not have a centre but comes from everywhere; it is not only repressive but also productive in that it produces identities, relations and capabilities (Sørensen and Torfing, 1999).

The case of a 'culture-house' in a Danish town

If power can be exercised through discourses it becomes difficult to place power with an actor that can be held responsible. How is democratic decision-making secured when networks predominate? The decision to build a 'house of culture' in a medium-size Danish town illustrates that, although power was exercised through a discourse, it was also possible to locate it with the mayor and thus to secure democratic accountability.[9] Because it was quite expensive and it was argued that money could have been better spent on, for example, improving the town's nursing home, it was a controversial decision to build the culture house, a place for art exhibitions and musical concerts. However, the decision was approved in the municipal council after a long struggle by a network of actors, comprising: a local public official named 'the culture worker', who was employed as a consultant; the trade and industry council; the mayor; and, not least, the cultural elite comprised of a group of resourceful individuals, who, for a long period of time, had been organizing a series of successful cultural events.

This network came into being as a consequence of a long period of crisis in the town of Skanderborg during the 1980s: the town hospital closed, as did the local cinema; unemployment rose; and a local, violent motorcycle gang was terrorizing the town. In 1991, a series of public meetings was held, and the trade and industry council, together with the local Rotary club and the municipal administration, decided to take initiatives to change things for the better. 'A community of fate' was created, in which many actors felt they were all in the same boat and should join forces to improve their town. In this collective effort it was realized that the town had to be attractive in an array of areas, such as culture, environment and infrastructure, in order to attract new investments. The town mayor was part of the network and worked energetically to create support for the culture house. The trade and industry council created sponsorships, while the cultural elite campaigned, wrote letters to the editor of the local newspaper, and arranged concerts in an old barn in order to demonstrate the need for a cultural house. Power in the case of the decision to build the cultural house was not, argue the authors, exercised by one person but resulted from a discourse that had emerged in the network, evolving around key words such as 'energy', 'community of fate', 'we are all in the same boat', 'we work together to turn the ship around', etc.

Was the decision to build the culture house taken democratically? Democracy means rule by the people (*demos* = people, *kratos* = rule). This meaning of course invokes many questions, like who are the people and what is it that should be ruled over (Held, 1987: 2–3), and since these questions have many answers, many models of democracy exist. In chapter 1 a distinction was made between two models. According to the aggregative model, a decision is roughly democratic if the aggregated interest of a society has been considered through a majority decision in a representative body. In the integrative understanding, a decision can be a consequence of a participatory process in which there has been a debate, and individual interests can be formed by such a debate. In the case of the culture house in Skanderborg, one can argue that the decision was democratic in both senses: it was democratic in an aggregative sense because the decision was taken in the elected municipal council by a large majority. And it was democratic in the participatory sense because a broad range of actors were involved in the debate, a series of public meetings were held, the local newspaper followed the debate, the actors in the governance network campaigned and talked to people on the street and in shopping malls.

However, if we look at how power was exercised, we might come to the conclusion that the decision was not so democratic after all. According to the *one-dimensional view*, we might ask who exercised visible power. The mayor used his position, and at a municipal council meeting he even threatened to resign if the decision was not taken. This sort of bullying is clearly a form of visible power easy to attribute to one person. According to the *two-dimensional view*, we may ask about decisions *not* taken. In Skanderborg, the rural areas of the municipality had long looked for funds to maintain and develop their small gathering places, but they were not considered. Further, the sports associations had wanted a new sports hall, which they did not get. The old people's home got reduced funding, and, finally, the local so-called 'citizen-house', where a majority of unemployed people spent their time, did not get funding for a new part-time administrator. These non-decisions were taken as a consequence of the fact that the culture network had more resources and hence was able to prevent others from affecting the agenda. Whether the *third dimension of power* had been exercised is more difficult to establish, but one of the cultural elites claimed in an interview that the mayor had asked them to *create a need* for the culture house: *if there is no need, you go out and create it*. Additionally, the real costs of constructing the culture house were kept secret. Finally, the *fourth version* points at the power existing *between* groups and individuals, in the powerful discourse of 'community of fate' referred to above.

The conclusion with regard to whether the decision was democratic or not must be that overall, yes, it was democratic both in the aggregative (majority decision) and integrative (active citizens, public debate) sense, but the process did not completely live up to democratic criteria, in that some groups and individuals were clearly excluded from affecting the political agenda, in other words, they did not have 'the exclusive opportunity to decide how matters are to be placed on the agenda of matters that are to be decided by means of a democratic process' (Dahl, 1989: 112–13). Also, if some facts about the costs of, and the need for, a culture house were kept secret, the process did not live up to Robert Dahl's criteria of 'enlightened understanding': 'Each citizen ought to have adequate and equal opportunities for discovering and validating ... the choice on the matter to be decided that would best serve the citizen's interests' (ibid.: 111–12).

The case illustrates how networks can mobilize resources, 'make things happen' and increase policy efficiency, but it also illustrates the point that where interests are concentrated in favour of a policy, with the costs borne by a large number of individuals as was the case with the culture house, networks should supplement rather than replace hierarchy if democracy is to be maintained.

Holding networks to account

The case of the culture house illustrates the democratic danger of networks: networks are very beneficial to the ones who are included because they tend to empower their members. But the networks also function to exclude some groups and individuals. This problem appears to be commonplace. It is, for example, referred to by Barbara Reid (1999: 142) in her study of housing policy, in which she quotes a director of a voluntary sector group: 'The danger with networks is that they're just a modern version of the old boy network. I think you need to pay attention to who's in the network, who's excluded, who's not invited to participate.'

Networks may be efficient in conceiving new policy ideas and realizing them, but they may also impede a democratic process. The democratic problem is that networks usually only serve some interests, and not the aggregated interest: the common will. Thus, there seems to be a need for structured forums, in which the common will can be determined, as a balance to the interests of the networks. New research, based on interviews with municipal councillors, documents that many councillors feel marginalized in the political process due to the influence of the networks (Sørensen, 2002). Their perception is that they are excluded from networks involving the administration and interest organizations, and many feel as if they are mere onlookers to the political process. They see this problem as exacerbated by the decentralization reforms that gave the service institutions (day care, schools, nursing homes) more autonomy. These reforms combined more self- and user-governance from below with centralized goal-steering from above. Thus, what seems to be needed is a redefined role for local councillors in order to strengthen democracy (Hansen, 2001).

It is hardly feasible to believe that the democratic deficits can be mended entirely by reasserting control at the centre. The new ways of organizing service delivery can hardly be rolling back 'governance to government'. One solution would be for local councillors to become co-governors: 'The traditional vertical political relations and interactions from above and below between elected councillors and voting citizens must be supplemented with lateral relations and interactions among institutions, professionals and users, who become politically integrated into, and made publicly accountable for, the common and public concerns of the municipality and the citizenry' (Hansen, 2001: 121; Sørensen, 2002). However, one may argue that if this were the only measure taken, local councillors could become so much part of the networks that they would fail to consider the common will of the municipality. So, an additional measure could be to strengthen centralized decision-making by setting up advisory deliberative forums to discuss issues of relevance to the community.

A deliberative forum is a formal public hearing, in which a representative group of the population is invited to debate a particular policy issue (Eriksen, 2001). The idea of a deliberative poll was introduced by the American James Fishkin. It combines two central elements of a democratic process: representation and deliberation. In a deliberative poll, the participants argue for their view on an issue, and they listen to other people's arguments. Examples of issues that have been discussed in deliberative polls are: crime in Great Britain; the question of a republic in Australia; and the Euro in Denmark. In the Danish poll, 364 participants discussed the issue of the Euro over a weekend. They debated in smaller groups as well as in plenary sessions and they had the opportunity to question political leaders and experts (Andersen and Hansen, 2002). A total of 25 per cent of the participants changed their mind on the Euro issue and the numbers of undetermined were reduced from 16 to 2 per cent. Thus, deliberation matters: it changes people's attitudes, it informs, it provides a forum in which all opinions can be expressed and it improves the basic knowledge upon which the decision is going to be taken (Eriksen, 2001: 35).

Deliberative polls cannot replace representative democracy, but they may strengthen it in a situation where the emergence of networks weakens the central elected bodies (Loftager, 2001). They can, arguably, strengthen a public space in which individuals act as citizens considering the common good, and thereby provide a counterweight to the networks, in which individuals act as users, clients or customers, considering their own particular interests rather than the public good. Experimenting with deliberative polls may thus be one strategy of meta-governance that political actors could choose in response to the new challenges posed to democratic control by self-organizing networks and increasing complexity.

Conclusion: governance in public administration and public policy

This chapter has outlined the traditional model of public administration, sketching both the challenges to the model and the new public management reforms undertaken in many countries. In the aftermath of the reforms, new networks emerged, and we have seen how they may deliver a more efficient service but also lead to fragmentation, providing a challenge to overall coordination.

In this context, the concept of governance has been used in at least two senses. The first, narrow sense, is network management. The focus here is on analysing the networks, their degree of closure, the type of actors within them, and how they may be managed. Thus Rhodes, for example, argues that 'leaders can respond by adding governance to their choice of governing structure and network management to their toolkit' (Rhodes, 1997b: 217). Governance of self-organizing networks can involve facilitating dialogue and consensus within the network, combined with understanding the characteristics of the network so as to better reach a joint decision. In this first sense, then, governance is synonymous with network management.

In the second sense, governance refers to a broader process of managing the rules by which public policy is formulated and implemented. This is what Bob Jessop has termed meta-governance and is not restricted to managing networks but covers the whole range of institutional set-ups that may characterize public policy-making. This understanding allows us to recognize that there are several ways to respond to the emergence of networks, and that the networks may also fail in both efficiency and accountability terms (Jessop, 2000). Governance in this sense is an analytical concept for addressing responses to the emergence of networks, but it is not a description of one particular response. It is about coordinating the plurality and complexity of hierarchies, markets and networks.

Governance theory in public administration and public policy often fails to distinguish between types of policy and the nature of interests at stake in different policy sectors, with the implications this may have for overall coordination and governance. When the benefits or costs of a particular policy are highly concentrated, network steering may fail to take account of the aggregated interest and instead be highly skewed towards a few powerful interests. Governance processes cannot, therefore, rely entirely on networks; they have to draw upon hierarchic structures as well.

3
Governance in International Relations: Governing in a Global Era

Global governance refers to more than the formal institutions and organizations through which the management of international affairs is or is not sustained ... [it]is conceived to include systems of rule at all levels of human activity ... in which the pursuit of goals through the exercise of control has transnational repercussions. (Rosenau, 1995: 13)

International relations were once seen as mainly an inter-*governmental* affair. Sovereign states conduct diplomacy, they wage war, they negotiate and they achieve peace agreements. They are the basic units in the international system. This neo-realist view was challenged by scholars, who observed that complex interdependence has a bearing on how states interact. Non-state actors are also important in international relations.

Interdependence has, argues liberalist scholars, accelerated to the extent that it makes sense to talk about globalization (Held and McGrew, 2000; Keohane and Nye, 2001). Globalization involves economic, political, sociocultural, environmental and military dimensions (Giddens, 1990; Keohane and Nye, 2001). Financial markets have become increasingly integrated; the information revolution and the World Wide Web have reduced distances in space; the explosive growth of the number of transnational non-governmental organizations has led some to talk of an emerging global civil society. These global changes may have led to an undermining of national constitutions, so that we now have many different systems of rule of transnational character, and 'governance without government' (Rosenau, 1992).

This statement may be exaggerated; indeed the degree to which globalization undermines state capacity is contested (Weiss, 2002). However, asking whether and how globalization is responded to is asking about governance. As Robert Keohane and Joseph Nye have phrased it: 'if laissez-faire is likely to be unstable in the long term, and networks of interdependence are stretching beyond the boundaries of the nation state, how is globalism to be governed?' (Keohane and Nye, 2001: 258). Global governance is thus about setting up global institutions that address the changes resulting from globalization.

This chapter starts by sketching the traditional model of international relations as found in the neo-realist paradigm. It then addresses the challenges to the traditional model, mostly as they were formulated by the paradigm of liberal institutionalism. Then it discusses the extent of change that has taken place, and asks whether globalization entails a declined role of the state, and whether and to what extent there is a need for global governance. It also sketches different visions of global governance. Most scholars have been concerned with how to increase the efficiency of global governance, but 'democratic globalists' also focus on how to democratize international institutions. The final section thus addresses a particular vision of global governance, that of global democracy.

The neo-realist model of international relations

The neo-realist model of international relations has often been referred to as a billiard ball model, because it views states as the single most important units, the billiard balls, in the international system (the configuration of all the balls).[1] The *states*, just like the balls, are equal units: they are all rational and pursue their national security interests; they seek to increase their relative capabilities, they are unitary (i.e. they speak with one voice); and a change in their foreign policy does not result from a change in the domestic political climate but from a change in the international system (Waltz, 1979: 40).

The *international system* is anarchic. There is no sovereign above the states, no world government to guarantee that law and order is upheld on a global level. Therefore, international politics and domestic politics are fundamentally different. Whereas international politics are dominated by power politics, self-help and anarchy, domestic politics are constitutionalized, i.e. characterized by law and order (Waltz, 1979; see also Jackson and Sørensen, 1999; or Viotti and Kauppi, 1987). In such a system, states are busy preparing for war, actively engaging in war, or recovering from one. The reason they go to war is that they fear other states will attack them. States find themselves in a security dilemma, because 'the means of security for one state are, in their very existence, the means by which other states are threatened' (Waltz, 1979: 64). Even if a state is sincerely arming only for defensive purposes, it is rational in a self-help system to assume the worst regarding an adversary's intentions and keep pace in any arms build-up. Causes of changes in international political outcomes should thus be found in the international system, not inside states.[2] Examples of such causes can be technological advances, transformations of weaponry or a disruption of alliances (Waltz, 1979: 67).

Thucydide's classical explanation of the war between Athens and Sparta is realist because it focused on the growth of Athenian power, together with the fear this created in Sparta. Sparta reacted by applying counter-measures to the growth of Athen's power through building up its own military strength. An arms race escalated that eventually led to war. The explanation of war is found in the nature of the international system: a change in the balance of power upsets stability, and can lead to war. Such a change is equivalent to a move of a billiard ball: it pushes the other balls around (war) but finally the balls will come to rest in a new balance of power. The notion of a balance of power is important to neo-realists because it explains why there is not constant war.

States negotiate, make alliances, and a balance will tend to occur in which no state feels immediately threatened by others because of the relatively even distribution of capabilities. Thus the basic assumption of the traditional model is that states are the most important actors on the international scene, and these states pursue power politics because of the absence of a world sovereign.

Challenges to the neo-realist model

Neo-realism has been challenged by a range of scholastic theories that can be subsumed under the label of liberalism.[3] Most liberalists do not question the importance of states as actors in the international arena, but they criticize the heavy focus neo-realists put on states and they argue that other actors are also important when trying to understand world politics. The other actors span from individuals who in general travel more and more, through to trade between companies, the emergence of transnational corporations, and the growth of international organizations such as the United Nations, the World Bank, the EU and others. International transactions, such as flows of money, goods, people, and messages across international boundaries, have increased significantly since the Second World War.

According to prominent liberalists, such as Robert Keohane and Joseph Nye, such transactions are important, but what is even more important is to understand that international relations can now be characterized by what they term complex interdependence, a concept that refers to a situation in which countries and economies are mutually dependent and where a multiplicity of reciprocities exist across borders (Keohane and Nye, 2001: 7–8). Table 3.1 summarizes the liberalists' main claims against neo-realists.

When focus is moved from the state to the many kinds of flows across borders, the unitary, rational billiard ball model of the state seems unlikely to reflect reality. Some liberalists have instead used the notion of a cobweb model to illustrate the transnational bonds over which states may have little control. Interdependence means that some states have

Table 3.1 Neo-realism versus liberalism

	Neo-realism	**Liberalism**
Actors	States are the dominant actors	States are not the only relevant actors
Instruments	Military force is most effective	Economic and other resources are also important means of power
Sources of peace	Balance of power	International relations are not only conflictual but also cooperative; peace derives from interdependence as well as from power balances
Foreign policy	Determined by the international system	Determined by intranational and transnational factors, as well as by systemic factors

Source: Compiled from Keohane and Nye (2001: 32); Jackson and Sørensen (1999); and Viotti and Kauppi (1987)

become so mutually integrated that war between them can practically be ruled out. This is the case, for instance, with America and Canada, or in Western Europe where, not many decades ago, Germany was at war with its neighbours. Sixty years after the Second World War, it seems highly unlikely that the European states should wage war against one another. Peace in these areas of the world does not derive from a balance of power; rather, it is a result of cooperative relations.[4]

The mutual dependence caused by trade and other trans-border flows may sometimes rule out military force as a viable instrument of foreign policy, for example, when settling an economic dispute between interdependent countries (Keohane and Nye, 2001: 22). Force is simply not appropriate for many of the economic, environmental or other issues that have become more prominent with modernization. This additionally means that states that are not strong militarily, such as Germany or Japan, may be great economic powers and therefore may to a large extent set the agenda. In other words, 'low politics' (regarding non-military issues) rather than 'high politics' (regarding military issues) can also prevail in setting the international agenda.

Finally, interdependence also means that the international system is not the only determinant of foreign policy. The distinction between what is domestic and what is foreign has become increasingly blurred, and a change of foreign policy can result from changes in domestic pressure or changes in transnational interactions as well as from changes in relative military power capabilities. Foreign policy is often a result of complex processes, involving international as well as domestic networks, and comprised of state as well as non-state actors.

Neo-realist reactions to the liberal claims against them basically boil down to the counter-argument that, even when states cooperate, they worry about *relative gains*. In other words, even if there are absolute gains in cooperation (that all parties involved do better), states worry about whether some parties may do even better still (Jackson and Sørensen, 1999: 131). Neo-realists do not believe that international institutions can change state behaviour and stop them from being short-term power-maximizers. For neo-realists, international institutions of cooperation reflect state calculations of self-interest, based primarily on concerns about relative power. Institutional outcomes will reflect the balance of power (Mearsheimer, 1995: 82). For example, the actions and declarations of the United Nation's Security Council reflect the security interests of the great powers rather than some aggregated global interest. Some liberalists, like Robert Keohane, have to a certain extent accepted the realist argument that relative gains have significance. Some neo-realists, on the other hand, have accepted that low politics and interdependence could sometimes be important. Thus, neo-realism and liberalism approached each other during the 1980s.

The end of the cold war ignited a new debate on globalization and governance. Interdependence was seen to accelerate into globalization, and this process called out for global governance. Governance became relevant in at least two ways. The first is the discussion about the *need* for global governance. What are the global changes about and do they call for global policy solutions? The second involves the political implications of the changes: whether they undermine the role of the state; and the extent to which *global* governance already exists. We will address the two ways in turn below.

The extent of changes: the need for governance in an era of globalization

> There is no alternative to working together and using collective power to create a better world. (Commission on Global Governance, 1995: 2)

Since the end of the cold war, *globalization* has become a buzzword, not only in the social sciences but also in the international political community. 'Globalization denotes the expanding scale, growing magnitude, speeding up and deepening impact of interregional flows and patterns of social interaction' (Held and McGrew, 2000: 4). 'A quiet revolution' is the term the UN secretary-general, Kofi Annan (1998), has used when describing post-cold war changes. Responses and interpretations of this development vary greatly. Neo-realists recognize that there are changes, but they do not think the changes are radical: a state's security interests still matter! On the other end, 'democratic globalists' claim it is now possible, and indeed worth striving for, to build a democratic global governance system. But what is globalization about?

Globalization is usually referred to as being multi-dimensional (Giddens, 1990; Held et al., 1999). Globalization, according to Giddens, involves the spread of the four institutional dimensions of modernity resulting in a global nation-state system, a world military order, a world capitalist economy and an international division of labour.[5] Held, et al. (1999) trace seven aspects of globalization historically in order to examine whether it is indeed possible to talk of a more globalized world, a question they answer in the affirmative. The seven aspects are: the political, including the spread of nation-states and the emergence of multi-layered governance; the expanding reach of organized violence, including war and arms production; global trade and markets; global finance; corporate power and global production networks, especially the rise of multinational corporations; global migration; cultural globalization; and, finally, environmental globalization. The Commission on Global Governance was an independent group of twenty-eight leaders that issued a report called 'Our Global Neighbourhood' in 1995 about the implication of globalization for global governance. Their conception of globalization, too, was one of several dimensions, including economic, security, environment, the emergence of global civil society, and uneven global development, including development aid.

In the present account of globalization, we will address economic, military, environmental and sociocultural globalization, and then in the following two sections deal with the political implications of these changes, for the state as well as for global governance.

Economic globalization

In order to be able to talk about globalization, rather than, say, regionalization, economic relations must have spread across the entire globe. An expansion in trade within the European Union, for example, would not qualify as globalization. However, if economic transactions, in the form of trade or financial flows, increase between continents, then it would be possible to talk about a process of globalization. Economic globalization involves: (i) an increase in the intercontinental networks and flows of trade; (ii) an increase in global financial flows; and (iii) a growth in the number and size of multinational corporations. Held et al. (1999: 149–82) find that both the extensity (the geographical reach) and the intensity (the magnitude) of trade has grown significantly since the Second World War. Indicators of more extensive world trade are, among others, that trade links between countries have become much more frequent since the war. In 1950, 64.4 per cent of maximum possible trade connectivity (every country trading with each other) involved a group of 68 countries, while in 1990, this share had risen to 95.3 per cent (Held et al., 1999: 167).

Some scholars have suggested that the increase in the number of trade links indicates a process of *regionalization* rather than globalization (Weiss, 1998: 176–7; Lauridsen, 1997). They argue that mutual trade is concentrated within three trade blocks: the American, the Asian and the European. Trade within the EU, according to Weiss (1998), is more important to Europe than trade with other regions, and intra-Asian trade has been growing more rapidly than trade between Asia and the US. Other scholars, however, have investigated trends in interregional trade that demonstrate a growth in trade *between* as well as *within* regions.[6] Their findings confirm that trade, especially between Asia and America, is growing. However, it is beyond doubt that the increase in trade links is uneven. Less developed regions are far less linked by trade than developed regions. So, although it may be possible to speak of a global increase in trade extensity, the increase is more marked among some regions than others.

A growth in trade *intensity* has also been observed. World exports, for example, have increased constantly since the 1970s, from less than 10 per cent of world GDP to over 15 per cent of GDP. For developed countries, both export and import shares of GDP have risen up from about 10 per cent in the 1950s to more than 20 per cent in the 1980s. Hirst and Thompson (1996) have argued that these trends mainly reflect a return to high levels of trade in the inter-war years; however, according to Held et al. (1999), trade has become even more dominant than in the inter-war period. Again, it can be argued that trade intensity is not even across the globe. In fact, rather than being integrated in the global economy, the African continent is increasingly marginalized. Africa's share of global manufactured exports is almost zero. The region accounts for barely 1 per cent of global GDP and about 2 per cent of world trade. Over the past years it has lost market shares in global trade, even in traditional primary products (World Bank, 2000b: 208). So, it is fair to say that although trade has become more extensive, the process is not entirely global. A few regions, most significantly the African region, are left out of trade globalization.

If there is one area in which it is possible to speak about globalization (save the less developed regions), it is that of finance. Enormous sums are constantly being transferred across the globe in a matter of split-seconds. World foreign-exchange trading averages $1,490 every working day (Held et al., 1999: 189). Even sceptics adhere to the view that international capital flows have reached 'spectacular levels' (Weiss, 1998: 178). International capital flows can be defined as cross-border flows of assets and loans, both long-term and short-term, and they are of several types, such as foreign direct investment, international bonds and bank lending, international equities, and international development assistance (Held et al., 1999: 190). These flows have grown considerably since the Second World War and especially since the 1970s. From the end of the war until 1971, the Bretton Woods system regulated capital flows, because exchange rates were fixed to the dollar, which again was fixed to gold at $35 an ounce. The system excluded the communist countries, but, within the system, the US authorities indirectly controlled international monetary supply (Held et al., 1999: 200). In the 1950s, the Soviets began to deposit their dollar holdings in European banks rather than American banks, and the European banks lent them out instead of converting them to national currency. This Eurodollar business put increasing strain on the dollar, and, in 1971, American president Nixon suspended the convertibility of the dollar into gold (ibid.; Keohane and Nye, 2001: ch. 6). This marked a new era, not of trade wars and a lack of regulation, but a period in which new rules about flexible exchange rates were agreed upon. In a flexible exchange-rate system, currency values are determined on a day-to-day basis, which encourages speculation in selling and buying financial assets. If enough speculators think a currency is going to devalue, the aggregated effect of speculators trying to sell may in fact cause a currency to devalue. Thus, the East Asian financial crisis of 1997 was partly caused by speculative activity on the international money market (Held et al., 1999: 209).

Many forms of investments have become more global in reach. Portfolio investments by institutional investors – insurance companies, pension funds, unit trusts – in stock markets increased markedly in the 1980s and early 1990s (Commission on Global Governance, 1995: 136). Foreign Direct Investment (FDI) has also grown, particularly in developed countries. For example, stocks of outward FDI by developed economies grew from 67.0 billion dollars in 1960 to 2,243 billion dollars in 1994 (Held et al., 1999: 247). With respect to the countries receiving FDI, the distribution is uneven, with developed countries receiving 73.8 per cent of inward FDI stocks and developing countries receiving only 25.3 per cent (Held et al., 1999: 249). Overall private investments in developing countries have risen, while overall development assistance has declined (Commission on Global Governance, 1995: 136). However, investment is concentrated in some developing countries, while others receive very little private investment. For example, private investments in Africa constituted practically the same share of GDP in 1997 as they did in 1964 (World Bank, 2000a: 20). In other words, the growth in FDI has completely bypassed that continent.

Growth in FDI is also an indicator of the third and final aspect of economic globalization, that of global production by multinational companies (MNCs). The MNC is a company with activities in more than one country. It produces and markets its goods in several countries, and it typically has one component for its product made in one place and other components in other places, according to where the cheapest or most efficient production sites are. A multinational enterprise thus does not leave one country for another, but rather it extends its activities across its homeland border.[7] The Ford Motor Company, for example, has evolved from a predominantly US company, with some overseas subsidiaries serving local markets, to an integrated operation around regional subsidiaries that in Europe serve the Single Market, producing a 'world car' through coordinated operations. In the post-war period, MNCs have acquired global presence, and stocks and flows of FDI have grown faster than world income. Overseas affiliates' production has grown from 4.5 per cent of world GDP to 7.5 per cent (Held, et al., 1999:

242–6). The United Nations has a 'transnationality index' that is calculated from the average ratio of foreign assets to total assets, foreign sales to total sales, and foreign employment to totals employment. The index is then calculated for a number of large companies, and for example, Nestlé, based in Switzerland, has an index of 94 while Japanese Sony's is 59.1. An increasing number of companies thus has a large multinational element. Most production is, however, concentrated in the developed world and Asia. The European Union houses 54,862 foreign affiliates, while Africa has a meagre 134 (Held et al., 1999: 245).

In all, although interpretations of the economic changes vary greatly, it is fair to conclude that we can talk about a real process of economic globalization in the post-war period, and in particular after 1989 when the communist bloc collapsed and became included in the world economy. Globalization is, however, extremely uneven, and tends to involve marginalization of some parts of the world. The income gap between rich and poor countries has increased with the process of globalization. We shall turn to the political implications on pages 78–98, but first look at other dimensions of globalization – the military and the sociocultural dimensions.

Military globalization

There is in a sense no Third World in respect of weaponry; only a First World, since most countries maintain stocks of technologically advanced armaments and have modernized the military in a thoroughgoing way (Giddens, 1990: 75). With the spread of modern weaponry, all citizens of the globe are potentially threatened, either by war which, with nuclear weapons, has enormous destructive potential, by oppressive states, or by international terrorism. The globalization of military power thus has to do with the spread of the war system and the spread of weaponry and arms technology throughout the globe (Giddens, 1990; Held et al., 1999).

The twentieth century saw two world wars that were of a global scale in that they involved all regions of the world, with unprecedented destructive and tragic consequences. Before that, conflicts had had a more limited character, being confined to a few neighbouring countries. During the cold war, the military system remained entirely global in the sense that Soviet–US relations affected the whole state system. While direct hot confrontation between the two powers was ruled out because of nuclear weapons' destructive potential, the conflict was fought by 'cold means' in various parts of the state system. The state system itself became globalized when the overseas colonies in Africa and the Oceanic area achieved independence. Superpower competition extended to these states and affected their internal political organization. For example, the Western powers repeatedly, and throughout the 1970s and 1980s, provided massive support to Mobutu Sese-Seko, Zaire's long-term dictator. The great power struggle was fought in regions like East Asia (particularly the Vietnam War), the Middle East, Central America, and Africa.

Since the end of the cold war, new types of conflict have emerged. The early years after the fall of the Berlin Wall in 1989 were characterized by great optimism, with the hope that a brighter, more peaceful future lay ahead. The United States' campaign against Iraq to liberate Kuwait in 1991 was often seen as a successful attempt to police the world and prevent states from embarking on military aggression towards other states. However, after a few years, it became clear that state collapse, civil war and local conflicts in the Second and Third Worlds were part of the post-cold war geo-political landscape. The tragedy in former Yugoslavia was but one example. Thus, in the years after the cold war, a picture of a bifurcated world began to emerge. On the one hand, in the North, a group of strong, rich states live peacefully together. These states are largely democratic in a liberal sense, and war among them has become almost unimaginable. The Northern military alliance, NATO, has not been dissolved with the disappearance of the Soviet enemy, but seems, in spite of occasional conflicts of interest, to be adapting to the changes and has invited several post-communist countries to become members.

On the other hand, a large group of states in the South are poor and weak. They have very few administrative powers and many of them are not able to deliver basic political goods, such as peace and stability, for their citizens. In fact, some of these states constitute a security threat to their own citizens as they repeatedly violate basic human rights (Zartman, 1995). In between these extremes, there are various regional security complexes (Buzan, 1991). For example, the Indian–Pakistani conflict continues even without superpower reinforcement, and China has territorial claims on Taiwan, which it refuses to recognize as a sovereign state (Sørensen, G., 2001). The military order, then, looks a lot less organized than during the cold war. However, this does not mean that the world military order has become any less global. As we shall see below on this page, the end of the cold war has opened up opportunities for new arms trade links, while the increased incidence of terrorist attacks has raised awareness that we all exist in a zone of risk, and in that sense we all live in one world. With the terrorist attacks on the World Trade Center, the symbol of Western capitalism in the heart of Manhattan, on 11 September 2001, the world entered an era in which the physical security of populations reappeared on top of the political agenda. As the one superpower in the world, the United States reacted by waging a war against one of the weakest and poorest states in the world, Afghanistan, where the al-Qaeda terrorist network had a strong base.

The global military order today is thus fragmented, but it is still global. Rich countries cannot afford to ignore the existence of weak and poor states, because conflict and poverty in these regions affect the wealthier nations, not only as breeding grounds for terrorism, but also as a source of political or economic refugees who often seek asylum in the North. The military order is also global because of international arms trade. While global exports of conventional weapons have declined since 1983, the numbers of countries supplying arms, particularly to the developing world, has more than doubled since 1960 (Held, et al., 1999: 112–13). Following the end of the cold war, the post-communist countries are to a large extent supplying arms to the Third World. Uganda's President Museveni, for example, travelled to White Russia to buy arms. Less officially, extensive trading takes place with resources available to Third World countries, such as diamonds, coltan and oil, paying for arms, weapons, helicopters and other war equipment. Angola's long-time civil war was kept alive for decades, partly because the Angolan government had access to oil while the rebel movement had access to diamonds (Hodges, 2001; Global Witness, 1998).

In all, military globalization involves global arms trading, regional and local conflicts, particularly in weak states, and an impact on the security of all populations that renders global governance urgent in the security area, a matter which shall be discussed on pages 81–98 in the section on global governance.

Environmental globalization

Ever since the 'Earth Summit' (UN Conference on Environment and Development) in Rio de Janeiro in 1992, global environmental problems have regularly been at the top of the international agenda. But how global is environmental degradation? Many problems of pollution are concentrated locally and only affect a confined area (Held, et al., 1999: 376). Yet most observers agree that some environmental problems are of a global nature and therefore call for global solutions (Roodman, 1999). Environmental degradation means the transformation of entire ecosystems, with consequences that have an adverse impact on the economic or demographic conditions of life and health for human beings (Held, et al., 1999: 377). Many see the entire planet as one single ecosystem, in which actions in some places affect the lives of people across the globe. A prominent example is the phenomenon of global warming. Global climate change has been identified as one of the greatest threats to our planet, because a global heating can cause melting of the ice caps, rising sea levels, flooding of low-lying lands and the spread of diseases such as malaria. Global warming is caused by the emission of greenhouse gases, most particularly CO_2. These gases create a heat trap, preventing the heat from leaving our system. Global carbon emissions have risen considerably since the 1950s, and this has set in motion a so-called greenhouse effect, i.e. a man-made global warming. The average global temperature has risen by approximately 0.3 degrees since 1975. The global temperature in 1998 was projected to be both the highest ever and to represent the largest annual increase ever recorded (Brown and Flavin, 1999: 14). Carbon emission derives mainly from the combustion of fossil fuels, such as coal and oil, and the developed countries are responsible for most of the increase in CO_2 (World Bank, 2003).

Thus, the development and energy consumption of the rich countries has affected the lives of many citizens in the South, for example, by causing floods in Bangladesh. And in the South, the hunt for mahogany trees has caused much destruction of rainforests in the Amazons. Deforestation also affects the global climate. In this way, populations in one area of the globe are affected by the behaviour of individuals in other areas of the globe, which has given rise to expressions such as the global commons and global public goods. If a healthy environment is a global public good, in the sense that nobody can be excluded from enjoying it, the provision of such a good requires global coordination. Even sceptical environmentalists agree that although the extent to which we should spend money on combating global warming can be debated, it should be debated in a global forum (Lomborg, 2001: 324).

In sum, although the degree to which our planet is seriously threatened by environmental degradation is continuously debated, no one seems to argue against the need for global environmental governance.

Sociocultural globalization

The term 'sociocultural globalization' gives rise to associations with such cultural icons as Coca-Cola, McDonalds, Hollywood and Madonna. And it is true that cultural globalization has a lot to do with the spread of Western norms, ideas and values, for example secularism, human rights, democracy or personal liberty. Some of these ideas naturally impinge on political matters, and therefore also belong to our discussion on pages 78–98 of the political implications of globalization. Some aspects of cultural globalization, such as the spread of world music, probably do not have as clear relevance to global governance as do environmental or economic issues. Nonetheless, to the extent that sociocultural globalization affects identities and gives rise to new cleavages or conflicts in the world, it does have implications for governance. Also, the increasing numbers of international non-governmental organizations, social movements and advocacy networks can be seen as a part of sociocultural globalization, although they are also political.

Nation-states and national cultures have been the *locus* of most cultural power in the modern era, but contemporary transformations challenge national cultures, national identities and their institutions (David Held et al., 1999: 328–75). These transformations include technological innovations, new progress in telecommunications, IT technology, and international media corporations such as, for example, the CNN. Cable and satellite voice paths over the Atlantic and the Pacific made communication cheaper and faster than with the old telex and telegraph networks. Global MNCs and sociocultural markets are bigger than ever, particularly in news broadcasting, music and cinema, and they are primarily based in the Western world. During the 1990s, the Internet gained prominence and provided new ways through which a global consciousness, a conception of the world as a single place, could be developed (Olesen, 2002b). The global infrastructures of culture and communication have contributed to increasingly dense transnational elite and professional cultures. For example the academic elite in one country may have more interaction or more in common with elites in other countries than with citizens of their own nationality. The global communications infrastructure has also increased the openness of information. For example, communist regimes could not prevent their citizens from watching Western satellite TV, which made them conscious of a potential alternative lifestyle and may have helped set in motion the large flows of people towards the West when Hungary opened its borders to Austria in the late 1980s. Although it is doubtful whether increased communication in itself can make a difference, it may increase the pace of social change.

However, it is far from clear that globalization reduces the strength of traditional identities. Rather, globalization may function through local and national spheres, and may even strengthen them by providing social actors with new arenas of contest and sources of support (Olesen, 2002b). National NGOs may, for example, bypass their state and ally with other states in order to exert greater pressure on their own state, a phenomenon Keck and Sikkink (1998: 12–13) have termed the Boomerang pattern. This has often been the case in human rights campaigns, but also indigenous peoples and environmental campaigns have followed a Boomerang pattern. In cases like the Indian government's damming of the Narmada River, international contacts significantly strengthened local organizations' demands (see chapter 7 on the World Bank). Social movements and international non-governmental organizations thus increasingly use links to the rest of the world in order to achieve their goals. For example, the Chiapas peasants' rebellion in Mexico started as a locally confined protest, but grew into a transnational network of Zapatismo by using modern methods of communication and formulating its goals in a language corresponding to a global anti-liberalist discourse used by people who demonstrated against the large multi-lateral economic organizations such as the WTO (Olesen, 2002b).

Resistance to globalization, i.e. the spread of neo-liberalism, is itself a part of globalization. Most movements are peaceful and rely on pressuring big organizations and governments. Others are violent. The perception of globalization as a Western affair, spreading a Western secular culture in which everything is allowed – including free production and marketing of pornography – is offensive to many. In particular, some Islamic groups have reacted strongly against Westernization. In Nigeria, in 2002, there were local Islamic protests and street riots against a Miss World contest where hundreds were killed, and the contest was eventually moved to London. Western groups also react to events that take place in other cultures. For instance, in 2002, when a Nigerian woman, Amina Lawal, was sentenced to death through stoning by a Sharia court of law, a widespread campaign through e-mail was set in motion, collecting thousands of signatures in a very short time.

Is globalization the same as Westernization? The understanding of globalization as the spread of neo-liberalism is widespread among anti-globalist social movements such as ATTAC, and the people who took to the streets in Seattle to demonstrate against the WTO meeting in 1999, causing what has come to be known as 'the battle in Seattle'. These movements express an anti-globalization attitude, but they understand globalization too narrowly when they equate it to a global neo-liberalist conquest. In reality these social movements are themselves part of what globalization is about: the extension of social relations across the globe. They represent a globalization 'from below', so to speak, and are only anti-globalists in the sense that they protest against capitalism's dehumanizing effects and argue for a more democratic world, for more political steering of the market forces, and therefore, as we shall see in the section on global governance (pages 78–98), for better governance (Falk, 1999: 127–37; Olesen, 2002a). Resistance to globalization can take different forms. The most violent and destructive is international terrorism, which showed its devastating consequences on 11 September 2001 when the twin towers of the World Trade Center were hit by passenger airplanes hijacked by suicide pilots. The attack was carried out by members of the al-Qaeda network, a transnational terror network that uses modern telecommunications to maintain links with other fundamentalist networks, such as Islamic jihad. Islamic terrorism has many causes, but most of them can be found in processes of globalization (Sørensen, 2002): economic marginalization and inequality, the existence of weak states with no ability to control their domestic domains, the secularization process of some Arab countries, like Saudi-Arabia, and maybe even the sociocultural clash between Western and Islamic civilizations (Huntington, 1997).

Sociocultural globalization is about the global spread of Western culture, but this does not necessarily mean that a single world culture will emerge or that other cultures will not affect Western culture. Sociocultural globalization does not necessarily erase local or national identities, but may even strengthen them. Nor does sociocultural globalization necessarily mean secularization, as it may even strengthen some religious identities. Finally, sociocultural globalization can lead to more harmony between nations that identify more easily with one another, but it can also generate clashes between cultures. To the extent that sociocultural globalization has political implications, it is of concern to proponents of global governance.

Globalization and the need for governance: summing up

'Globaloneys' think globalization processes are profound and truly transform the world into a global village. Sceptics think the changes do not lead to a qualitatively different world. In the globalization version given here, a balanced account is attempted, placing it among the 'transformationalists'. It is indeed possible to talk of an accelerated economic, social, sociocultural and environmental interdependence, and it is fair to call this process globalization, although it is highly uneven and entails marginalization of some regions. However, even people in marginalized areas are a part of globalization when they become aware of the lifestyles of the rich countries through CNN and Western TV shows, and this may cause increased migration.

Whether a 'globalonist', a 'sceptic' or a 'transformationalist' viewpoint is held, all agree that global changes have occurred. We will now turn to the political implications of these processes: globalization has been described as a 'juggernaut', a powerful runaway wagon that nobody can control unless collective action is taken. 'The juggernaut crushes those who resist it, and while it sometimes seems to have a steady path, there are times when it veers away erratically in directions we cannot foresee' (Giddens, 1990: 139). But are we really powerless in the face of an all-encompassing globalization? Differing views exist. There are two aspects of the political implications of globalization, which we will discuss in turn. The first concerns the implications for the role of the state, the second the implications for global governance.

Is the state's role in global governance declining?

Has the policy-making autonomy of nation-states declined? Do states no longer have the authority they used to have? David Held et al. (1999: 189) argue that the worldwide trading of currencies and government bonds means that

Table 3.2 Views on the role of the state in an era of globalization

	Economics most important	Politics most important
Comparative national development	Neo-liberal economists (Milton Friedman, international financial institutions)	The regulatory state (Linda Weiss, Peter Evans)
International relations	Strong liberalism (James Rosenau, Richard Falk)	Neo-realism (Kenneth Waltz, Stephen Krasner)

exchange rates and interest rates are determined within the context of global financial markets, and that states have no power to set the rates themselves. All states have to conform to the global financial markets, whether they want to or not. On the other hand, Linda Weiss (1998: 184) counter-argues that financial integration may not continue unabated, and that it is not certain that uniformly passive or undifferentiated national responses will prevail. Thus, there are differing views with regard to the continued importance of the state.

The differing views on globalization's impact on the power of the state can be found in two debates. One is the comparative national development debate, which is mainly between political scientists, who argue for the importance of the state in economic development (Weiss and Hobson, 1995; Weiss, 1998; Wade, 1990; Evans, 1996), and economists, who argue for neo-liberal economic policies. Another is the debate in international relations as to whether national interests still matter most when important stakes are at play, or whether increased globalization and integration can prevent national interests from dominating international relations (Rosenau, 1995; Keohane and Nye, 2000; Waltz, 1999). Both debates, however, are basically about differing views of the importance of economics or politics, as shown in table 3.2.

Neo-liberal economists argue that states should provide enabling frameworks for the free market. With no state intervention, global trade will lead to economic growth and secure welfare for all. On the other hand, political scientists argue that national economies have often done well *because of* state interventions to protect infant industries or guide local industries in new directions. Thus, states are important when meeting the challenges of globalization, and, in a competitive system, state capacity matters more, not less (Weiss, 1998).

Liberalists in international relations argue that economic globalization may weaken the power of states. James Rosenau (1995: 18), for example, observes that shifts in the 'location of authority and the site of control systems' have taken place and 'in some cases the shifts have transferred authority away from the political realm and into the economic and social realms' (see also Mathews, 1997). Contrast his words with those of Kenneth Waltz (1999: 699), whose baseline is that 'politics prevails over economics'. Waltz argues that economic globalization did not happen by itself; rather, it was the policies of nation-states that set in motion the processes of economic globalization through deregulation and agreements of international trade rules. But not only were states important in setting globalization in motion; they remain important because they exist in a competitive system in which they try to survive – they compete, adapt, protect themselves and imitate states that have been successful. 'States perform essential political social-economic functions and no other organization appears as a possible competitor to them' (ibid.: 697).

Thus, if politics are viewed as more important than economics, the position is that states remain dominant actors, and if economics are seen to prevail over politics, the position is that states are in decline. In between these positions are 'transformationalists' (Held et al., 1999; Sørensen, G., 2001), who believe that rather than to talk of state decline, it is more appropriate to talk about state transformations. In some areas, such as monetary policy, states may be losing authority, but they still have authority in other areas, such as social or military expenditure. They are so far the only organizations that can uphold the rule of law within a given territory (Hirst and Thompson, 1995). Moreover, international forces shape different kinds of state differently. The end of the cold war may have signified greater economic and political interaction between post-communist countries and the Western world, but it also saw a number of weak states collapse, such as Somalia, or Yugoslavia.

In sum, has the role of states declined? Not necessarily. The potential for collective action by states may have *increased* with globalization. States can organize within multi-lateral organizations such as the EU, they can regulate international trade through the WTO, and they can intervene in crisis situations through the United Nations Security Council. Multi-lateral arrangements can provide mechanisms that protect individual countries from some of the threats of globalization. For example, the European Monetary Union is a macroeconomic mechanism that will offer an effective shield for its member states from international speculation against the individual country's currency rate (Pierre and Peters, 2000: 102). Also, many transnational networks are in fact trans*governmental*, consisting of contacts between national courts and banks, etc., all over the world. States are, in this sense, not disappearing but their relations to the world have become more complex (Slaughter, 1997).

International politics is not necessarily a zero-sum game in which more global governance means less national governance and vice-versa. Because of the different ways in which states manage external challenges, global and national are not necessarily competing principles of organization, but may be complementary as well (Weiss, 1999b). We will now turn to the political implications of globalization at the global level.

What is the character of global governance?

> Globalism is here to stay. How it will be governed is the question. (Keohane and Nye, 2000: 38)

There are many different views regarding the political implications of globalization, and therefore about what global governance is or could be about. At least three perceptions of governance can thus be identified in IR: a narrow perception of governance that refers to practically all activities in transnational networks; a broader perception of global governance as a 'meta' affair, the process of coordinating the sum of transnational and intergovernmental activities; and third, the minimal definition of neo-realism that equates it with world government and therefore dismisses it as naive.

The disagreements are basically about how efficient global governance can be in a global system where states may refuse to comply. Neo-realists maintain that states prevent efficient international institutions, while others believe in such institutions to varying degrees. Here, we add the models of pluralism and of global democracy to the neo-realist and the liberal models (table 3.3).

Neo-realism and pluralism

The differing views have much to do with the different perceptions of the extent to which rules bind the behaviour of states. Neo-realists argue that states cannot be bound by rules (Mearsheimer, 1995). If rules of sovereignty (mainly that states should respect the territorial integrity of other states) were to guide state behaviour, why have these rules been broken repeatedly, neo-realists would ask. Stephen Krasner (1999), for example, argues that although states sometimes seem to adapt to rules and do what is considered appropriate, they nonetheless seldom hesitate in violating those rules if this suits their security interests best. For example, the United States, under President Bush Junior, defected from the Kyoto Agreement on greenhouse gas emissions because it was not willing to go against domestic industrial interests.

Although individual human rights on a global basis would be better secured by a more effective international judicial system, the United States refused to ratify the Rome Statute establishing the International Criminal Court, and, although the United States advocates free trade on the grounds that it benefits growth and welfare worldwide, it imposed protective tariffs on agricultural products and steel against WTO pressure. These unilateral actions show that the United States is concerned about relative, not absolute, gains, which is perfectly predictable in an anarchic system with no global

Table 3.3 Views on global governance

	Neo-realism	Pluralism	Liberalism/solidarism	Global democracy
Proponents	Mearsheimer, Krasner, Waltz	Bull, Jackson	Rosenau, Annan, Commission on Global Governance, Wheeler.	Held, Archibugi, Falk
Evaluation of existing global governance	There is no global governance; the international system is anarchic in spite of increasing globalization	International law upholds the principles of sovereignty and non-intervention	International regimes are an important part of global governance; governance at the sub-national, national and supra-national levels dampens the effects of anarchy	The existence of global civil society and a global citizenry call for more democratic global governance
Vision of global governance	Achieving a stable balance of power through alliances is the only realistic characteristic of global governance	A legal framework based on pluralist norms; a world of dialogue between separate but recognized political others	Global governance in many areas, not only the military, is required; a legal framework based on solidarist norms and with inbuilt enforcement mechanisms; solidarist norms place individual rights as high as sovereignty rights	Cosmopolitan democracy involves a global constitution and the recasting of territorial boundaries

governance. Global governance in this framework is the equivalent of some sort of world government built by states, and, since what ultimately counts is the national interest, it is neither realistic nor desirable.

Pluralists (the English School of international relations), on the contrary, argue that states may indeed be bound by rules. The international norm of sovereignty and the principle of non-intervention are effective with regard to securing international peace and order (Jackson, 2000). These rules challenge the assumption of international anarchy and emphasize that power balancing need not be the only source of international order. On the contrary, there has been an international society of states acting in accordance with mutually accepted norms and rules ever since the European Westphalian Peace in 1648 (Jackson, 2000: 11). These rules 'have waxed and waned. They have been attacked and defended, violated and upheld. But even though they have on several occasions been trampled upon, they have always been restored afterwards' (ibid.). Although the UN Security Council was unable to reach an agreement on a Resolution to invade Iraq in 2003, this is not a reason for the Security Council to cease to exist. In the post-Second World War period, these rules, embodied in what Robert Jackson (2000: 13) terms 'the global covenant', extended beyond the Western world, when decolonization gave rise to a world system of sovereign states. The global covenant is, according to Jackson, the first attempt in world history to construct a society of states that operates within a doctrine of recognition and non-intervention, bridging different cultures around the world. In that sense, global governance is very much present, and it has been around for a while.

The global covenant provides a normative guarantee of political independence but it does not guarantee that international freedom will be used wisely or effectively (ibid.: 410). The global covenant gives peoples the opportunity to build a 'good state', but it is entirely in the hands of peoples whether they do so or not. The global covenant does not steer the forces of economic, social and environmental globalization and nor should it, but it does provide a guarantee that peoples can pursue their happiness without external interference.

However, according to this view, there is a limit to how far global governance can extend beyond agreeing on an international norm of sovereignty. If the sovereignty norm were to be sacrificed in favour of human rights, international order would no longer prevail. Favouring human rights would imply breaking the rule of non-intervention, which would disturb international order. The Commission on Global Governance concludes that individuals' human rights should stand above the sovereign rights of states. It believes the Charter of the United Nations should be changed accordingly (Commission on Global Governance, 1995: 132). Jackson (2000: 389), however, criticizes the Commission's conclusions on the grounds that abandonment of the sovereignty norm would imply a threat to international order:

> The globalization thesis is a useful sociological account of important international changes that obviously are occurring widely at the present time. The problem is the mistaken political inference drawn from those changes by the commission, which has erroneously concluded that the socio-economic changes captured by the globalization thesis necessitate corresponding changes of a normative kind to alter state sovereignty.

To uphold a norm of human security would, according to Jackson (ibid.: 214), imply enforcement, and this is unrealistic since no great power would be prepared to sacrifice its own citizens to save citizens of other, far-away countries.

In sum, neo-realism and pluralism have in common the view that states remain the most important actors in the international system and that global governance is no more than what governments can agree upon; what distinguishes them is the extent to which they consider states to be bound by rules. Neo-realists reject the idea that states can be bound by global governance, whereas pluralists believe that the pluralist norms of sovereignty and non-intervention are in place and, although they constitute a system of global governance that may be far from efficient, it nonetheless works most of the time. According to pluralists, this system is the best we can get.

Liberalism/solidarism: The extent of existing global governance

Liberalists generally believe there are plenty of global governance processes under way, which go beyond the exchanges between governments (Keohane, 2001; Koremenos, Lipson and Snidal, 2001). The independent Commission on Global Governance is of the view that nearly all transnational activities concern global governance. 'Global governance has been viewed primarily as intergovernmental relationships, but it must now be understood as also involving non-governmental organizations (NGOs) Citizens' movements, multinational corporations, and the global capital market' (Commission on Global Governance, 1995: 2). The Commission seems to be of the opinion that the activities of economic actors (i.e. multinational corporations) are a part of governance, but this is not the view taken here. Economic activities are part of globalism and form part of the need for governance.

The general use of global governance in the paradigm of liberalism refers to *political* not economic activities. The definition used by the Centre for the Study of Global Governance is illustrative of the way liberalist IR scholars understand governance: not as government but as a minimum framework of rules necessary to tackle global problems, guaranteed by a set of institutions including both international organizations and national governments.[8] Global governance is about the setting, application and enforcement of rules for global politics.

Global governance in the liberalist view refers to more than just the norms of sovereignty and non-intervention; it covers political activities on sub-national, national and supra-national levels. Governance has grown since the Second World War, but became global in scope after the end of the cold war.

The growth in the number of international regimes is an important part of global governance. International regimes can be defined as principles, norms, rules and decision-making procedures, around which actor expectations converge in a given issue-area (Krasner, 1982). International regimes arise because states recognize that globalization necessitates international cooperation. For instance, in the environmental area, negotiation and decision-making procedures to address global environmental problems have taken place. One example is the UN Framework Convention for Climate Change, signed in Rio in 1992, in order to stabilize greenhouse gas concentrations in the atmosphere. A first step to reduce emissions was taken with the signing of the Kyoto Protocol in 1997. An often told success story with regard to global environmental governance is the reduction of chlorofluorocarbons (CFCs) that are known to break down ozone molecules. The ozone layer in the upper atmosphere protects living creatures from the sun's harmful ultraviolet rays. In the 1980s, a hole in the ozone layer above the Antarctic was discovered, which was connected to the emission of CFCs. A series of international agreements, starting with the Montreal Protocol, then succeeded in reducing the production of CFC gases; it is assumed that the ozone layer will now regenerate slowly over the next fifty years. It is doubtful, however, if CFCs can be taken as a representative case in order to offer general statements about the feasibility of global environmental regulation, because implementing the ban on CFCs was relatively cheap and it was easy to find substitutes.

The WTO (former GATT) is another example of an important international regime. Its purpose is to establish international trade rules in order to lower trade barriers and thereby secure free trade. It promotes norms such as reciprocity, i.e. that a country enjoying another country's lowering of tariffs should reciprocate; liberalism, i.e. the reduction of barriers; or economic development (Finlayson and Zacher, 1983, see also www.wto.org). The extent to which WTO really does promote development has been debated, and the organization has been criticized, for example, for not allowing the least developed countries to follow the same protectionist strategies as the developed countries have done. In addition, there are frequent complaints about countries breaking WTO rules, for example, by dumping the prices of goods produced in developing countries. No matter how imperfect, however, the WTO has set up a number of trade rules, negotiated with its 146 members, and therefore qualifies as an international regime.

The definition of an international regime does not specify whether regimes are always inter*governmental*. However, the IR literature often seems to refer to regimes as being about governance carried out by governments (Krasner, 1983; Rosenau, 2000). However, liberalists in IR stress that international norms and practices of global public policy can also be affected by non-governmental actors. A good example is the international campaign against landmines, which has been a successful case of global agenda setting. In the early 1990s, there was consensus among states that landmines were legal. But, in a number of countries, citizens could hardly go for a walk or farmers tend to their fields without fear of stepping on a landmine. The international campaign to ban landmines in 1992 united a host of NGOs with a common interest in banning them. Within a few years, the campaign succeeded in changing the norms surrounding landmine use. Through extensive publicity campaigns, the use of landmines became a humanitarian issue and, in 1997, 122 countries signed the Ottawa Treaty to ban anti-personnel landmines.[9] In this instance, NGOs effectively contributed to a change in governments' perceptions about landmines.

International environmental NGOs, such as Greenpeace, have fought successfully to raise awareness about environmental issues. Human Rights Watch, or Transparency International, are other examples of NGOs that have contributed to a change in public and media awareness in the areas of human rights and corruption. Transparency International has successfully set corruption on the global agenda (Rosenau and Wang, 2001). Human rights organizations, such as Amnesty International, have regularly succeeded in pressurizing governments to release political prisoners or to place important human rights issues, such as the death penalty, on the agenda. Some networks are loose and flexible at the beginning, but gradually acquire a more institutionalized form. Some governance forms resemble corporatism at a global level because they include representatives of governments (for example, the World Bank), business and global civil society. An example would be the World Commission on Dams, an independent Commission set up to discuss environmental consequences of large irrigation projects, with participation by all three types of actors (Ottaway, 2001).

The definition of global governance in relation to the concept of international regime is not quite clear, and the two are sometimes used interchangeably. Like governance, regimes include governmental as well as non-governmental actors, formal as well as informal rules. However, regimes or networks are confined to one cause or issue, such as campaigning for human rights, or regulating trade, while governance also covers the cross-cutting of these issues, with the steering of the totality of networks and regimes (Rosenau, 1992).

Some liberalists, such as James Rosenau (2000), reject the tendency of the regime literature to assume that authority is state-based. In much theorizing about regimes, the actors that bring about a change in rules and norms are implicitly or explicitly assumed to be governments. However, as illustrated by the examples above, other actors are also involved in governance processes. The tendency to equate governance with government in international relations theory should be abandoned. In light of the increasingly complex and multi-layered nature of transnational relations, the term 'international' itself should be rejected in favour of terms that capture the nature of change, such as global politics or politics on a global scale (Rosenau, 2000: 171). In addition, processes of globalization and governance should lead international relations scholars to focus less on internecine warfare, and instead turn their attention towards ways of governing complex relations and effectively addressing pressing problems such as drug-trafficking, pollution, corruption or terrorism. When addressing such issues, reliance upon top-down, hierarchic solutions are not likely to help; rather, inclusion of transnational NGOs, in networks comprising a multiplicity of actors who rely on dialogue, is a wiser strategy. The emergence of a global civil society, involved in global politics and pressurizing for a global agenda, is a change that should be taken seriously and incorporated into our view of international relations.

Liberalism/solidarism: visions of global governance

The liberalist paradigm in international relations theory is not particularly concerned with setting up visions of global governance. Liberalists' main concern is to analyse how international institutions function and how they may be designed. They analyse the impact of international institutions in the social and economic realms, such as trade regimes or human rights organizations.

Solidarists look more to the military than to the social or economic realms.[10] They argue that cases of global governance already exist, where humanitarian intervention has promoted human security rather than guarded the sovereign rights of states. For instance, although the intervention in Kosovo can be interpreted as a failure of the UN to provide a basis for global governance, the intervention nonetheless took place with reference to the minimum standards of humanity as contained in international law, for instance, the UN Charter, the 1948 Genocide Convention and the Geneva Conventions. There are principles in international law on which humanitarian intervention can be based (Knudsen, 2001). Solidarism builds on the assumption of solidarity of states when it comes to law enforcement.

Contrary to pluralists, who believe that enforcement of international law in favour of human security is not realistic, solidarists believe that it is both realistic and desirable to set up a system in which the international community has an obligation to support any state or group of individuals whose rights have been violated (ibid.; see also Wheeler and Dunne, 1996). Thus, solidarists often argue for a reform of the United Nations, especially the abandonment of the veto-right in the Security Council. Removal of the veto-right will make decisions about humanitarian intervention easier. In addition, many argue that the membership of the council should be expanded and made geographically equitable, to avoid the tendency for intervention to occur only when it is in the interest of the Western powers (Ayoob, 2001).

In sum, liberalists are concerned with the rise of institutions of global governance regarding a plurality of issues, while solidarists are more concerned with the enforcement of international law, and with military interventions. They have different conceptions of what global governance is about. Solidarists focus on global governance as the collective action of *states*. They make no mention of non-state actors, unlike liberalists, who clearly consider governance as referring to something broader than government. However, this is not a fundamental disagreement. It is rather a matter of different foci. Solidarists are concerned with human security and therefore focus on the enforcement of international law. Such enforcement occurs through the action of states. Liberalists are more concerned with how globalization is governed in all realms, and they therefore adopt a broader analysis of governance.

The critique of solidarists and liberalists has come from two camps. The neo-realist critique of solidarism that it would not be in the national interest of a state to delegate power to supranational organs, such as the security council, does *not* favour a decision to abandon the veto-right. In addition, prioritizing human rights over sovereignty rights would put international order at risk. The neo-realist critique of liberalism would emphasize that international regimes are dependent upon a hegemon, a strong power, and therefore they are not indicators of global governance but rather instruments of one power to promote its national interests. Although neo-realists recognize that transnational activities occur, they attribute importance to them only to the extent that they affect state behaviour, not as processes that could potentially affect norms and rules outside the reach of states.

Another critique has come from the neo-Marxist, or the 'structuralist' camp (Strange, 1983, 1996). This critique finds that the liberal approach to global governance neglects power differences among actors. The liberal approach sees mostly harmonious relations and benefits from free trade rather than conflict. It sees mutual dependence rather than skewed economic dependence relations. It finds that the focus is still overwhelmingly on state authority and regrets the lack of attention to economic forces and non-state sources of authority. Thus, rather than a system of global governance, we have a 'ramshackle assembly of conflicting sources of authority' (Strange, 1996). Alternative sources of authority could be the firm or a social movement. Firms and big corporations have a large say, and sometimes a larger say than states, in who gets what in the international economy.

Thus, when neo-realists and pluralists maintain a focus on *order*, strong liberalists such as James Rosenau focus more on *efficiency* and how to steer in a situation of increased complexity and disaggregated authority, while the 'structuralist' approach represented by Susan Strange brings to the fore issues such as *justice* and legitimacy.

The final model to be considered takes up the question of *democratic legitimacy* and focuses as much on the input as on the output side of global policy-making. It discusses the normative but relevant question of how democratic accountability is strengthened within the structure of the politics taking place at the global scale.

Democratic global governance

> Globalization presents modern democratic theory with a daunting task: how to reconcile the principle of rule by the people with a world in which power is exercised increasingly on a transnational, or even global scale. (McGrew, 1997: 231)

Democracy means rule by the people. However, the increase of global policy problems raises concerns about how to define 'the people'. According to Robert Dahl (1989), 'the *demos*' should be all those who are affected by a decision. The point is that the nature of some decisions means that the *demos* cannot be confined to a certain nation or a few specific nations. To combat terrorism, to control greenhouse gases, or to combat diseases such as AIDS and malaria, involves political decisions that affect people of many nations. When the American government decides to defect from the Kyoto agreement, for example, gas emissions may not be reduced enough to avoid floods in Bangladesh. When the *demos* include all citizens around the world, in theory, they should all have an opportunity to influence a decision affecting them.

Due to these concerns, it has been argued that democracy should be rethought at the global level. Democratic global institutions are, according to this argument, a pre-condition for democracy at the local or national levels (Held, 1993: 27). From a normative democratic point of view, rather than being a guarantee of international peace, the sovereignty norm may actually impede global democracy. This is because global solutions should be implemented without the obstruction of states claiming the right of non-intervention.

Global democracy is not about abolishing nation-states and removing the sovereignty right (Archibugi, 1998; Held, 1998). Rather, it is about democratization at three political levels: democracy inside states, democracy between states, and global democracy. 'Democracy inside states' builds on the premise that the state exists at the consent of its citizens, and that the state should be the caretaker of individual human rights (Archibugi, 1998; see also O'Byrne, 2003). It is difficult to imagine a democratic international system consisting of only autocratic states. 'Democracy among states' requires respect for reciprocal sovereignty, but also strengthened inter-state cooperation. Finally, the concern of 'global democracy' is to address global problems and find a way in which all citizens can be represented in global affairs (Archibugi, 1998: 211). David Held and Daniele Archibugi use the term 'cosmopolitan democracy' to create a vision for a democratic world order.

In a cosmopolitan democracy, cosmopolitan institutions would coexist with a system of states but would override states in certain clearly defined spheres of activity (Archibugi, 1998: 216). Sovereignty would in some cases be subordinate to international law. The individual is a global citizen who has rights and duties, not only in relation to a state but in relation to a global institution. 'The cosmopolitan system envisages not only the existence of universal human rights protected by states, but also the creation of a mandatory core of rights which individuals may claim, as well as duties vis-à-vis global institutions' (Archibugi, 1998: 217).

The most important institutional features of a cosmopolitan democracy are listed below (Held, 1993, 1998; Archibugi, 1998; Falk, 1995):

- A strengthened regional level, with a democratic European Union, but also strengthening and democratizing other regions in the world to give them independent administrative and political resources.
- A strengthened global level with resources independent from the states and more administrative capacity.

- Civil society to be represented in an elected global parliament with consultative powers. A first step could be the election of a UN second chamber.
- International court of justice and of human rights, and a criminal court with compulsory jurisdiction and sanctionary powers.
- Growing shift of coercive capacity from nation-states to regional and global institutions, and the establishment of a standing and accountable international military force.
- Reform of the UN security council to include more states and removal of veto-power.

In sum, the vision of global democracy rests on the notion that global institutions have to be built because some regional and global processes easily escape democratic control and are beyond the reach of national states.

These visions have been criticized as naive and idealistic, and neo-realists as well as pluralists would argue that subordinating sovereignty rights to human rights means sacrificing international order, which is a precondition for any democratization efforts to take place at all. Also, the problem of representation at a global level is difficult to solve. The rule of one state, one vote is not democratic because small states with a few million inhabitants would have as large a say as very populous states. However, to treat the world as a single global constituency with majority rule would mean that more than 2 billion Indians and Chinese could usually get their way (Nye, 2001). Additionally, in a multi-centred and complex world a global parliament may not be the answer to problems of accountability. Adding another political layer could even increase the steering problems posed by globalization. Finally, constructing democratic institutions at the global level presupposes the existence of one global locus of popular decision-making (Hirst, 2000: 16). Yet the very essence of modern globalized society is that there is no one political community, but multiple centres and layers of authority.

Hence, we might be better off exploring ways to increase the democratic accountability of existing institutions and networks. A growing literature does address this important issue but from somewhat different viewpoints (Masicotte, 1999; Woods, 1999; Woods and Narlikar, 2001; Helleiner, 2001;

Ottaway, 2001; Cox, 1996; Strange, 1996). One angle is to focus on the nature of the international political economy. Scholars adopting this viewpoint generally argue that the world economy is becoming ever more unequal, with an increasing gap between rich and poor. The *locus* of economic power has moved away from states towards firms and big multi-lateral corporations (Cox, 1996; Strange, 1996). It is difficult to know how to ameliorate this problem, but Robert Cox sees the rise of self-help organizations and the strengthening of the international labour movement as potential counter strategies to the neo-liberal wave (Cox, 1996: 516–34). Also Gerald Helleiner (2001) sees the world economy as severely under-governed. He views current governance arrangements as being dominated by the interests of the industrial countries, and is concerned that sustainable development and global poverty will be low on the global agenda. Although he is sceptical about reform, he nonetheless argues that current international economic institutions, such as the G7, the IMF, the World Bank and the WTO, should become more representative, to reflect the interests of all nations rather than merely the rich.

A slightly different angle is to focus more narrowly at specific international organizations, such as those just mentioned, and examine their degree of accountability and the feasibility of increasing their reform. These institutions cannot be characterized as generally illegitimate. They have had some degree of success in securing efficient outputs. After the Second World War, the IMF secured stability on international financial markets, and the GATT was successful in setting up rules that served to avoid trade wars and a financial crash like the one in 1929. Thus, output legitimacy probably is or has been quite high. However, regardless of their success, these institutions have been characterized by a low degree of accountability. They have not been responsible to a particular body when taking a decision. Their input legitimacy is therefore probably quite low. The lack of accountability is partly a consequence of a lack of clear knowledge about to whom or what these organizations should be accountable – for example, to member states, people directly affected by decisions, or a global civil society (see chapter 7).

The degree of accountability of these organizations differs. In a sense, the WTO is more accountable than the World Bank or the IMF because it is based on consensus and therefore cannot implement decisions without the consent of all its member states (Woods and Narlikar, 2001). The World Bank and the IMF are both primarily accountable to their shareholders, of which the largest is the United States. This means that they tend to support pro-capitalist economic strategies and policies.

It can thus reasonably be argued that the poorer member states of the World Bank and the IMF should have a larger say in policy decisions. Also, attention could be paid to the views of people who are affected by programmes of these institutions. For instance, World Bank support for big infrastructural projects, such as dams, can be questioned on the grounds that they involve moving thousands of human beings who live in the area.

But focusing on the issue of listening to people affected by programmes also raises the question of exactly who is affected and who should represent such people. Lots of NGOs who fight for 'good' causes are not necessarily representative of the groups of people they claim to represent. The third angle on accountability in global politics is thus the one pointing to transnational NGOs. The fact that NGOs act for particular constituencies is good in the sense that they give voice to groups who often lack the resources to organize on their own. Yet, it is the second-best solution in that the NGOs act as a substitute for the imperfect way in which states represent their own peoples. Further, there is no knowledge about which NGOs actually represent marginalized groups and which NGOs are financially motivated or represent powerful groups. Thus, international NGOs should be subject to the same standards of transparency that many of them demand from international institutions (Nye, 2001).

Conclusion: governance in international relations

The neo-realist model of international relations builds upon the assumption that states are the most important actors on the international scene and that they are rational and unitary actors. This model was questioned by liberalists, who argued that interdependence challenged many of the core assumptions of neo-realism. With the entry of globalization on the agenda, 'strong' liberalists (and neo-Marxists) claim that the increased importance of multinational actors and transnational networks weakens the authority of states. International regimes govern transnational relations in a range of issue areas from landmines to trade. Some IR scholars still see governments as the components of regimes, but others stress the multi-centred and multi-layered nature of the global political space, rejecting the centrality of nation-state as the sole *locus* of governance. While neo-realists equate global governance with global government and therefore dismiss it as unrealistic, strong liberalists often describe global governance taking place without government.

There is thus disagreement about the importance of – and the amount of attention which should be given to – nation-states. However, using the concept of global governance does not necessarily imply neglecting the centrality of states, but rather questions the actors involved in setting, applying and enforcing the rules of the game. A concern with governance does not presume a decline of the state, rather it leaves open to empirical investigation the extent to which the authority of states increases or decreases.

Additionally, it seems important to distinguish between sectors. In the security area, states still tend to act unilaterally when they perceive a threat, and hence the neo-realist approach rejecting global governance may have a case. However, in other areas, such as the environmental or the economic, governance is much more realistic and, no matter how faulty, it is already a feature of the modern world. The globalization juggernaut has not run entirely loose, the direction it takes is affected by state and non-state actors alike.

The main issue for global governance theory has been output-efficiency: how to make nation-states comply with international rules, and how to find better solutions to global problems. However, an increasing number of scholars have been concerned with the input-side, on how to establish procedures of global democracy. Some have created visions of cosmopolitan democracy. While this is an important normative discussion, the literature on cosmopolitan democracy tends to presume that a global political locus of decision-making exists. However, the very nature of the modern world is one of multiple centres and fragmented authority. Therefore, a more realistic way to promote democracy in the twenty-first century may be to explore how the democratic accountability of existing international institutions can be increased.

4
European Governance: Between International Relations and Public Policy

What will happen to the nation-state in the emerging European Community? 'There will be a continued drift toward supra-nationality,' answered Ernst B. Haas in the 1960s (Haas, 1964: 492). 'No,' sounded the reply from others, 'the nation state is far from obsolete, it is preserved as the basic unit in Europe' (Hoffman, 1966: 862, 910).

The two answers are representative of a long-standing debate on European integration between, on the one hand, *neo-functionalism*, which maintains that integration is a process that naturally follows increasing interdependence and will eventually result in a new political community that obscures current state boundaries, and, on the other hand, *intergovernmentalism*, arguing that European integration can best be seen as a successful intergovernmental regime, in which national leaders only give away as much sovereignty as they consider to be in their interest. The debate is parallel to the general debate in IR theory between liberalism and realism; it has the same opposing views about the fate of the nation-state.

The governance approach to studying the European Union represents a move away from the IR debate. Scholars focusing on multi-level governance in Europe consider this debate to be stuck in opposing trenches, without contributing much to the understanding of the character of policy-making in the EU. Instead of perceiving European integration as a dependent variable, driven either by negotiations of government leaders guarding their sovereignty or by processes of modernization and interdependence, the governance approach considers the EU *as a polity* and studies it as such. The EU then becomes an independent variable, affecting policy-making in the member states. The governance approach thus introduces public administration and public policy to EU studies.

The purpose of this chapter is to give an overview of the most important contributions to the debate on European governance. It starts by briefly sketching the neo-functionalist and intergovernmentalist strands, together with an outline of the history of European integration. It then goes on to address the contributions to the literature on governance in the EU. Further, it discusses the often emphasized democratic deficit of the EU and the proposed remedies. Finally, it argues that European governance is about regulating hierarchies, networks and markets at the supra-national, national and sub-national levels, but it is also about setting the political rules of the game, thereby providing much-needed democratic legitimacy to the Union.

The emergence of the European Community (Union) and the IR debate

The European Community arose almost like a phoenix out of the ashes of the Second World War, as part of the efforts to reconstruct institutions and revitalize the collapsed economy. The European countries had been devastated by the war and were willing to cooperate peacefully, realizing that cooperation (rather than protection) would promote growth, and, hopefully, prevent West Germany from rebuilding its war-machine. Hence West Germany, France, Holland, Belgium, Luxembourg and Italy agreed to establish the Coal and Steel Community in 1951 (Friis, 2001; Wallace and Wallace, 2000). They pledged to pool their coal and steel resources, remove restrictions on imports and exports and make common policies through a 'High Authority', which later became the European Commission. The endeavour soon proved successful, with increasing iron and steel production during the 1950s. In 1957, cooperation was expanded with the establishment of the European Economic Community (EEC) and the European Atomic Energy Community in the Treaty of Rome. The treaty established a common market, a common agricultural policy and a customs union. The aim was to work towards an economic and, ultimately, a political union; a union that would guarantee peace in Europe.

Neo-functionalism was inspired by and developed in tandem with European integration, and its fate became linked to that enterprise (Tranholm-Mikkelsen, 1991). Neo-functionalists saw peace as an important effect of integration, but they had a different conception of peace from realists. Whereas realists considered peace as the absence of war, neo-functionalists perceived peace in more positive terms: 'not a peace that would keep nations apart, but a peace that would bring them actively together'.[1] The practical implication was that 'working peace-making efforts should address themselves first and foremost to economic and social reform; to the joint management of scarce resources, unemployment, commodity price fluctuations, labour standards, and public health' (Haas, 1964: 11). Hence, economic integration would promote peace.

The basic argument of neo-functionalism is that integration in one sector will tend to expand to other areas and therefore set in motion dynamics of integration that eventually lead to the blurring of nation-state boundaries. Integration is thus understood as a process (not a condition) towards a supra-national political community (Haas, 1964: 26–9). Such a community does not necessarily entail a common constitutional arrangement, such as federalism or a unitary state, but it does mean that political loyalties are at least partly shifted to the new supra-national entity, which acquires powers to make legally binding decisions. The expansion of integration thus occurs through processes of *spill-over*, a central term in neo-functionalism, referring to the effects of integration of one sector creating new needs for integration in other sectors, together with new perceptions among political elites about the need for further integration (Haas, 1958: 283–317; Tranholm-Mikkelsen, 1991).

European developments in the 1950s did indeed support neo-functionalist assumptions, as cooperation in the steel and coal sector spilled over into wider economic integration and the creation of the EEC. However, the integration process lost its initial momentum during the 1960s and 1970s, having reached a turning point in 1957; it was almost thirty years before a new European treaty was signed. One reason for the formal stagnation of the integration process was that the Rome Treaty provided a skeleton that member states had to build upon. This process took all the time and energy of the members, so they did not give attention to negotiating new treaties. However, while this is part of the explanation, national interests, most notably claimed by French president de Gaulle, also played a role in killing the initial Euro-optimism. In 1963, de Gaulle blocked the entry of Britain into the Community and, during the 1965–6 crisis, he strongly resisted budgetary and institutional reforms aimed at giving the Commission more power in budgetary decisions and introducing majority decisions in the council. With de Gaulle's resistance, the integration process entered a period which has been called the 'dark ages', due to the lack of progress. De Gaulle's departure from the political scene in 1969 made little difference to the integration process, mainly because the economic decline of the 1970s kept the members busy saving their own economies, and because the new member states (Britain, Denmark and Ireland) were reluctant to give away sovereignty, not least the Euro-sceptic Margaret Thatcher, who came to power in 1979. In the beginning of the 1980s, the London journal *The Economist* even featured a gravestone for Europe on the front page.

The European stalemate triggered much criticism of neo-functionalism. Its teleological and rather deterministic assumptions about ever-increasing integration were criticized and, most significantly, scholars representing intergovernmentalism claimed that neo-functionalists had ignored the power logic of the international system. External influences would trigger different responses from European states and therefore constitute a disintegrating source (Hoffman, 1966, 1982). For example, France's stance in the bipolar order of the cold war was different from that of the other West European states, in that it preferred to stay outside the full NATO framework. Neo-functionalism was also criticized for ignoring the power of resistance to integration. Haas had argued that integration would be likely to proceed even against the interests of individual leaders. But reality showed that a de Gaulle could pose a serious obstacle to the process. Finally, intergovernmentalists emphasized the distinction between 'high' and 'low' politics, and the obstacles raised by zero-sum bargaining when national interests – high politics – were at stake. The 'pooling' of sovereignty was possible only in areas that were not considered of importance to national security.

For these reasons, Stanley Hoffman argued, 'the best way of analyzing Europe is not in the traditional terms of integration theory, which assumes that the members are engaged in the formation of a new, supranational political entity superseding the old nations' (Hoffman, 1982: 33), but rather to look at the EEC as an international regime with shared rules and norms. Increasing cooperation and the pooling of sovereignty in some economic areas does not necessarily lead to the overall decline of national sovereignty. On the contrary, participation in a regime can enable states to adapt to a changing world economy. Hence, the EEC has helped preserve the nation-state as a basic unit in Europe, according to Hoffman. Member states have, for example, referred to EEC directives when they were too weak to take unpopular measures on their own, and the EEC has helped members to modernize their economies, thereby upgrading competitiveness, and, ultimately, the EEC has strengthened the nation-state's capacity to act both at home and abroad (Hoffman, 1982: 35). The response of neo-functionalism, and its leading proponent, Ernst Haas, was first to attempt the adaptation of the theory to the criticism. For example, he tried to incorporate 'the phenomenon of a de Gaulle' by specifying the circumstances of spill-over (Tranholm-Mikkelsen, 1991: 9). But by the end of the 1970s, even Ernst Haas gave up and declared neo-functionalism obsolete in Western Europe.

However, during the 1980s, European integration gained pace and gave rise to a new wave of Euro-optimism. A dynamic new president of the European Commission, Jacques Delors (1985–95), presided over the first treaty reform since Rome, and the signing of the Single European Act, which spelled out further measures to be taken towards a common market allowing for the free movement of people, services, goods and capital. In addition, the European Parliament was strengthened and more majority decisions were introduced in the Council. The act also included social and environmental measures, as well as reform of the structural funds in order to even out regional imbalances in the EU.

The end of the cold war brought a new situation to Europe, in which the reunified Germany suddenly overpowered France and Britain with its economic might (30 per cent of EEC GDP) and 80 million inhabitants. French president Mitterrand considered further integration as a means to control Germany, and Chancellor Kohl also expressed his desire for a 'European Germany' rather than a 'German Europe'. The road was paved for the Treaty of the European Union, signed in the Dutch town of Maastricht in 1991, which renamed the community the European Union. The new union was to consist of three pillars. The most important pillar is about the common market, the union citizenship, the monetary union, a social protocol, and new policy areas such as the environment. This pillar takes more steps towards supra-nationality due to an increase both in the number of majority decisions and in the powers of the European Parliament.[2] The second pillar deals with a common security and foreign policy, and the third with justice and home affairs. The two latter pillars are entirely intergovernmental affairs, with decisions to be taken unanimously by the council.

The new momentum continued throughout the 1990s, with the deepening of integration being supplemented by a debate on European enlargement. With Greece, Portugal and Spain having joined in the 1980s, and Finland, Sweden and Austria in 1995, the EU now had fifteen members. The end of the cold war had raised the question of the post-communist European countries and their fate. The EU leadership agreed that co-opting these countries into the EU was the best way to contribute to their stabilization (in the aftermath of the Yugoslavia crisis) and further democratization. This required a discussion of decision-making rules in a larger Union, the number of commissioners, the number of representatives in the European Parliament, and the number and areas of majority decisions. A new treaty was signed in Amsterdam in 1997, building upon the Maastricht Treaty, and spelling out the Schengen agreement on removal of border controls, but no final agreements were reached on decision-making rules other than to meet again at a new intergovernmental conference.

The conference took place in Nice in 2000. A new treaty was signed in which decision-making procedures preparing the EU for enlargement were agreed upon. Also, the Nice Treaty gave the president of the Commission more powers, and introduced an increase in the use of qualified majority voting. The Treaty of Nice came into force in February 2003, and additionally, in 2003, a Treaty admitting the first ten candidates (Poland, Hungary, Estonia, Slovenia, The Czech Republic, Cyprus, Malta, Lithuania, Latvia, Slovakia) to accession was signed. Finally, the issue of a European Constitution has been raised, with a new framework to be discussed at an intergovernmental conference in 2004.[3]

The new wave of integration gave rise to calls for the revival of neo-functionalism. Some scholars pointed to examples of spill-over, such as the economic logic evident in the creation of the EMU (monetary union), the role of interest groups with positive orientations towards the EU, the innovative actions of the Delors Commission, or the increasing importance of the rulings of the European Court of Justice (Tranholm-Mikkelsen, 1991; Burley and Mattli, 1993; Rosamund, 1999). It was, however, agreed that neo-functionalism could not work as a grand theory of integration, and that the concept of spill-over could explain some but not all aspects of integration. For example, Wayne Sandholtz (1993) argues that to explain why European leaders agreed on the EMU, focusing on spill-over is a necessary, but not sufficient, condition. It is necessary, not because adoption of the monetary union was a functional logic from the viewpoint of internal market dynamics, but because the enthusiasm created by Maastricht led to a positive atmosphere in which it was easier to agree about a monetary union. However, according to Sandholtz, additional theories are necessary to explain why the EMU was adopted. These should focus on the need for individual member states to have a voice in monetary policies vis-à-vis Germany, on the changed international system after the cold war with Germany's willingness to make a European commitment, and on the proposition that a monetary union would simply be the optimum way to achieve the common goal of low inflation.

Neo-functionalism was, according to many EU scholars, far from obsolete; yet it could not provide sufficient explanations for European integration. Some therefore argued for a revival of federalism in order to find analytical tools to understand the supra-national institutions of the EU, while others were more anti-neo-functionalist and maintained, in line with Hoffman's argument, that the EU should be studied as 'a successful intergovernmental regime designed to manage economic interdependence through negotiated policy co-ordination' (Moravcsik, 1993: 474). According to Andrew Moravscik, in order to understand European monetary integration it is necessary to look at *both* the convergence of policy preferences arising from economic interdependence, *and* the relative capability and bargaining power of individual states that affected the precise terms under which monetary cooperation would take place (ibid.: 482).

In all, the debate in international relations has circled around the important question of whether states are losing their importance on the European scene, and how European integration can be explained (Cornett and Caporaso, 1992). According to many non-IR scholars, this debate, although valuable, does not make clear all the important aspects of the EU. The EU is both supra-national (the Commission, the European Court of Justice, the European Parliament) and intergovernmental (the Council of Ministers, particularly in the second and third pillars). Rather than discussing the driving forces of integration, the real issue for these scholars is the character of policy-making in the EU. Instead of asking how it came about, these scholars, who are to be found mainly in the tradition of comparative public policy, treat the EU as a polity and study its effects rather than its determinants (Rosamund, 1999; Wallace and Wallace, 2000; Hix, 1998; Jachtenfuchs, 2001). The EU, then, is treated more as an independent than a dependent variable; the focus is the process of policy-making in different policy sectors rather than the process and extent of integration.

Policy-making and governance in the European Union

> The Modern state (. . .) was defined by its unitary character.
> Post-modern European states operate within a much more
> complex, cross-cutting network of governance, based upon
> the breakdown of the distinction between domestic and
> foreign affairs, on increasing mutual transparency, and on the
> emergence of a sufficiently strong sense of community to
> guarantee mutual security. (Wallace, 1999: 519)

For international relations scholars, the 1970s and early
1980s were seen as the dark ages due to the failure of neo-
functionalism to explain integration. But in the field of public
policy, a growing number of studies focusing on the EU *as a
polity* was emerging, among which Wallace's *Policy-making
in the European Union* of 1977 (now in its fourth edition
– Wallace and Wallace, 2000) is a prime example. In addition, studies of public opinion and political parties grew in
number, all using concepts and categories developed in the
fields of comparative politics, public administration and
public policy (Jachtenfuchs, 2001). None of these studies was
particularly interested in the character of the nation-state.
Their concern was not for sovereignty, but for politics at the
European level.

After 1985 and the new integration impetus, the question
of whether the distinction between domestic politics and
external influences could be upheld became increasingly
important. Students of domestic politics or international relations no longer dealt with entirely separate fields of inquiry.
Whereas previously nation-states had largely been perceived
as sovereign, i.e. with complete control over domestic affairs,
European states to an increasing extent now shared sovereignty (Wallace, 1999; Marks, Hooghe and Blank, 1996). EU
regulations had an increasing impact upon national and sub-
national policies, and in many policy areas member states
could no longer legislate against EU law (Majone, 1992). The
EU attracted the attention of scholars, who saw it as a political system rather than a process of integration. A seminal

work was Fritz Scharpf's (1988). He compared German federalist decision-making with that of the EU and found that the processes were similar: decisions in the Council required bargaining and unanimity, which also characterized the German 'Bundesrat', where the states – *Länder* – are represented.

Thus, the way the EU worked as a political system and the way it impacted as a polity on national policy-making came into focus, and governance, or multi-level governance, emerged on the EU scholars' agenda. The concept of governance as applied to European studies was adopted from public administration and public policy literature, where governance referred to processes of steering and pursuing common goals that involved state and non-state actors at societal, sub-national and even supra-national levels (Kooiman, 1993; Rhodes, 1996).

There are two main ways in which the concept of governance is applied in European studies. One is as multi-level governance (MLG), connoting a new policy mode in the EU in which regions, states and the EU are involved. The other way in which the concept of governance has been applied in European studies is broader than MLG and may simply be termed 'European Governance'. European Governance refers to the complex, non-hierarchical nature of policy-making, but does not presume this governance to be necessarily multi-level, i.e. to involve the regional, the state and the EU level. A move away from 'old governance', involving top-down steering and control, towards a 'new governance', involving horizontal networking, is identified (Peters, 2000; Hix, 1998), but this does not necessarily mean that hierarchic steering has disappeared from the repertoire of governance strategies.

Both MLG and European Governance approaches distance themselves from intergovernmentalism, which emphasizes the continued dominance of the nation-state in a controlled hierarchical setting (Hix, 1998; Jachtenfuchs, 2001). Scholars applying the concept of governance assume that policy-making in the EU involves a move *beyond* the state, but this does not necessarily mean that policy-making takes place primarily *above* the state, implying that a new state is constructed at a higher institutional level (Jachtenfuchs,

1997: 41). However, governance does imply a move away from national government to a situation in which many actors are involved in pursuing public goals.

Multi-level governance

MLG refers to an evolving policy mode in the EU, in which the state no longer monopolizes EU policy-making (Marks, Hooghe and Blank, 1996). MLG is a model in which decision-making competencies are shared. The Commission devises programmes in partnership with local and regional authorities. Individual state executives lose a significant degree of control over rule enforcement, and sub-national arenas are not restricted to acting only within the limits of the state. The regions act increasingly at the EU level, they have established their own offices in Brussels, and they also pressure the Commission through the European Parliament (Marks, Hooghe and Blank, 1996: 246; Wallace and Wallace, 2000: 32).

The study of MLG involves examining the relationship between sub-national, national and supra-national actors without an a priori assumption that states are the dominant actors (Marks, 1996; Hofhansel, 1999). Many scholars have found the concept of policy networks appropriate for this purpose (Rhodes, Bache and George, 1996; Rhodes, 1997a: 137–62; Hooghe, 1996). A policy network is a set of resource-dependent organizations. The number of members can be large or small, the interaction among members can be frequent or more occasional, power balances can be equal or unequal. The point is, according to these scholars, that much policy-making in the EU can be described by the network concept.

The concern with MLG and multi-level networks arose with the development of EU policies to focus on regulation to involve distributional policy-making (Wallace and Wallace, 2000: 31–2). After the single market began to be pushed forward in the 1980s, discussions about economic inequalities among regions in Europe became commonplace. The term 'cohesion' was used to denote a commitment among European policy-makers to pay attention to economic and social divergence, and to introduce a more planned redistribution of European resources.

The EU cohesion policy is thus the area in which multi-level policy networks are said to be most characteristic. The policy aims at reducing regional and social disparities in the region through the structural funds. In 1988, cohesion policy went through a major reform. Before 1988, there was not much of the policy that was common: it consisted mainly of the Commission writing a cheque to be cashed by individual states, who then decided how to administer it. But after the 1988 reform, in addition to a doubling of budget allocations, a uniform regulatory framework was imposed on different national settings, stressing that the design and implementation of the EU funded programmes should be carried out in close collaboration between regions, states and the EU. Therefore, EU cohesion policy is 'bound to affect territorial relations in member states by empowering sub-national authorities' (Hooghe, 1996: 5). Also, the new rules are found to have promoted the regional level as a new institutional partner for the Commission (Nanetti, 1996), thus giving the sub-national level direct access to the EU. Many regions now have offices in Brussels for lobbying purposes. Thus, in addition to affecting the content of cohesion policy, the reform had the significant effect of changing boundary rules, by widening the circle of policy participants, and decision rules, by introducing horizontal co-decisions (Hooghe, 1996: 12). Hierarchy was repudiated and networking promoted.

European governance

The question is whether multi-level governance is a concept which can be applied to all policy sectors or whether it is unique to cohesion policy. The 'European governance' approach has a broader perception of governance than MLG and examines varying types of governance in the EU. The policy-network approach was developed in relation to public administration and service delivery. Thus, Rod Rhodes (1996: 658) refers directly to 'the term network as describing the several interdependent actors involved in delivering services'. Yet the EU is *not* mainly about welfare and redistribution. The EU is predominantly about *regulating markets* (Sbragia, 2000; Majone, 1992). The EU budget remains tiny in comparison with the budgets of national governments, and it does not significantly affect national legislation in areas such as poverty, family policy, urban policy or old age. On the contrary, 70 per cent of all business administration in the UK is authorized in Brussels (Sbragia: 2000: 225), and EU regulation has gained tremendous importance in 'so many areas of economic and social life, from banking and technical standardization to environmental and consumer protection' (Majone, 1992: 303). In addition, EU regulation, when agreed by the Council, does have primacy over national legislation.

What kind of governance characterizes the regulatory area? Different kinds of regulatory policies exist, and the type of governance and the effectiveness of problem-solving can vary from one area to the other. Fritz Scharpf (1997a), for example, draws attention to the fact that European regulation is most successful in harmonizing product standards. Such agreements can be difficult to reach in intergovernmental bargains, but the Single European Act delegated the task to the Commission, which has committee procedures where national representatives participate. This 'comitology' arrangement greatly facilitated reaching unanimity (ibid.: 528).

In the area of *industrial relations*, a pattern of interest representation may be emerging which does not resemble a horizontal network of many members. National collective bargaining still prevails, and the national institutional frameworks differ greatly. For example, the state does not interfere in British labour relations, while in other countries corporatist bargaining arrangements, involving employers' associations, unions and state representatives, prevail. However, when national boundary control declines as a consequence of the common market, states and unions are no longer capable of shaping the conditions under which the capitalist economy operates (Scharpf, 1996). If national governments in agreement with labour interests decide to create jobs by lowering interest rates, the result is likely to be capital flight rather than job creation. Thus, as national regulatory capacity declines, unions hope to gain more influence at the European level.

Tripartite arrangements resembling corporatism may thus be emerging at the European level (Schmitter, 1996). They are involved in processes of collective bargaining to determine wages, working hours and employment conditions in the EU (European Commission, 2002: 29). Thus, interest representation in the EU does not necessarily take the character of 'new governance', but may be characterized by the hierarchic, non-competitive traits of corporatism (Schmitter, 1974: 93).

EU regulation may thus be as much about 'old' as about 'new' governance, in the sense that there is as much top-down steering as network coordination. Alberta Sbragia (2000) argues that the Union is able to steer, not through the application of force, which characterizes the ultimate instrument available for nation-states to secure compliance, but through the European Court of Justice. The provisions of the Court are supreme in many areas, and therefore the Court actually steers and regulates markets, hierarchies and networks. The Court 'implements the norm of economic liberalization, has access to a wide range of information, and has taken a vow of fiscal (but not regulatory) poverty' (ibid.: 234). Yet the fact that the Court steers in a traditional sense does not preclude the existence of 'new' governance. On the contrary, 'it is clear that policy networks . . . exist in a wide range of policy arenas' (ibid.: 234). The Union typically views these networks as assets rather than as impediments to change, with the Commission actually encouraging the establishment of new networks. This type of governance has been labelled 'policy coordination and benchmarking' because policy coordination among the groups in the Council, specialist committees in the European Parliament and independent experts has served as a mechanism of transition from nationally rooted policy-making to a collective regime (Wallace and Wallace, 2000: 32).

Policy coordination through what the EU calls 'the open method' has been identified as a new type of governance in the EU, particularly in *economic policy* (Hodson and Maher, 2001). The open method of coordination is about consensus-forming among member states, involving a common assessment of the economic situation, agreement of the appropriate policy response, acceptance of peer pressure and, where necessary, adjustment of the policies being pursued. The process of the open method involves a Council Committee (for example, the Economic and Finance Committee) that sets guidelines, establishes performance indicators and benchmarks tailored to each member state, and monitors periodically through peer review, with the emphasis placed on a process of mutual learning. The targets are not legally binding, but they are a result of policy learning and policy transfer between member states. This type of governance thus involves member states in policy areas where there is *no* transfer of power to the EU. Yet it represents a sort of deliberative supra-nationalism, in that inter-administrative governance leads to common ideas among a club of national ministers and key officials (Hodson and Maher, 2001: 740). Hence, network governance in this case can involve *more*, not less government, and policy learning may improve the economic policies of individual member states.

Helen Wallace identifies a particular type of governance, which she terms 'transgovernmental', in policy areas that are normally perceived as being intergovernmental, such as *foreign* and *security policy*. Her point is that even if this type of policy formulation takes place outside the EU institutional framework, it is nevertheless an understatement to call it 'intergovernmental'. The reason is that collaboration among representatives is so close and intense, involving the setting up of special arrangements for managing cooperation, that it is more than just bargaining between individual states. Similarly, Knud Erik Jørgensen (1997) argues that an interpretation of the Common Foreign and Security Policy (CFSP) which focuses exclusively on intergovernmental features is 'grossly misleading', but it is even more mistaken to interpret it as a supra-national affair. Jørgensen argues that, although far from efficient, the CFSP can best be understood as a system of European governance, in that a process of socialization and organizational adaptation has taken place, along with a fusion of world views, in which national policy-makers alter decision-making processes to bring them more into line with a common policy (ibid.: 178).

Finally, in the area of *export control of dual use products* (i.e. products that can be used for productive purposes in industry, but also for destructive purposes in war), Claus

Hofhansel (1999) makes the case for recognizing the EU as a system of multi-level governance (MLG), rather than to use neo-functionalist or intergovernmentalist theories. While the policy decision on control of dual-use exports resembled intergovernmental bargaining, neo-functionalism could better capture the judicial process in the dual-use area. However, rather than argue for one of the two perspectives, MLG, according to Hofhansel, describes a system in which 'the relative weight and influence of actors varies depending on whether we are concerned with policy initiation, legislative decision making, policy implementation, or judicial policy-making' (ibid.: 229).

In sum, there are two ways in which governance has been used in European studies. MLG refers to a particular policy model involving three levels (region, state and EU), and the bargaining networks among them. 'European Governance', more broadly, refers to the steering and coordinating of rules of the game, be they networks, markets or hierarchies. Understood in this latter sense, governance leaves open the character of policy-making in the EU, not all of which is characterized by multi-level networks. The network concept was developed in the context of national policy-making, with a focus on service delivery. But, as we have seen, there are many types of European governance and they vary with each policy sector. Many of the governance types involve network coordination, but this does not necessarily imply a reduced role for national governments. On the contrary, policy coordination can strengthen member states on some counts. European governance is thus much broader than govern*ment*, but it does not take place without governments.

Finally, the governance approach has the virtue of moving European studies beyond the debate about integration as a supra-national or intergovernmental affair. Instead, the governance approach takes our attention to what happens, not only at the intergovernmental conferences where treaties are signed, but during policy implementation and, ultimately, in the everyday lives of European citizens. Instead of asking about the extent of integration (how far has it proceeded?), the governance approach identifies the actors involved in the EU policy process and analyses the impact on national policy-making (what are its consequences?). Hence, the governance approach simply captures an important part of the policy process, which is not seen by the IR debate.

However, in addition to its virtues, some critiques of the governance approach in EU studies can be raised. The first is a neo-realist (intergovernmentalist) critique; the second is a critique more related to democratic theory and is concerned with the emphasis on output efficiency inherent in the governance approach. The neo-realist would not question the existence of networks or the findings that the EU polity affects national policy-making. But the neo-realist would point to the fact that external influences trigger different national responses in Europe, no matter how entrenched the European governments are in formal or informal horizontal networks. Thus, systems of governance and 'fused world views' do not effectively prevent states from reacting differently to issues that are perceived to affect security. An example would be the February 2003 NATO crisis caused by Germany, Belgium and France's refusal to send aid to Turkey, should it be attacked by Iraq in a potential war. The USA, Britain and other NATO members felt it was necessary to use all means to make a credible threat against Iraq in order for it to let UN inspectors detect all its weapons of mass destruction, while the position of Germany and France was to enable the inspections by giving them more resources. The crisis affected the EU because it impeded a common EU stand on the question of a war in Iraq. Most notably, after France and Germany's explicit reluctance, Britain, Italy and Denmark, among others, signed a letter of support for the US policy towards Iraq, thus exacerbating the cleavage in Europe around this issue.[4] Neo-realists would argue that the different reactions to the Iraqi question are predictable, and that these differences recur whenever security issues become pressing. The EU works well in the area of 'low politics', but 'high politics' can easily create divisions within the Union (Hoffman, 1966).

The second critique has to do with power and how the exercise of power is legitimized. The overall concern of scholars studying governance in the EU is with efficiency and, therefore, with the output side of policy. Since the main questions are about the capacity to solve problems, to regulate, to steer and to affect policy-making in the EU, democratic legitimacy becomes less important. Questions of power and rule are almost completely ignored (Jachtenfuchs, 2001: 258). It seems to be implicitly assumed that legitimacy of the EU institutions will increase if policy problems are solved and decisions implemented effectively (Hix, 1998: 51). Although the EU has been efficient in securing outputs, for example, securing food safety or specific common-market policies, this alone does not secure legitimacy. More democratic input procedures need to be established as well. Although the input side has been under-emphasized in the governance literature, it does point to one important feature of democracy in the EU: because politics are exercised at several levels, the 'democratic deficit' of the EU is not solved by democratizing one level only. Hence, the insights provided by governance have important implications for the debate on democracy in the European Union.

Democratizing the EU

In a nation-state, the *demos* have the ultimate authority. Ideally, the *demos* rule through an elected parliament that makes laws to be executed by the government. The EU, however, is not a state. EU directives are agreed upon by member states through majority decisions or through unanimity, or by member states and the European Parliament together. They are executed by the Commission, the member states or the European Court of Justice. EU policy-making is thus more complicated than national policy-making. Governance scholars emphasize that there are many different actors and levels of government involved in EU policy-making. Consequently, it is difficult to identify one power centre and to hold any particular group or person accountable. Governance scholars would thus find it difficult to transfer recipes of democracy prescribed for the nation-state to the EU polity.

However, the fact that power is difficult to localize should not prevent a discussion of democratic accountability. Indeed, the insights from studies of European governance are important to the debate on Europe's democratic deficit, because they imply that democratization efforts should be directed, not just at one level, but simultaneously at many levels.

If the normative principle that individuals should have an opportunity to affect decisions concerning their own lives is accepted (Held, 1987), or merely on the ground that European decision-making institutions need to be legitimated in order to function, it is highly relevant to discuss ways in which democracy could be strengthened in the EU. Many European citizens find the EU to be bureaucratic and distant, and referendums in, for example, France, Denmark and Ireland have shown that a large portion of the citizens are sceptical regarding further integration. A gap between the European political elite that is very much in favour of integration and a sceptical European population can thus be discerned. European leaders are asking what they can do to give the Union project more legitimacy. For example, the decision to introduce EU citizenship, allowing citizens from EU countries to vote in local elections in the EU country in which they reside, should be seen as an attempt to give the EU a more democratic face (Friis, 2001).

In 2003/04, a new intergovernmental conference is taking place at which a possible constitution for Europe is being discussed. A 'convention for the future of Europe', headed by French ex-president Giscard d'Estaing, was set up to debate the content of such a constitution. Naturally, there has been much resistance to the draft constitution. Some find them 'too federal', leaving too little power for the nation-states, while others feel that more powers should be given to supra-national institutions. These opposing views reflect, among other things, different opinions about democracy. At least two models for democratic accountability in Europe exist:

Democratic control through national parliaments: This is a model preferred by the most Euro-sceptic members, such as Britain or Denmark. In this model, majority decisions in the EU should be kept at a minimum in order for national governments to be able to veto decisions in the Council of Ministers. National parliaments can then give mandates to their governments on how to vote in the council, and, in that way, citizens in member states can retain some control over the decision-making process. The problem with the model is, of course, that the issues the EU deals with (market regulation, environmental, etc.) are of such a nature that they can no longer be solved at the nation-state level. And the most efficient way to solve these problems is by introducing majority decisions. Since majority decision-making is already a fact, how do parliaments claim control? How does a parliament react when a veto, which it has mandated its government to enact, gets overruled? In addition, it is probably not feasible for parliaments to keep track of hundreds of directives decided in the EU when they are also occupied with national legislation. So, although a national parliament is certainly a crucial instrument of democratic control, it cannot remain the only instrument.

Democratic control through federal institutions: This model finds the solution to the democratic deficit in reconstituting representative institutions at the EU level (Goodman, 1997). It sketches an EU model under which EU institutions, not those of the member states, would be the primary units of democracy, and with a two-chamber EU parliament: one chamber with representatives from member governments, which would replace the Council of Ministers; and one chamber which is directly representative of the European people. There could be a directly elected chairman of the Commission, and the Commission would be appointed by the chairman and approved by parliament. There would be pan-European parties that selected candidates for parliamentary elections, and European-wide elections could be held. The model is clearly attractive in that it strengthens control of decisions taken at the EU level. However, it seems to have two flaws. One is that it involves greater centralization at a time when citizens are strongly opposed to the distant and bureaucratic nature of the EU. More centralization would in itself probably not serve to legitimize the EU. Second, the insights from governance scholars that politics and policy-making take place at many levels are ignored in an entirely federal model. While it is certainly desirable to democratize EU institutions, this is only one measure towards democratizing all levels of European governance.

The two models of democracy in the EU can be criticized on the grounds that they address democracy at only one level; hence the insights from governance theory are not adequately taken into account. A *cosmopolitan* model of democracy has been suggested as a way to democratize the European Union that would more effectively target several levels (Held, 1993; Held, 1998; Goodman, 1997; Linklater, 1998; McGrew, 2002). Cosmopolitan democracy addresses the implications of the 'fact that nation-states are enmeshed today in complex interconnected relations' (Held, 1998: 24). Principles of cosmopolitan democracy build upon three core features: i) democracy inside nations; ii) democracy among nations; and iii) global democracy. Transferred to the EU, this implies that democracy should be strengthened at all levels, including the regional level. It does not imply a 'Europe of the regions', in which only the sub- and the supra-national levels have power while the national level is bypassed. In the cosmopolitan model, 'strengthened institutions at one "level" does not imply weakened institutions at other levels; on the contrary, the overall "quantity" of democracy rises as democratic accountability increases across the various levels' (Goodman, 1997: 183). James Goodman (1997: 184–94) argues that the pan-European parliament, as well as national assemblies, sub-state authorities and pan-European social movements, are all potential vehicles for EU cosmopolitan democracy because they are all oriented towards pan-European agendas. For example, environmental movements have contributed to an increasing amount of EU directives addressing environmental issues, and even to institutional initiatives such as the establishment of the European Environmental Protection Agency.

In sum, different models of democratizing the European Union exist. Since democratic theory is basically normative, this is how it should be, and a continued and strengthened debate between various visions of democracy in Europe is desirable. However, it is possible to get a little closer to a European model of democracy than the ones sketched above. With some help from the long-standing democratic theorist, Robert A. Dahl, one can ask about the criteria for a truly democratic process. Dahl (1989: 109–20) sets up five ideal criteria:

- *Effective participation*: citizens should have adequate and equal opportunity to express their preferences throughout the process of making binding decisions.
- *Enlightened understanding*: citizens should have an opportunity to validate the choice on the matter to be decided. This implies the existence of a free public discourse between the members of a society.
- *Control of the agenda*: the members of the community are the ones who have the exclusive opportunity to decide how matters are to be placed on the agenda.
- *Voting equality at the decisive stage*: the interests of the members of the community should be considered equally at the decision stage (no one individual should have more weight than others).
- *Members of the association*: the *demos* should include all adults subject to the binding collective decisions of the association.

All these are relevant to the debate on democratizing the EU, but the last point, the 'categorical principle', is of particular relevance here as it addresses the problem of inclusion: who should be included in the *demos*? According to Dahl's categorical principle, all those who are bound by the decisions are members. He modifies the principle by exempting children, transients and mentally handicapped persons (ibid.: 129). However, with regard to the EU, citizens are primarily members of their own national political communities, but they are also EU citizens. If they move to another European country, they immediately acquire the right to vote in the municipal elections of that country. Inhabitants in the European Union are clearly bound and regulated by EU decisions as much as by the decisions taken by their own governments. So, if we were to follow Dahl's fifth criteria, EU citizens should have the opportunity to enjoy the other four criteria of participation, agenda-setting, enlightenment and equality. The extent to which they do so is highly questionable. In particular, free public discourse is lacking in a European space with fifteen national public spheres and significant language barriers. The principle of enlightened understanding is most probably not met. In addition, participation is limited to election for the EU parliament, which has limited powers. More effective participation would require, for example, more European-wide social movements or perhaps European-wide referendums. Similarly, it is also debatable whether all interests are considered equally or all have access to the European political agenda.

The democratic problems can be addressed partly through the measures suggested by cosmopolitan democracy, the most important of which would be to strengthen the EU parliament while simultaneously strengthening the influence of national parliaments on EU decisions. However, in order to promote a free public pan-European debate, initiatives beyond the establishment of European social movements would arguably be necessary. Social movements are for people who have the resources to get involved, and they do not guarantee an encompassing debate. More deliberation in a wide range of forums, across nations and language barriers, would have to be promoted. The debate regarding a possible constitution at the Convention on Europe's future is an opportunity to strengthen a pan-European discourse. A number of initiatives of a deliberative nature have been taken which could contribute to more cross-national deliberation in Europe. One such measure was the Youth 2002 meeting, which was held in June 2002 on the initiative of a number of Danish high schools and a Danish news think-tank.[5] The purpose of the youth meeting was to draft a constitution for the EU, with 1,000 young people from all over Europe participating. The meeting was preceded by a nine-week web dialogue – a virtual EU parliament – and the event itself consisted of two weeks of courses and debate. Finally, the draft constitution was presented to the EU presidency, as well as to the 'real' convention headed by d'Estaing; it was also translated into twenty-five languages and sent to 30,000 organizations and decision-makers.

Setting up deliberative forums at the European level does not imply weakening *national* publics, but rather an additional strengthening of a European public sphere. In this sense, European governance is not only about managing markets, hierarchies and networks, but also about *political* rules of the game: about setting the rules so they can allow equal access to decision-making and thereby inject much needed legitimacy into the European political order.[6]

Conclusion: governance in the EU

Research on the European Community, and later Union, was initially undertaken mostly by international relations scholars. Hence, European integration was seen as something to be explained, and the debate centred on whether integration was driven by nation-states guarding their sovereignty, or whether it was driven by underlying economic and technological developments that necessitated supra-national political cooperation.

Students of public policy, however, became interested in studying the EU *as a polity*. Rather than explain integration, they wanted to examine EU policy-making and its effects on national policy-making. Hence, governance came to denote the management of complex policy-making structures at all levels in the EU, be they hierarchies, markets or networks. Using governance as an analytical framework in European studies does not entail that national policy-making is ignored. Rather, governance focuses on the formal and informal institutions that frame decision-making: and these institutions can allow national, as well as sub-national or supra-national, influence by the actors. Using governance should not entail ignoring questions of rule and power; rather, it should mean identifying who affects the rules about access to power, and how. The points made by students of European governance are helpful to the debate on democracy in the EU because they imply democratization at many levels. Thus, governance in the EU refers to rules guiding the entire EU policy process; it is about looking at boundary rules – who has access to policy decisions, alongside rules regarding the actors that are involved in policy implementation.

5
Governance in Comparative Politics I: The State and Economic Development

Argentina and Australia were at the same level of development and among the richest countries in the world in the 1920s. Yet, by 1977, Australia was nearly five times richer than Argentina. The East Asian tigers successfully pursued interventionist economic policies, but the same strategy failed in many Latin American countries. Botswana has enjoyed annual growth rates of over 10 per cent of GDP, while practically all other African countries have found themselves in permanent economic crisis. And Germany's economy boomed after the Second World War, while Britain's declined.

What can explain these differences? The answers, claim an increasing number of studies, are to be found in the character of state and politics. The successful countries do not have the same kinds of political regime. Some of them have been authoritarian, others democracies. What they do have in common are fairly strong states with ability to direct development initiatives, and a particular kind of state–society relation that is conducive to economic development.

This chapter outlines approaches to the role of the state in economic development and describes how they have used the concept of governance. The chapter starts by briefly sketching the society-centred approaches dominant from the period after the Second World War until the mid-1980s. It then outlines 'bringing the state back in' approaches that entered the stage during the 1980s and 1990s. Very few of these were entirely state-centred. The debate quickly came to circle around which type of state–society interaction would best promote economic development and which type of institutions would most encourage innovation and investment. Governance was brought into the debate with reference to the way in which institutions spanning the state–society divide were set up. The role of the state in economic development should not be restricted to being merely an enabling environment for the market, nor should the economy be entirely planned. Rather, the role of networks including public and private actors should be emphasized.

The chapter gives an example of this by looking at how the developmental state of East Asia was theorized. By drawing upon evidence from these states, it was argued that good governance was far from the neo-liberal image of good governance applied by the World Bank or Western bilateral donors. It did not denote a minimalist state. On the contrary, governance referred to more state-directed efforts to include societal actors in common efforts to promote economic development. Studies of successful governance enabled scholars to demonstrate the benefits of a regulating role in development for the state and state–society networks. Further, they ignited a debate about whether such governance models could be transferred to weak states in the developing world.

Societal approaches to the state

In the pre-Second World War era, political scientists were primarily concerned with studying and comparing the formal, legal institutions of political systems, not the features of the societies in which the constitutions worked. Around the turn of the twentieth century, some studies, most notably Woodrow Wilson's *Congressional Government*, attempted to broaden the focus by studying the constitution in operation – how it works in reality – by including political parties, and later also pressure groups, in the analysis, but the analytical focus remained on the formal institutions of the state.

After the Second World War, attention shifted away from formal state institutions to the behaviour of individuals and groups in society (Rasmussen, 1971: 53–62). Behavioralists were not at all keen on the concept of state; they preferred the concept of political system. David Easton, for example, introduced his systems analysis as a way to move beyond state institutions and instead study political behaviour (Easton, 1965: 79). The focus was on 'inputs' to the political system, such as demands from different interest groups, and on the 'outputs' of the political system in the form of public policy. What happened in the process of transforming inputs to outputs was not an object of inquiry. The state was considered a neutral arbiter of a plurality of societal interests, and it was not considered to generate interests of its own. For example, Robert Dahl's (1961) *pluralist* study of politics in New Haven concluded that there was not one strong interest group with power, but that a plurality of interests existed. The mayor in New Haven took all these existing preferences into consideration when deciding on a particular policy (ibid.: 214). Thus, the mayor's 'strong individual initiatives for urban renewal were extensively documented but not grounded in any overall state-centered analysis of the potential for certain kinds of mayors to make new uses of federal funding' (Evans, Rueschemeyer and Skocpol, 1985: 4). In other words, the mayor's interests were not considered to be institutionally derived.

Structural-functionalist scholars were not occupied with state features but focused on identifying the main functions of political systems. The most important functions mentioned by structural-functionalists are political socialization, interest articulation, interest aggregation, policy-making and policy implementation. Inputs from the environment are aggregated and transformed to outputs (Almond et al., 2000). If the system fails to perform these functions it is likely to collapse in the long term. The existence of the political system is, so to speak, explained by the functions it performs. But the nature of the state is seldom in focus as a separate object of study, and the concept of state itself is rarely used.

Marxist approaches did not concur with pluralist or structural-functionalist approaches that the state was a neutral arbiter of a plurality of interests. On the contrary, the main point of Marxist scholars was that the state represented one strong interest group: the bourgeoisie. The state was thus unable to take initiatives that would be against the preferences of the capitalist class. Some neo-Marxist studies introduced the concept of 'relative autonomy' to refer to the ability of states to act autonomously. Thus, different capitalist states may pursue different economic policies depending on the relative strength of social classes. However, according to Skocpol, neo-Marxist writers remain founded in 'society-centered assumptions, not allowing themselves to doubt that, at base, states are inherently shaped by classes or class struggles and function to preserve and expand modes of production' (Evans, Rueschemeyer and Skocpol, 1985: 5).

Neo-Marxist scholars considered the role of the state in economic development to be roughly in line with the interests of the bourgeoisie, while pluralist scholars tend to see the state as more of a neutral arbiter between competing interests. Society-centred scholars, be they Marxist or pluralist, were criticized for ignoring the many cases in which states have been observed to act autonomously against dominant interests in society. In particular, society-centred analyses failed to account for the numerous instances of state intervention that went beyond the narrow roles they had prescribed to the state.

Bringing the state back in

Since the mid-1980s, a return to the state has been prominent in political science (Barkey and Parikh, 1991). Whereas society-centred theories had been of a Marxist, pluralist or structural-functionalist slant, these neo-statist studies adopt a Weberian approach. State-centred analyses conceptualize the state as an actor able to formulate independent goals and to shape societal outcomes. In this way, they see state institutions as independent explanatory variables in societal change.

Neo-statist scholars thus maintain that states have autonomy: the state is not merely a reflection of the most dominant societal groups; on the contrary, 'states conceived as organizations claiming control over territories and people may formulate and pursue goals that are not simply reflective of the demands or interests of social groups, classes, or society' (Evans, Rueschemeyer and Skocpol, 1985: 9). Changes in public policy should not be explained merely by a change in the relative power of societal pressure groups, for instance, but could as well be a result of the influence of interests generated within the state. For example, the change of policy paradigm from a Keynesian to a monetarist ideology in Britain around 1980 has been explained as a result of policy networks of public officials, politicians, journalists and researchers adopting the monetarist prescription for improving the economy (Wolfe, 1991; Hall, 1993). Although the degree of autonomy varies with the character of networks, the change to monetarism nonetheless took place in spite of massive resistance from trade unions and other influential groups.

States' *autonomy* often derives from their *capacity*, according to neo-statist scholars. Capacity is the ability to formulate and implement policies, and it increases with increasing differentiation and specialization. Capacity requires an efficient bureaucratic organization that has Weberian characteristics, such as corporate cohesion of the organization, differentiation and insulation from its social environment, unambiguous location of decision-making and channels of authority, and internal features of merit recruitment and merit promotion (Evans, Rueschemeyer and Skocpol, 1985: 50). An efficient bureaucracy, according to Max Weber, could not be dominated by private interests as in patrimonial societies, where the state is ruled as if it were the ruler's private domain (Weber, 1978).

The state's autonomy also derives from its centralization and territorial boundedness. Michael Mann (1988: 29) argues that 'societies need some of their activities to be regulated over a centralized territory. So do dominant economic classes, churches and other ideological power movements, and military elites. They, therefore, entrust power resources to state elites which they are incapable of fully recovering, precisely because their own socio-spatial basis of organization is not centralized and territorial.' Hence, the autonomy of the state derives from the fact that it alone meets external threats to domestic order. Inter-state warfare has, in the case of European states, been a major driving force in development of state autonomy and capacity; war created an impetus for the state elite to generate domestic revenue, to strengthen state administration and to promote domestic production. In particular, the state pursued and supported the development of weapons technology and production, and thereby indirectly generated further industrial development (Giddens, 1985). The impetus to build efficient state apparatuses is thus seen to derive from war: conquest means that state actors expand their administration over new territories. And preparation for war leads to efforts to increase resource extraction. As a by-product of preparations for war, rulers initiated activities and organizations that eventually resulted in the materialization of modern bureaucracy: courts, treasuries, tax systems, regional administration and public assemblies (Tilly, 1990: 75). Thus, the capacity and autonomy of the state is a consequence of historically/geo-politically formed elite orientations (Weiss, 1998: 44).

Models of economic governance

Neo-statist scholars argue that a market economy cannot be entirely self-regulating; it needs some intervention from the state. For instance, anti-trust laws are necessary to prevent large monopolies from blocking the market mechanism. This was pointed out as early as 1944 by Karl Polanyi in his famous *The Great Transformation* (Polanyi, 1944, repr. 1957: particularly pp. 135–51). Polanyi's work was a critique of the *economic liberalist* model of governance, which spread from Britain to much of the Western world during the nineteenth century.

The basic idea in the liberalist model was that markets, through prices, would be able to allocate goods, labour and land efficiently. The 'invisible hand' of the market would ensure equilibrium and increase the wealth of societies. However, as Polanyi showed, laissez-faire proved to be insufficient, and markets needed to be sustained by state regulation. In addition to trade union laws and anti-trust legislation, states also provide public goods that will be under-supplied under market conditions. Public goods are defined by two features: (i) if the good is provided for one individual, it cannot be withheld from anybody else's consumption; and (ii) one individual's use of the public good does not detract from anybody else's use. National defence, or clean air, are public goods. Public goods will not be provided in a market because there is an incentive to free ride: people will not pay for them when they know others can enjoy them without having paid. States may additionally play a role in the case of externalities, which occur when an economic activity produces costs that are not borne by any of the parties in that activity. An example could be pollution caused by a factory's emission. States can regulate so as to diminish externalities.

Neo-statist scholars argue that state autonomy may be important for capital accumulation. Providing property rights and public goods is frequently not sufficient to maintain a growth momentum. Left to private actors, capital accumulation may stagnate as oligarchs prefer to maintain the status quo (Rueschemeyer and Evans, 1985: 45). These oligarchs may prefer to stick to their own sector, which they consider safe, rather than direct surplus capital to new areas. Thus state initiatives that are not necessarily in line with the dominant economic interests of society may be needed to promote entrepreneurship. In addition, innovation and new technologies may not occur if left to the market because large capital injections for research and development are required. The state may be the only actor able to produce such capital.

The second model of economic governance was the *Keynesian* model, which was dominant for most of the twentieth century. In part it was based on the mentioned arguments regarding the need for regulation, but it also emerged as a remedy to the great depression of the 1930s. The model was based upon the ideas of the British economist John Maynard Keynes, which were basically that the government could alleviate economic crises by expanding fiscal expenditure and thereby re-establish a growth momentum. During the 1930s and 1940s, a number of Western governments successfully pursued Keynesian policies. President Roosevelt, for example, used expansionary fiscal policies to improve conditions for business and agriculture and to reduce unemployment. He also introduced relief to the unemployed and measures to avoid social marginalization and impoverishment.

In the Western countries, over two decades of growth and prosperity following the end of the Second World War confirmed the idea that the state could alleviate crises, ensure near full employment and welfare. However, two oil crises during the 1970s and 1980s, and a period of economic recession with runaway inflation and rising unemployment, marked the crisis of the Keynesian welfare state. Increased government spending was no longer enough to ameliorate crisis. The collapse of the Soviet Union and its planned economy further revealed that 'state failure' could be even more detrimental to economic growth than 'market failure'. Hence a new period set in from the 1980s, which was dominated by a third model of economic governance: the *neo-liberal doctrine* of minimizing the state. This model was based on monetarist ideas that government should give priority to controlling inflation, deregulating the private sector, and reducing public spending and taxation.[1] The model particularly aimed at reducing the role of corporatist arrangements, in which wage-bargaining was centrally managed, although this did not happen everywhere. Hence, the dominance of the neo-liberal doctrine has not eliminated the existence of more intervening states. Coordinated capitalism is still characteristic of many political economies, for example, those of Austria, Germany or Scandinavia (Hall and Soskice, 2001), and the overall degree of coordination is larger than a century ago in all countries, including the Anglo-American ones.

To some extent, the neo-liberal model apparently revived the British and American economies (Gamble, 2000); however, it has also been proved to fail in some aspects (Jessop, 1998, 2002b). The old sources of market failure in the liberal model still appeared. Privatization programmes and processes of rolling back the state needed steering, and calls for regulation re-emerged. For example, dismantling the Soviet state did not automatically lead to a well-functioning market economy. Corruption and mafia-like behaviour penetrated privatization programmes, and party posses or other influential persons obtained ownership of former state assets. The

Russian experience demonstrated that markets need state regulation. In addition, the free movement of financial capital across borders proved to be a destabilizing force to such an extent that calls for regulation, for example through a tax on currency trades, have become more frequent.[2] Market strategies did not solve all the problems of economic governance.

The debate between liberalists and 'statists' seemed to become somewhat locked as neither state nor market solutions proved optimal. Additionally, a sharp distinction between the public and the private sectors was upheld in the debate: for economic liberals, the solution for state failure is more market, while proponents for state intervention see the solution for market failure to be more state. A zero-sum perception seemed to prevail, in which more state meant less market and vice versa. However, the move to a post-industrial society involved the emergence of other types of governance, relying more on networks and on horizontal dialogue between individuals on both sides of the public–private divide. Governance theorists thus reject the sharp dichotomies in the market or state approaches. Bob Jessop (2002b: 224–30), for example, identifies a third way between market anarchy and state imperative coordination as 'heterarchy', 'which comprises horizontal self-organization among mutually interdependent actors' (ibid.: 228). Heterarchic governance has become widespread in post-industrial society, which is more complex and more specialized than industrial society. Hence, networking, negotiation and partnerships are part of modern economic strategies.

Heterarchy, however, has its own sources of failure (Jessop, 1998, 2002b). Since the point with heterarchic governance is that 'goals will be modified in and through ongoing negotiation and reflection', failure may occur when goals are not successfully redefined and if consensus is not found. Moreover, the basic conflicts of interests inherent in capitalist society do not disappear with the rise of self-organizing networks (Jessop, 2002b). Systems of heterarchy may not in all cases provide the best mechanisms through which to resolve conflicts, since they do not have the legitimate authority of the democratic nation-state, which emerged with the exact purpose of arbitrating between conflicting interests (Hirst, 2000). There are thus grounds to argue that an important role for the state remains: that of setting the rules of overall coordination among a plurality of organizational forms. This is what governance is about. Heterarchic governance refers to the self-regulating networks, but, in general, governance is about overall coordination.

To sum up, there have been three main models of economic governance during the last three centuries: the economic liberal, the Keynesian and the neo-liberal. The debate about models often assumed a dichotomy between the state and the market, but, with increasing complexity of economy and society, networks have achieved more attention and blurred the distinction between state and market, or between public and private. Economic governance is about setting rules that induce economic actors to cooperate more effectively with each other, and that support the implementation of economic policy. In Andrew Gamble's (2000) words, it is about setting an economic constitution, i.e. the rules, constraints and norms which economic agents accept as binding upon them. Economic governance is not prescribed to a particular setting, for example the nation-state, because many actors take part in it. However, the state has an important role in coordinating a plurality of institutional arrangements in economic policy-making.

Since socio-political institutional settings differ across countries, the economic constitution must vary accordingly. A particular economic policy may fail in one institutional setting but succeed in another. For example, a policy to upgrade skills through vocational training, relying on co-ordination between many firms and workers' unions, may fail in an institutional setting that relies on market forces, such as the UK, where there are few inter-firm networks to draw upon. On the contrary, such a policy may succeed in a more coordinated economy (Hall and Soskice, 2001: 45–7).

The debate about how the *type* of governance may vary with the *object* of governance is particularly relevant to the discussion about how the least developed countries in the world should achieve economic growth. This discussion has also theorized about networks and governance across the public–private divide.

The developmental state

During the 1950s and 1960s development theory had been dominated by the 'structuralist' school, which claimed that the state had a large role to play in promoting growth in less developed countries. In the 1980s, with the rise of the neo-liberal paradigm, this school was attacked on three counts: (i) extensive state intervention to promote import-substituting industrialization had generated inefficient industries, requiring permanent subsidies to survive; (ii) extensive government intervention tended to generate rent-seeking and corruption; and (iii) empirical evidence showed extraordinary growth rates for countries that had used an outward-oriented model driven by market incentives and a strong private sector, particularly from four East Asian countries – Taiwan, South Korea, Hong Kong, and Singapore (Onis, 1991).

East Asian countries had experienced a remarkable economic boom during the 1960s and 1970s, clearly overtaking other developing regions (World Bank, 1993). Neo-liberals interpreted the boom as a result of *un*guided markets, assuming that exports expanded because prices were undistorted by government measures (Weiss and Hobson, 1995: 139–40). However, a number of studies revealed that the East Asian successes were not ungoverned. On the contrary, the studies documented that synergetic interaction between state and economic agents had led to economic growth. They saw markets and exports as essential elements of growth, but did not take this to imply that state intervention should be kept at a minimum. They thus refused to be put in either the structuralist state-centred box or the neo-liberal society-centred box.

Chalmers Johnson (1982) was the first to introduce the concept of the developmental state in his classic study of Japanese industrial policy. Defining development in terms of growth, productivity and competitiveness, he argues that the developmental state has an overriding goal of achieving national economic development (rather than merely advancing capitalist interests). The developmental state is devoted to the free market and to export-led growth; however, it guides the market by the hands of a small elite economic bureaucracy recruited from the best managerial talent available.

Japanese academics called the model 'state monopoly capitalism'. By this, they meant the activities of the state to supply capital or other funds to industry on terms not available in the private sector and for specific, state-determined policy objectives (ibid.: 211). Johnson emphasizes that a developmental state has a pilot agency, a driving force in the economic bureaucracy, such as the Japanese MITI (Ministry of International Trade and Industry), that can formulate and implement policy. Crucially, this agency does not act without being informed of what goes on in different industries. On the contrary, close institutionalized links are established between the elite bureaucracy and private business for consultation and cooperation (Johnson, 1982; Onis, 1991).

Subsequent studies found economic institutions similar to Japan's in South Korea and Taiwan (Amsden, 1989; Wade, 1990, 1993). Wade (1993) finds that Taiwan has departed significantly from a free-trade regime. Taiwan supported some industries more than others through tariff rebates on imports of capital equipment and it also used quantitative restrictions, such as import quotas, extensively. Central to Taiwan's and Korea's success, according to Amsden and Wade, is the establishment of an incentive system that links public support to performance standards. Subsidies, or other support measures, are not just handed out but are given only if certain output targets are met. Such performance-oriented policy, note Weiss and Hobson (1995: 151), is very different from the 'hand-out character of the subsidies that have typified so much of European and Anglo-American assistance for industry'. Britain's industrial decline, they argue, is to a large part a consequence of a lack of the coordination capacity that has characterized Asia. Another prominent feature of East Asian industrial and trade policy has been its selectivity – targeting specifically chosen industrial sectors. The countries did not stay in the areas considered to be their comparative advantage due to cheap labor, but directed support to such sectors as ship-building, state-sponsored development of industrial electronics, synthetic fibres and machine tools. Thus, in 1983, Korea's output in the field of tanker construction was five times larger than Sweden's, a country whose output was 230 times that of South Korea only ten years earlier (Woo, 1991; Amsden, 1989; Weiss and Hobson,

1995). The coordinated economies in East Asia, then, have not been similar to the Western Keynesian welfare states. In East Asia, state intervention was more performance-oriented and targeted than in Western countries.

Specifying state–society interaction: embedded autonomy and governed interdependence

The puzzle for a political scientist in relation to these findings is why such large degrees of state economic management did not lead to corruption and self-seeking by state officials (Wade, 1993). In other countries where the same policies had been pursued (import-substitution, import quotas, tariffs), misuse and waste had frequently been the result. Import licences were handed out to political supporters or to relatives of public officials without any regard to economic performance. The bureaucracy became dominated by political imperatives, penetrated by particularistic interests or dominated by local strongmen (Bates, 1981; Migdal, 1988).

The reason why this did not happen in East Asia should, according to Peter Evans (1995), be found in the bureaucracy's 'Weberianness'. Japan's MITI, for example, was a very prestigious place to be employed. It attracted top graduates from top universities, and its officials had the 'special status that Weber felt was essential to a true bureaucracy' (Evans, 1995: 49). These officials followed long-term career paths, and pursuing and fulfilling the goals of the organization would in general mean maximizing individual interests as well, since this would mean improving career opportunities.

However, in addition to the Weberian characteristics, the Japanese bureaucracy was also characterized by the existence of numerous informal networks, both *internal* and *external* to the organization. Ties among classmates from elite universities were emphasized by Johnson (1982) to be central to the organization's internal coherence, a coherence that meritocracy alone could not provide. Internal networks reinforce 'Weberianism' in a way that increases overall efficiency.

External networks connecting the state and civil society were found to be at least as important as internal networks. Evans (ibid.: 49) found Japanese industrial policy to depend on a 'maze of ties' between industrialists and ministries. For example, 'deliberation councils' join bureaucrats and business people in rounds of data-gathering and policy formation regarding a series of issues. Bureaucratic coherence and external networks are not mutually contradictive; on the contrary, 'internal bureaucratic coherence should be seen as an essential precondition for the state's effective participation in external networks' (Evans, 1995: 50). This is essentially what Evans's concept of 'embedded autonomy' is about: a developmental state not only needs to be able to intervene authoritatively in the economy, above particular interests, i.e. to be autonomous, but to coordinate with societal actors. 'A state that was only autonomous would lack both sources of intelligence and the ability to rely on decentralized private implementation' (ibid.: 12). On the contrary, states that are overly embedded in society and lack autonomy fall prey to individual incumbents' pursuance of their own goals. However, embeddedness is needed because ties with society provide information and facilitate implementation. Hence, 'only when embeddedness and autonomy are joined together can the state be called developmental' (ibid.: 12).

The concept 'embedded autonomy' does not go very far in theorizing the particular kinds of interaction among state–society actors that promote industrial development. By introducing the notion of 'governed interdependence' (GI), however, Linda Weiss further examines these linkages. GI refers to a distinctive kind of institutionalized linkage between state and society that does not focus solely on the 'strength' or 'embeddedness' of a state, but rather on how states share power with society: 'in a system of GI, as described for Japan and the NICs, the question of "who initiates" loses much of its meaning and importance. Both the state and industry can and do take policy initiatives, but this takes place within a negotiated relationship in which the state retains a guiding role, exercising leadership either directly or by delegation to industry' (ibid.: 71).

There can be several forms of governed interdependence. Setting performance-targets and supporting selective industries are examples that were mentioned above. Weiss, however, adds a third form of governed interdependence called private sector governance. This is about 'teasing out of economic society the capacity for self-governance' (1998: 76). Private sector governance can be seen as a kind of delegated industrial policy-making which, according to Weiss, is particularly well developed in Germany but may also be found in Japan. For example, the printed circuit board industry in Japan has, through delegation from MITI, assumed responsibility for framing and administering public programmes which specify detailed targets to be reached by the industry, such as those for technology upgrading (ibid.: 76). Another example was Taiwan's textile industry, which had been in decline when the industry itself proposed a strategy based on more design-intensive production to increase value-added. The government supported the initiative, which proved to be successful.

Finally, the fourth form of GI may be public–private innovation alliances that are a form of coordination associated with policies for acquiring, developing, upgrading and diffusing technology. For example, in Taiwan, special 'technology alliances' have proliferated; they constitute a network which is state-led and supported, but to which each joining company contributes resources such as capital and senior engineer support. The networks then develop new products in areas such as high-definition TV or Power PC-based computers (ibid.: 78). In sum, these public–private networks are institutionalized in a sense not discussed by Peter Evans. The essence is that in systems of GI, the question of 'who pushes whom around', state or society, is irrelevant, since it is a win–win situation that in the end is beneficial to both state and society.

In sum, the concepts of embedded autonomy and governed interdependence go beyond the confines of the state–society dichotomy, by introducing the crucial roles of public–private partnerships, state-induced self-governance and para-public policy networks in economic policy-making. However, the developmental state model they are illustrating tends to highlight this 'heterarchic' kind of economic governance as the optimum solution to economic performance. There is an implicit assumption that wherever you find successful industrial growth, you will find embedded autonomy or governed interdependence. Yet there are several ways to achieve growth. In the Western world, both liberal economies and coordinated economies have had high growth rates, but in different ways and through different institutional mechanisms (Hall and Soskice, 2001). Hence, it seems that effective economic governance involves a careful evaluation of the particular institutional setting to which it is applied. This point is especially relevant to the debate about the way donors attempt to apply 'good governance' to developing countries. Neo-statist theorists thus draw upon the East Asian experience when criticizing the neo-liberal assumptions of the international financial institutions. They do not believe the neo-liberal model to be optimal. They also criticize neo-liberals for recommending complete trade liberalization when, at the same time, the developed economies have followed quite protectionist policies while they were developing into advanced industrialist economies (Chang, 2003). The question is, however, whether the developmental model can be transferred to another institutional setting.

'Good governance' in the development community

In development studies there has been a critique of the donor community for imposing neo-liberal models of governance on the developing world. The argument is that the donors' concept of governance is ideological and based on 'the currently dominant Anglo-American/liberal/pluralist sociopolitical doctrine' (Moore, 1993: 41; see also Moore, 1995). The World Bank's governance concept, for example, is not based on an empirical study of the type of governance that has actually worked in promoting development, argues Mick Moore: such an empirical assessment would force recognition of the factors that have promoted economic development in East Asia.

Good governance was introduced on the agenda by the World Bank (1989) because it needed to explain why a number of countries failed to develop, in spite of the fact that they had adopted the neo-liberal adjustment policies imposed on them by the International Monetary Fund and the World Bank. The answer was 'bad governance', understood as self-serving public officials and corruption in the public service (ibid.: 60). Thus, the recipe for the developing countries was to increase transparency and accountability in the public sector. The overall model to be 'transferred' was one of expenditure reduction, privatization and public service reform, i.e. not only less, but also better government. During the 1990s, the bilateral donors also put increasing pressure on recipient governments to hold democratic elections. Hence, the model of good governance promoted by the donors and international financial institutions was built upon the Anglo-American liberal-democratic states.

The key notion of accountability inherent in this governance model was one of *outward* accountability: the governments' responsibility towards parliaments and citizens. However, this notion of accountability can be criticized. Hilton Root (1996), for example, points at other important kinds of accountability such as fiscal accountability, i.e. responsibility for the management of public funds; or programme accountability, i.e. responsibility for carrying out a programme; or outcome accountability, i.e. responsibility for results (Root, 1996: 45; see also Day and Klein, 1987; and chapter 1). Root argues that the East Asian states may have been undemocratic, but they rank high on these other kinds of accountabilities, that may be termed *internal* or hierarchic accountabilities. They also rank high on criteria such as transparency and predictability of the public sector.

Such features can characterize states even when they are not democratic in the Western liberal sense. In fact, 'regime type does not provide a clue' as to why some countries develop and others do not (Root, 1996: 170). The ability to formulate and implement economic policies in an effective and accountable manner matters more. To ensure more efficient outputs, donors should support measures aimed at strengthening those policy-making abilities. In addition, the East Asian experience offers ground to argue that the neo-liberal economic policies supported by the financial institutions may not be the best available. When tying loans to such policy conditions as retrenchment of public employees, they should give careful consideration to how this may affect the ability to formulate and implement policies effectively.

In sum, the East Asian experience calls into question the way donors use the concept of governance. It questions whether democracy is a necessary precondition for a developmental state, and it also raises doubts about whether the IMF strategy of minimizing the state through privatization and expenditure cuts is always such a good idea.[3] However, the question is whether the East Asian model of governance can be transferred to other settings where state-led development was tried without success. In other words, can a unique best model of good governance be identified or does the type of economic governance vary with the object of governance?

Governance in weak states: can the developmental state model be transferred?

Governance in weak states is often an uphill task. Economic governance in these states is about managing institutions that have often developed in such a way that they constitute obstacles to development, and they may be difficult to change for state and societal actors. In other words, the object of governance in weak states is very different from that of the developed economies.

In this final section, we will first outline the institutional conditions of governance in weak states and explain why reform is difficult. Then we shall see that although reform is difficult, it is not impossible and, even in weak states, we find successful cases of governance. These cases are not identical to the East Asian model, although they share core features. The conclusion is that 'good' governance is possible even under adverse conditions.

The concept of weak states refers to the states in parts of Africa and South Asia that lack the ability to provide political goods to their populations (Jackson and Rosberg, 1982). Political goods are basic conditions that are necessary to enable citizens to go about their daily lives: peace, security, and law and order. Rarely are weak states able to provide social or economic goods such as development and welfare. Weak states often have autonomy, i.e. the state elite can take whatever policy decision it likes, but they lack the ability to implement the policy and make a difference to society.

Weak states lack the development-oriented political elite and the pilot agencies that were found to be crucial to development in East Asia. This is because they have different historical/geo-political backgrounds. Weak states are often ex-colonies. They did not emerge out of inter-state warfare, as in Europe, but were handed sovereignty by the United Nations after the Second World War. While European states would have to possess basic qualities of statehood, such as national self-defence, the only criterion for recognition of the new states was that they had been under colonial administration. Thus, they had juridical sovereignty in the form of recognition from international society, but they lacked positive features of statehood (Jackson, 1990). The elite felt no urge to promote national development because there was no need to strengthen the state when sovereignty had been served to them on a silver plate. The political elites were often in charge of vast territories with impenetrable rainforest and low population density. The costs of broadcasting power under such circumstances were extremely high (Herbst, 2000), which provided an additional disincentive to state consolidation.

Third, weak states often have economies with a large share of subsistence production, which is hard to tax. A subsistence economy has fundamentally different cleavages from a capitalist economy, where cleavages emerge around economic groupings such as labour and the bourgeoisie, and political parties reflect these interests (Rokkan, 1981). In a subsistence economy cleavages are drawn between ethnic groups or clans and, consequently, the political elite sacrifices national economic development in order to take care of particular regions or groups in society. As long as this type of economy remains predominant in Africa, argues Goran Hyden (1983: 60), the hidden social base of power holders will be networks based on ethnicity or region, and 'the state will serve merely as an arena of rivalry among political clans'.

Fourth, the international economy is not conducive to growth for two reasons. First, the terms of trade for developing countries have slowly but steadily been deteriorating in the post-independence period. World market prices for primary commodities that developing economies depend on exporting have declined, while the prices for manufactured goods have risen. Second, the governments that receive loans and grants have had to remove all trade barriers, and have therefore not had the option to protect infant industries or to lead the kind of state-directed development policies found in East Asia.

Finally, weak states tend to be characterized by political institutions that many scholars term neo-patrimonial (Jackson and Rosberg, 1982; Bratton and van de Walle, 1997; van de Walle, 2001). The concept of neo-patrimonialism derives from Weber's old definition of a patrimonial state as one in which the ruler governs the state as if it were his own household. The neo-patrimonial state is a hybrid form of state between the modern bureaucratic state and a traditional patrimonial state. Neo-patrimonial institutions are characterized by presidentialism, i.e. the tendency of power to be concentrated in the hands of one person, and clientelism, i.e. power is legitimized by appointing important persons, clients, to important positions in the state. Governance in weak states is about managing neo-patrimonial institutions that are often adverse to national development. Clientelism, nepotism and corruption prevent genuine reform (Chabal and Daloz, 1999).

Yet the picture of weak states drawn in neo-patrimonialist approaches is rather static and tends to be pessimistic about the prospects of reform. The particular culture and the lack of institutions to limit misuse of power prevent donor money from being spent efficiently and, although some reform may appear at the surface, the underlying informal system of politics will remain. The picture, however, neglects cases where reform has actually taken place. These cases demonstrate that reform is difficult, but it is not impossible. The reason why reform is difficult is that, even if the political leadership is genuinely committed, opposition to reform is likely to emerge among societal interest groups (Haggard and Kaufman, 1992, 1995; Nelson, 1994; Rakner, 1998), or among client groups within the state (Bienen and Herbst, 1996; van de Walle, 2001). Such opposition has often served to block attempts at economic reform in Latin America,

Eastern Europe and Africa. Simultaneous democratization and economic liberalization can be difficult because elections allow access to groups that oppose reform (Ndulu and van de Walle, 1996).

The reason why reform is not impossible is that, in spite of the fact that many states remain neo-patrimonial, they have changed during the 1990s; a few of them have changed for the worse and collapsed into chaos and civil war (Zartman, 1995). Many of them remain as weak as they were prior to the 1990s. But some have strengthened basic capacities, such as the ability to maintain macroeconomic stability (Brautigam, 1996; Grindle, 1996), and some, such as Botswana and Mauritius, moved from being weak states to an African type of developmental state as early as the 1970s. What characterizes governance in these more successful countries, and which conditions are necessary?

Conditions for effective governance

Mauritius and Botswana are Africa's only truly successful developers. In the 1960s they did not have any particular advantages over other African countries and thus faced roughly the same adverse conditions to governance as did other weak states. However, in the 1990s they had overtaken many Latin American or post-communist countries and belonged in the middle- rather than low-income group of countries. Botswana and Mauritius share many features of the developmental state, such as a strong, relatively incorruptible economic bureaucracy, but they are also consolidated democracies and have had regular free elections since independence. Hence, they are not identical to the developmental state, and they give support to the argument that democracy may be a pre-condition for growth in Africa, where the lack of external threats and the existence of guaranteed sovereignty do not give elites any incentive to develop. A democratic process could open a channel for the population to put pressure on the elite to develop.

How did Mauritius and Botswana manage their economies to promote broad-based growth while simultaneously reinforcing democracy? On the basis of Mauritius' case, Deborah Brautigam (1999: 138) argues that three initial factors are necessary: (i) an institutional design that promotes coalition building and compromise; (ii) an initial set of economic and social policy choices that creates constituencies for broad-based growth; and (iii) limits on the power of the landed elite and the military. Like most African countries, Mauritius is a plural society with different languages and ethnic groups, and at independence was entirely dependent upon export of one primary commodity: sugar. However, the government succeeded in establishing institutions during the independence period that were important to subsequent developments. These institutions included: an electoral system that enabled compromise and coalition formation; legislation that established an export-processing zone, which became crucial for diversifying exports; and the decision *not* to establish a standing army (ibid.: 144). Institutional choices were important to economic development.

Adopting Mauritius' approach to governance in other African countries is not easy, and there is certainly not a shortcut to economic growth. However, the study of Africa's and East Asia's successful developers indicates that some strategies are wiser than others and that some factors are crucial to create state capacity and growth (Brautigam, 1996; Ndulu and van de Walle, 1996). First, a *leadership* committed to building state capacity and promoting development has characterized all successful developers. Although societal actors are important participants in processes of governance, rulers are the ones who guide the process. They can enable self-governance of economic agents, and they can protect important state agencies from political pressures. If dedicated, political leaders may support the establishment of pilot agencies free of corruption, Korea under Syngman Rhee and Park Chung Hee may be a case in point. Although Rhee's reign was known to be inefficient and corrupt, he created the basis for development, argues Jung-en Woo (1991), because he was above the clan and patronage politics of previous leaders. He built a powerful patronage constituency consisting of industrialists. These industrialists provided money for Rhee's party, and the state in return provided capital, import licenses and the like. These practices were characterized by excessive rent-seeking and corruption, but, as Woo explains, 'the dynamics of Korean political economy were such that economic efficiency lost in rent-seeking was recovered in the political realm, with the state and business sustaining each other like Siamese twins, buttressed by the police and a huge bureaucracy' (ibid.: 69). Thus, Rhee's regime gave rise to the political capitalists who would become an essential part of the 'Korea Inc.', established by Park Chung Hee, who imposed new rules and sanctions within the bureaucracy. Under Park, meritocratic recruitment became the norm, and internal promotions became the principal means of filling higher ranks. Park's reformist drive built the Korean developmental state upon a foundation already established by Rhee.

Second, *consultation with non-governmental agents* and *involvement of society* has proved to be an elemental part of economic policy-making. This is true for East Asian developmental states and has also been observed in Botswana (Holm and Molutsi, 1990, 1992). Dialogue and consensus-seeking are key strategies in this regard. Ignoring interest groups and networks may block policy implementation, while consultation ideally eases implementation because it secures the cooperation of economic agents. Kenya under Jomo Kenyatta provides an example of how societal organization was encouraged. Kenya had a tradition for self-governance through local self-help organizations called Harambee. Kenyatta encouraged these organizations to proliferate in order to relieve pressure on the government, and the spread of Harambee established clear norms of social interaction between state and society as well as within local communities (Barkan, 1992). Therefore, Harambee improved governance and promoted economic growth.[4]

Third, *a social coalition for growth* is important to the adoption of pro-growth strategies (Ndulu and van de Walle, 1996: 224). Such a coalition may be encouraged by the government, but it may also emerge out of dissatisfaction with the traditional anti-developmental policies. Such a coalition could consist of senior public servants, cash-crop farmers, exporters and businessmen, and it has been observed in nascent forms in some African countries such as Ghana. Technocrats in the ministries of finance have also been observed to emerge as supporters of reform, and many countries have indeed improved their capacity for maintaining macroeconomic stability (Grindle, 1996; Therkildsen, 2000; Kjær, 2002).

Finally, in some weak states, processes of *decentralization* have been observed to improve public services, to increase participation and thereby, it is hoped, enable new development initiatives (Villadsen, 1999; Enemuo, 2000; Nsibambi, 1998). Many weak states have been overly centralized and have killed a large number of development initiatives taken by non-government agents, simply by taking over the project and monopolizing it. Weak states have thus jealously guarded their authority and controls, afraid to let any independent organization, economic or social, acquire too much power. Therefore, the problem in weak states has often been the lack of *societal* autonomy, rather than the lack of *state* autonomy (Tripp, 2000). Decentralization transfers power and resources to local governments and non-governmental groups. Thereby, it may promote development initiatives that involve collaboration between state and society actors.

However, the virtues of decentralization can be exaggerated. If central government transfers all powers and functions to lower levels, its capacity to coordinate policies may disappear. On the basis of a study of successful government programmes in the Brazilian state Céara, Judith Tendler thus concludes that civic and other non-governmental associations were indeed important, but success was achieved as much because of an active central government. She argues that 'improvements in local government turned out to be less a result of decentralization than they were of a three way dynamic among local government, civil society, and an active central government' (Tendler, 1997: 145). Decentralization in itself is not enough to strengthen the state. Tendler's findings do confirm, however, the importance of involving society in development initiatives. In the case of school furniture, for example, Tendler observes how the State Department of Industry and Commerce, the Small Enterprise Assistance Service, the Association of Small Furniture-makers *and* Parent–Teacher Associations successfully collaborated to improve the quality and quantity of school furniture (ibid.: 102–34). Such development programmes can create a type of state–society synergy at the local level that may spread to other sectors or other local governments (Evans, 1996).

In sum, there are numerous obstacles to reform in weak states and hence economic governance is not easy. However, even under adverse conditions, cases of effective governance can be found, which induces grounds for careful optimism: at the general level, it is indeed possible to transfer elements of the developmental state, such as the creation of state–society synergy, to other policy environments. At the general level, developing countries may learn from strategies relying upon dialogue, consensus-seeking and inclusion, rather than coercion, raw power and exclusion. But at the more specific level, economic governance must be fitted to the particular policy setting in question.

Conclusion

The literature on the role of the state in development has had two outer positions; the neo-liberal position claiming the state should have no role at all and leave development to the market; and the structuralist position claiming the state should take the lead. In between these two, heterarchic governance refers to the management of self-organizing networks. Narrowly defined, governance refers to these networks. More broadly, however, economic governance is about setting and enforcing an economic constitution that may involve a plurality of organizational forms – state, market or networks.

In comparative political economy, the challenge is to examine the conditions and consequences of economic governance. This is a complicated task, since cause and effect are difficult to identify. Subsistence economies in weak states, for example, may be more ungovernable than other economies; on the other hand, the reasons why they remain subsistence economies may be an effect of poor governance arrangements. The best way to tackle this problem would be to study countries with similar economic structures and different governance arrangements, and explore how governance may make a difference. Another solution would be to study similar models of economic governance in different economic settings and investigate the effectiveness of governance in each. It appears that there is no one optimal model of economic governance, since diverse governance arrangements can lead to economic growth and increasing welfare. However, as indicated, some general elements of economic governance can be found in developed and developmental, as well as in developing, states: strategies of dialogue and cooperation in networks spanning the public–private divide gain increasing importance in a globalized economy. A plurality of state and non-state actors are increasingly involved in economic governance. However, an important role for the state remains. In developed countries, this role is about governing the increasing complexity of organizational structures involved in the move from national industrial economies to globalized post-industrial economies. For developing countries, it is about how to incorporate societal actors in order to gain the capacity to formulate and implement efficient economic policies. While the starting point for developed economies is more one of redefining governance in light of globalization, the starting point for developing economies is how to strengthen economic governance in a context of weak state institutions and economic dependency. Although networks and public–private partnership characterize governance in developed as well as developing economies, their governance challenges differ.

6
Governance in Comparative Politics II: Theories of Democratization

Great Britain moved towards democracy during the nineteenth century, but Germany did not. Portugal, Greece and Spain democratized in the 1970s, while democratic Chile became a dictatorship after a military coup in 1973. The authoritarian regimes in the communist bloc collapsed around 1990; some, like Hungary, made moves towards democracy, while others, such as Belarus, did not. What accounts for these differences? Under what circumstances do countries become democratic? Why and when do authoritarian leaders give in to demands for political liberalization, and how come some regime transitions are halted by authoritarian setbacks while others consolidate successfully?

These questions have occupied scholars in comparative politics for a long time. This chapter will sketch the debates in democratization theory and look at how different approaches have answered the questions posed about democracy. Modernization scholars believed that democracy followed economic growth. This basic argument was criticized for not taking account of the role of actors in regime transitions. Hence, transition scholars counterbalance modernization theory and look at regime transitions from an actor-perspective; they argue that political leaders can decide to introduce democracy at any level of economic growth, and they focus on the political conflicts that characterize authoritarian breakdown and subsequent moves towards democracy. Institutional theory attempts to tread a middle ground and studies the role of institutional choice in transition processes; it argues that some types of political or social institutions are more important for the promotion of democracy than others. Most of these approaches do not take external factors in regime transitions into account, but, as we shall see, these too are important and may affect democratization negatively as well as positively.

Theories of democratization therefore discuss the structures, actors and institutions affecting democratic governance. Yet some scholars argued that 'governance' was too narrowly identified with 'democracy' and tried to apply governance in a more analytic way, separating it from its normative, Western-liberal contents. As an analytical concept, governance was introduced as an extension of the institutionalist approach to democratization. It was also a reaction against the conception of governance promoted by donors and international financial institutions. The governance concept is relevant to a wider range of regime types than that of democracy, because it shifts the attention away from a pre-defined set of ideal institutions towards examining ways in which legitimacy for the public realm is affected (Hyden, 1992, 2002). A governance approach studies the processes by which regime rules change. Transition theory assumes that regime transitions have a specific outcome, that of a liberal democracy, i.e. a regime guaranteeing basic civil and political rights. Using the framework of governance leaves the outcome of a transition process open. Hence governance was introduced, as in other political science sub-fields, as a reaction to perceived fallacies in existing approaches.

Modernization theory and democratization

Modernization theorists assume that the causes of processes of democratization can be found in systemic features of the economy and society. Their main argument is that democratization is the likely outcome of a broader process of modernization, in which the economy industrializes, roles get more specialized, and values and orientations change. Seymor

Martin Lipset (1959: 75), to mention one very prominent modernization theorist, put forward his famous claim that 'the more well to do a nation, the greater the chances that it will sustain democracy'. He argued that economic development and political legitimacy were structural pre-conditions for a stable democracy and showed that the average wealth, the degree of industrialization and urbanization, and the level of education were much higher in democratic countries than in non-democracies. According to Lipset, 'Education broadens men's outlooks, enables them to understand the need for norms of tolerance, restrains them from adhering to extremist and monistic doctrines, and increases their capacity to make rational electoral choices' (Lipset, 1959: 75). Education therefore fosters democratic values, and a nation's increasing wealth will enable it to educate its citizens better.

While Lipset saw education as the link between wealth and values, others focused more directly on the type of values and the kind of political culture that underpins democratic governance. On the basis of a large cross-national study, Almond and Verba in 1963 argued that a so-called civic culture was necessary for maintaining a stable and effective democratic political process (Almond and Verba, 1963: 493). These scholars defined political culture as the particular distribution of patterns of orientation towards political objects among the members of a nation (ibid.: 15). They argued that a civic culture has both traditional and modern elements. There were three types of culture, according to Almond and Verba. A *parochial* culture has members who are only vaguely aware of the political system in which they live; a *subject* political culture has members who are well aware of the system but act as subjects, obeying rules without participating in their making, as with people living under a dictatorship. And, finally, a *participant* culture has members who are participants, fully aware that they have the ability to influence the policies of the political system in which they live. Almond and Verba's idea was that democracy is likely to be most stable in societies where a participant political culture is balanced by the survival of subject and parochial attitudes. The development of a civic culture, according to the authors, does not happen in the space of a few years. It develops gradually over a long period of political and social development.

Modernization theory was criticized for being too teleological and deterministic. It studied the modernization
process in the West and took for granted that the new developing nations would follow the same path of modernization towards a common end: the Western liberal model of
democracy. An early critique was formulated by Samuel P.
Huntington (1965) in a seminal article, where he observed
that the real patterns of political change were far from the
stable, linear processes predicted by modernization optimists:

> Instead of a trend toward competitiveness and democracy,
> there has been an 'erosion of democracy' and a tendency to
> autocratic military regimes and one-party regimes. Instead of
> stability, there have been repeated coups and revolts. Instead
> of a unifying nationalism and nation-building, there have been
> repeated ethnic conflicts and civil wars. Instead of institu-
> tional rationalization and differentiation, there has frequently
> been a decay of the administrative organizations inherited
> from the colonial era and a weakening and disruption of the
> political organizations developed during the struggle for
> independence.[1]

Huntington demonstrated that political development is not
unidirectional and he 'opened the door to meaningful empirical inquiry about the relationship between socioeconomic
change and political outcomes' (Remmer, 1997: 35).

Since then, many studies have tried to develop modernization theory further, without falling into the deterministic
or the teleological trap. Modernization theory focuses mainly
on structural factors when identifying the conditions for
democratic governance. Structural factors are underlying
systemic features of state, economy and society that are
beyond the reach of individual agents (Bratton and van de
Walle, 1997).[2] Many scholars within the modernization paradigm retain the focus on structural factors, but try to avoid
the determinism of early modernization theory. Pointing to
certain social structures that promote democracy does not
necessarily entail predicting that democracy will occur, but
the structural factors can be interpreted as conditions that
will increase the likelihood of a successful democratization
process, should the political actors choose to initiate such
process.[3]

Some scholars have found that studying crude indicators of socio-economic development is not enough to predict democracy. In addition, the distribution of power resources and the relative strength of social classes must also be taken into consideration. In his search for the social origins of dictatorship and democracy, Barrington Moore Jr found that a strong, landed upper class is not conducive to the development of democracy because it has an interest in retaining its privileges and continuing to extract rents from peasants who are tied to the land (Moore, 1967: 7, 42–3). However, if the nobility adapts to modernization by commercializing agriculture and starts producing for profit, as in England, the likelihood of democracy increases. The main source of democracy, however, is to be found in the existence of strong urban areas and the growth of capitalism. In England, wealthier townsmen turned against royal monopolies because they felt these prevented them from carrying out their business. Thus, Barrington Moore concludes that 'a vigorous and independent class of town dwellers has been an indispensable element in the growth of parliamentary democracy. No bourgeois, no democracy' (ibid.: 418).

This statement has not been left unchallenged. It has been argued that oppressed classes, rather than the bourgeoisie, have fought for democracy (Therborn, 1983: 271; Rueschemeyer, Stephens and Stephens, 1992). Rueschemeyer et al. thus challenge Barrington Moore and argue that the development of a strong working class is the key to democratization. Collier (1999) examines a number of democratic transitions and finds that, although the working class has often played an important role, its importance can be exaggerated. She argues that 'although democracy may be a class project, it is not necessarily the project of a single class' (ibid.: 193). Political outcomes depend on class alliances and the ways in which interests are altered during the process of class struggle, not just on the struggle of one class. All seem to agree, however, that a strong landowner class is a serious obstacle to democracy. The Finnish political scientist Tatu Vanhanen (1990, 1997) also modifies modernization theory by looking at the allocation of resources. He argues that, rather than modernization, the spread of power resources can be used to explain the emergence of democracy in a particular state. The more inclusive the process of growth, the greater is the likelihood of democracy.[4] Thus, it is not just modernization, but the specific character of modernization that matters.

A different type of approach focuses directly on the nature of the revenue base of a country, and how this may affect the prospects for democratic governance (Hyden, 1983; Moore, 1997; Bates, 1999). The argument is that if the state does not depend on its citizens for income, there is no incentive for leaders to be accountable to the citizens. This is because leaders tend to be accountable towards their source of income. Some European monarchs, for example, bargained with their citizens in order to obtain revenue, because they depended upon income and profit tax in early capitalism.[5] The resource base consisted of mobile as well as fixed capital. Mobile capital, i.e. goods or capital that can be transferred from place to place, is more difficult to tax than fixed property (such as land) because it can be concealed from the authorities. Taxing mobile capital therefore requires the cooperation of the owners, and, to induce capital owners to cooperate, governments have to bargain with them. 'In contrast with other regions in the world, Africa lacks capital, and it is relatively abundantly endowed with land. In the search for public resources, those in control of the state therefore encounter little reason to bargain; they have felt little need to exchange control over public policy for receipts of public revenues' (Bates, 1999: 86). African leaders have had no incentive to be responsive towards their citizens. Accordingly, African political systems are authoritarian, and political change is unlikely.[6] Theories about rentier states, e.g. many Middle Eastern states dependent on oil for income, and therefore with no reason to bargain with their citizens for revenue, follow the same line of argument (Beblawi and Luciani, 1987).

The common problem with modernization approaches (the early as well as the modified versions) is that they cannot explain the character of a specific transition. As Georg Sørensen (1993a: ch.2) has put it: 'the formulation of a law about democracy: "if x,y,n, structural preconditions are present, democracy will or will not emerge" is not possible'. The approach is not fruitful when the desire is to explain and understand the dynamics of change. Why is change taking place now? How did it come about? The validity of the approach is that, by pointing to structural features, it enables us to identify why change is difficult, and why a democratic outcome is likely or unlikely; but when change does take place, these features often do not help us in understanding exactly how or why. Thus, the gradual degradation of the Soviet economy may have paved the way for the radical political changes taking place around 1990, but it does not explain much of the exact process of change or what set it in motion.[7] In order to understand changes better, actors and their choices must enter the stage.

Transition theories

The study of regime transitions focus on sequences leading from authoritarian collapse to democracy. Here, political actors, their conflicts and bargains are central (Johannsen, 2002). Dankwart Rustow (1970) made a major contribution to the study of regime transitions when he argued that introducing democratic reform is a *decision* to be made by political actors. Rustow emphasizes that the transition to democracy does not follow a uniform pattern worldwide, and it does not always involve the same social classes. On the contrary 'a wide variety of social conflicts and of political contents can be combined with democracy' (Rustow, 1970: 345).

Rustow distinguishes between different phases of transition. This is important because the factors that keep a democracy stable may not be the ones that brought it about (ibid.: 346). He points to a single background condition for a democratic transition, that of *national unity*, and then goes on to identify three phases:[8] (i) the *preparatory phase* in which the protagonists are involved in a prolonged and inconclusive political struggle (ibid.: 352); (ii) the *decision phase* in which political leaders take a deliberate decision to 'accept the existence of diversity in unity' and therefore to institutionalize democratic procedures (ibid.: 355); and (iii) finally, in the *habituation phase* political actors learn to live with and accept democratic procedures. Democracy becomes the only game in town. Rustow thus split democratization into several analytically distinct categories, and taught us that modernization approaches may say something about the likelihood of consolidation (habituation) but not much about the preceding phases.

Transition theory builds upon Rustow's seminal article and the main assumption that regime change is brought about by political actors. Adam Przeworski (1991), for example, has argued that whereas the degree of economic growth can help us evaluate the chances of survival of the new democracies, it tells us nothing about the chances of regime change. He maintains that democracy can be decided in any country at any level of economic development, and he investigates what makes political elites agree to democratic procedures when these procedures may result in them losing power. It is essential, Przeworski argues, that the institutions that are negotiated are the outcome of a compromise, or a pact, that reflects the basic interests of the most important actors. The persons in power must have some guarantee that they will not be prosecuted by a new government, and they must also believe that they have a good chance of continued influence.[9] Thus it is often 'an agreement among a select set of actors which seeks to define rules governing the exercise of power on the basis of mutual guarantees for the *vital interests* of those entering into it' (O'Donnel and Schmitter, 1986: 37) that opens up the possibility of a democratic development.

A common feature of all the transition approaches is that they bring political agents back on stage. But there are two distinct problems with these approaches. The first problem is that if all outcomes depend upon individual agents and their negotiations, making any kind of prediction becomes very difficult. If outcomes of political struggles were truly uncertain, it would not be possible to claim any predictive or explanatory power for theories at all. Truly, actor-oriented approaches should be seen as complementary to, rather than contradictory to, more structural theories (Bates, 1997). The second problem is that transition theory does not help us identify the institutional constraints faced by political actors struggling to define the rules of the game. As pointed out by Karl and Schmitter (1991: 271), the focus on strategic choices has the advantage of stressing political interactions that have been underemphasized in the search for preconditions for democracy. Yet a focus on choice may underspecify the conditions under which choices are made. 'Even in the midst of tremendous uncertainty provoked by a regime change, the decisions made by various actors respond to, and are conditioned by, socio-economic structures and political institutions already present, or existing in people's memories' (ibid.). This critique of transition theory inspired a range of scholars to adopt approaches that enabled them to identify institutional constraints.

Institutional approaches to democratic governance

The focus on institutions was an attempt to tread a middle ground between structures and actors. Terry Lynn Karl (1990), for example, argues that since the search for democracy's preconditions is bound to be futile, the task is rather to 'develop an interactive approach that seeks to relate structural constraints to the shaping of contingent choice' (ibid.: 1). Certain social structures make some choices difficult but enable other choices. For example, the presence of a strong landowner elite that engages in labour-repressive agriculture and prefers authoritarian rule can block democratization processes. In Chile and Venezuela, dependence upon minerals (copper and petroleum) for exports made landowners sell their land, whereby they became part of a commercial bourgeoisie and no longer needed the state to maintain their privileges. This meant that Chile and Venezuela were able to institutionalize democratic agreements. Karl argues that, in this way, 'it should be possible to demonstrate how the range of options available to decision makers at a given point in time is a function of structures put in place in an earlier period and, concomitantly, how such decisions are conditioned by institutions established in the past' (ibid.: 7).

The institutional approach includes scholars focusing on political as well as on social institutions. With regard to *political institutions*, the importance of a particular institutional set-up, consociational democracy, has been argued to be relevant for plural societies (Lijphart, 1977). It is difficult to maintain democratic governance in pluralist societies, argues Arend Lijphart, because they have deep structural cleavages of a religious, regional or ethnical nature. However, he maintains, it is not at all impossible. He argues that if democratic institutions are designed on the basis of a consociational model, stable democracy will have a chance of success even in pluralist societies. Consociational democracy refers, in Lijphart's parlance, to institutionalizing the cooperation of segmented elites.

Parliamentary institutions have also been emphasized as a means of promoting democratic governance better than presidential systems (Linz, 1990a; 1990b).[10] By examining fifty-three non-OECD countries (and thereby controlling for economic structure), Alfred Stepan and Cindy Skach (1993) find that parliamentary democracies had a rate of survival more than three times higher than that of presidential democracies. This is because of parliamentarism's

> greater propensity for governments to have majorities to implement their programs; its greater ability to rule in a multi-party setting; its lower propensity for executives to rule at the edge of the constitution and its greater facility for moving a chief executive who does so; its lower susceptibility for military coup; and its greater tendency to provide long party-government careers, which add loyalty and experience to political society. (ibid.: 22)

Similarly, Lars Johannsen (2000) finds that in post-communist countries economic modernization predicts much of the democratic development, but that constitutional choice does matter, particularly in poor countries.

In addition to political institutions, *civil-society institutions* have been noted as important to democracy. The term 'civil society' normally refers to an intermediate associational realm between state and family populated by organizations which are separate from the state, enjoy autonomy in relation to the state and are formed voluntarily by members of society to protect and advance their interests or values (White, 1996: 182). Civil society lies in between the state and the private sphere. It does not include parochial relations,

relations of kin or other inward-looking groups, such as groups getting together for entertainment or religious worship. It also excludes economic activities (Diamond, 1999: 221). 'Civil society' is distinct from 'society' in general, in that it involves citizens acting collectively in a public sphere to express their interests and to make demands on the state. Society, then, refers to everything that is not the state, whereas civil society is only concerned with public ends.

Democratic transitions are not necessarily initiated by civil-society organizations. They may be initiated by the political elite. Transitions are complex processes in which civil society raises demands for reform, and the elite may or may not react to such pressure. If the elite introduce reform, civil society may push for further reform. O'Donnel and Schmitter (1986: 48–56) have argued that transitions are often initiated by the elite, but the opening can lead to a revitalization of civil society – a popular upsurge, as they call it. However, this conclusion regarding the sequence of democratization has been challenged. It has been demonstrated that many Southern European and Latin American transitions were initially triggered by protests and strikes by trade unions; they were *not* initiated from within the regime (Diamond, 1999: 234). Similarly, Bratton and van de Walle (1997) find a strong relation between a pluralist civil society, popular political protest and transitions in Africa. Also, in Asia, civil society has sometimes played a crucial role in pushing for a democratic opening. For example, in South Korea in 1987, student and worker demonstrations combined with the less radical middle-class business and professional groups and opposition politicians to force the authoritarian regime to yield to demands for change (Diamond, 1999: 235).

Democratization scholars assume civil society to be instrumental in *bringing about* a democratic transition and to increase the likelihood of *consolidating* democracy. For example, civil society can play a disciplinary role in relation to the state, by holding it accountable and making sure it abides by the rules (White, 1996: 186). The media can expose cases of corruption or election malpractices; or civic associations can watch whether the police respect human rights. Civil society also plays an intermediary role between state and society. It supplements political parties in aggregating interests and channelling demands; it helps recruit and generate new political leaders; and it educates citizens for democracy. If organizations and associations are broad, and cross ethnic or religious cleavages, it can also ameliorate political conflict (Diamond, 1999: 245).

An important aspect of the institution of civil society is the degree of civicness. Robert Putnam (1994) argues that a high degree of civicness, or social capital, is essential to democratic governance. He defines social capital as 'features of social organization, such as trust, norms, and networks, that can improve the efficiency of society by facilitating coordinated actions' (Putnam, 1994: 167). In his study of regional governments in Italy, Putnam found that vibrant civil societies in the North enabled the regional government to solve collective action dilemmas much better than Southern regional governments, where there were low degrees of social capital. Democracy, according to Putnam, will fare poorly in societies with low degrees of social capital, simply because they are difficult to govern.

There are probably limits to the virtues of civil society. Civil society itself is not always democratic. Some groups may have more power than others and be able to exclude marginalized groups entirely from participation in the public sphere. Some non-governmental organizations may exist not because they want to promote a common cause, but simply because the opportunity for international funding exists (these are the so-called 'brief-case NGOs'). In addition, a civil society does not just occur out of nowhere – it develops in interaction with government, and if government authorities are repressive, civil society may be destroyed. However, these caveats do not alter the consensus that civil society *can* 'play a central role in building and consolidating democracy' (Diamond, 1999: 260).

The role of external factors in the process of democratization

The approaches sketched so far see democratization as primarily a domestic affair. However, states have never had clear boundaries, and domestic political developments do not take place in splendid isolation from international society. Laurence Whitehead (1996) lists three ways in which international factors may influence regime transitions. One is *contagion*, in which one country's transition simply initiates a kind of domino effect that sets in motion other transitions. This is what Huntington (1991) has called the 'snowballing effect'. The rapid political changes in Africa and in countries like Nepal, for example, have often been seen as influenced by what happened in Eastern Europe after the fall of the Berlin Wall (Sørensen, 1993a). The second way in which international influences play a role is through *control*. Control occurs when democracy is imposed by more powerful states on less powerful ones by deliberate acts of imposition. Whitehead mentions the role of US forces in some Central American countries, or that of the British, who exported their Westminister model to former colonies. Since 1989, one may also mention the donor countries' demands of democracy and respect for human rights. The threat of withdrawal of aid funds was an important catalyst for Kenya's 1992 elections and Arap Moi's decision to allow multiple political parties.

The outcomes of such transitions are at best mixed, since domestic political groups may not be willing or ready to democratize. The final influence is through *consent*. According to Whitehead, international forces contribute to the generation of domestic consent to democratization by a variety of mechanisms, for example, through regional blocks such as the European Union that may encourage democracy in its member states, or by supporting groups in exile who are in opposition to an authoritarian regime. These groups may regain power and push for renewed democratization. In addition, globalization and the spread of liberal-democratic ideology means that hardly any state leaders argue against democracy any longer. Thus, the world opinion is generally in favour of democracy, and more regimes have experienced democratic progress than authoritarian setbacks (Plattner, 2002: 57).

Yet the positive influence of external factors is not at all clear. External factors may affect democratization adversely.

For example, external aid funds may be used by the incumbent regime to buy political loyalty. Or donors may turn a blind eye towards the defunct democracy if economic adjustment goes well. This was the case with Ghana and Uganda, who were both good adjusters but for many years were (and in Uganda's case still is) semi-authoritarian. Many observers have argued that the presence of donors in developing states has the unfortunate effect of turning accountability outwards, so that accountability becomes a matter between governments and donors rather than a matter between the government and its citizens.[11] Although the donors claim to support good governance and participatory development, government policy is often negotiated between the International Monetary Fund and government technocrats in closed sessions. Democracy may suffer when liberal economic policy and the removal of regulation prevail (Plattner, 2002).

The impact of external factors on domestic transition processes is far from clear. Indeed, it may be argued that the separation of internal and external is analytical and therefore artificial, and that the whole transition process evolves with complex interaction between the two. However, in conclusion, it must be emphasized that democratization is first and foremost a process that takes place within the boundaries of a political system. It is possible to distinguish between domestic actors and actors exogenous to the system. The relative strength of domestic groupings depends not only on their alliances with external actors, but also on domestic traditions and resource allocations.

In sum, there are different approaches to the study of processes of democratization. Modernization theory focuses on the structural prerequisites for democracy, while transition theory focuses more on political actors and their strategic interaction in the transition period. Modernization theory may be able to point out prospects for consolidation, while transition theory can explain how the transition came about. Institutional approaches take a middle ground, and look at how certain political and social institutions may increase the likelihood of democratic outcomes. They maintain that, although some societies are less governable than others, institutional choices do matter. This is the starting point for the governance approach to regime transition.

Governance and regime transitions

Governance was introduced as a reaction against dominant perceptions both in the academic democratization debate and in the practical debate by the development community. In democratization theory, 'good' governance implicitly equalled democratic governance and, therefore, a need to introduce a less normative concept was identified. In the development community, the concept of good governance had been introduced by the World Bank as referring to predictable and efficient government practices. Bad governance was seen to denote corruption and patronage practices in the public services of developing countries (World Bank, 1989: 60). However, the concept soon came to denote a broader list of accountability, transparency, responsiveness, a strong civil society and clean government (World Bank, 1994). In particular, the bilateral donors emphasized the importance of democracy and respect for human rights. In both democratization theory and the development community, then, 'democratic' and 'governance' were tightly connected.

An early attempt at clarifying the concept of governance by separating it from the concept of democracy was made by Goran Hyden (1992), in an edited volume with Michael Bratton. His point of departure is clearly institutional: politics and institutional choice matter. Hyden is not happy with the concept of democracy when focusing on regime changes. First, he is concerned that democracy is associated with dominant Western norms and values. Second, he points out that the outcome of the many transitions is far from certain and, therefore, it seems prudent to choose a concept that is less loaded. This point is in line with the common critique of transition theory's assumption that any country moving *away* from dictatorial rule can be considered a country in transition *towards* democracy (Carothers: 2002: 6). Third, Hyden maintains that, even when democratic institutions are established, countries may still be characterized by bad politics. Governance focuses on the nature of the public realm in all political systems, democratic or not.

Consequently, the concept of governance is more appropriate than that of democracy when analysing regime transitions. Governance is 'the conscious management of regime structures with a view to enhancing the legitimacy of the public realm' (Hyden, 1992: 7). A regime is constituted by the explicit or implicit rules that define who the relevant political actors are, and through what channels and with what resources they actively seek political positions (ibid.). A governance realm is bounded by four characteristics:

1 *Authority* refers to legitimate power. If government uses raw and arbitrary power, for instance by cracking down hard on particular groups of the population, the public realm is damaged and people may exit from the system rather than act collectively (Hyden, 1999).
2 *Reciprocity* is a form of social interaction that generates new forms of consensus about basic rules of politics. Reciprocity is different from exchange because an exchange relationship is more immediate, and it is not based upon future expectations of returns. A reciprocal relationship is more continuous. The difference may be hard to understand. An exchange situation involves an immediate exchange, with no expectation of future contact: you may buy a chocolate bar in a kiosk and then think no more of it. In a reciprocal relationship, you will expect some future interaction: you may watch your neighbors' children and expect them to watch yours when you may need it.
3 *Trust* refers to trust within families and kinship groups, but also to a broader, more impersonal trust between different groupings and towards public authorities.
4 *Accountability* is mainly about the responsiveness of public authorities towards citizens and the extent to which citizens can hold public authorities to account.

The more regime management is characterized by authority, reciprocity, trust and accountability, the more it generates legitimacy for the political system, and the more people will participate in the public realm with enthusiasm.

Governance acknowledges institutional constraints on individual behaviour. However, during periods when institutions are in flux, individuals and groups have potentially large influence on new institutions. Governance is defined as the setting, application and enforcement of regime rules, but the focus is on the setting of rules, precisely because a transition implies a move away from one institutional set-up towards another. Governance in democratization theory is thus, in a sense, meta-policy-making: it refers to the setting of rules that guide rule-making (Hyden, 1999).

The governance approach brings several new issues to the fore. In transition theory there is a focus on the choices of political elites. The governance concept includes trust and reciprocity, and thereby emphasizes the importance of social capital and civil society institutions in legitimizing the public realm. Hence, adopting the governance concept means abandoning the sharp focus on the political elite in favour of an approach that includes institutions crossing the state–society divide. As in other sub-fields, governance thus denotes something broader than government: societal as well as government actors may affect processes of rule change. This conception implies abandoning the assumptions about the location of power that are found in concepts such as government or leadership. Concentrations of power may be found outside as well as inside the state apparatus.

In addition, the introduction of governance has the advantage of not excluding external actors from the domestic political scene. Although Hyden does not explicitly deal with this issue, the influence of international financial institutions and bilateral donors may very well affect the formal and informal rules of the political game. Interactions between external and domestic political actors, for example, may alter existing power relations. In addition, donor support for opposition parties may weaken the government. Or outside pressure to introduce economic reforms that are politically costly may induce domestic conflicts over access to resources. As a concept, governance, rather than democracy, is better placed to capture transnational reciprocity and exchange.

Finally, introducing the concept of governance removes the assumption found in the transition paradigm that all countries undergoing regime change are on their way towards democracy. As pointed out by Thomas Carothers (2002: 14), the political trajectories of most third-wave countries call into 'serious doubt' the transition paradigm.[12] Many of these countries have not democratized at all, and to consider them to be in transition towards democracy has often been 'inaccurate and misleading'. Carothers argues that, when looking at a country that has recently moved away from authoritarianism, one should not start by asking 'How is its transition going?' Instead, a more open-ended query, 'What is happening politically?' should be formulated (ibid.: 18). This is what governance does.

Electoral governance is an emerging sub-field of the study of democratization which is worth noting. Its point of departure is that electoral governance matters for the credibility of institutions, and for the transition and consolidation of new democracies (Elklit and Reynolds, 2002; Mozaffar and Schedler, 2002). It identifies the provision of procedural certainty to secure the substantive uncertainty of democratic elections as the principal task of electoral governance (Mozaffar and Schedler, 2002: 5). How is this done? The choices of powerful individuals and groups are important. These choices relate to a range of electoral issues, such as the organizational structure of the central Electoral Management Body, its political independence, its own internal motivations and transparency of the organization (Elklit and Reynolds, 2002: 90).

Elklit and Reynolds (2002: 92–6) identify twelve important steps in the electoral process:

   (i)   Legal framework.
   (ii)   Election management.
   (iii) Constituency and polling strict demarcation.
   (iv)   Voter education.
   (v)   Voter registration.
   (vi)   Access to, and design of, the ballot, nomination and registration of parties and candidates.
   (vii) Campaign regulation.
   (viii) Polling.
   (ix)   Counting and tabulating the vote.
   (x)   Resolving election related disputes and complaints, verification of final results.
   (xi)   Election result implementation.
   (xii) Post-election procedures.

They argue that what happens *prior* to the actual polling, i.e. steps (i) to (vii), is at least as important as the actual polling (step viii), in order to gain support and credibility for the electoral process.

Hence the assumption of transition theory that elections in themselves will increase political legitimacy and broaden political participation is avoided (Carothers, 2002: 8). Elklit and Reynolds examine eight African countries, and find that electoral governance matters more for the perceived legitimacy of the process than the choice of electoral system (first past the post or proportional representation). They find that the unsuccessful cases (the ones with a low legitimacy) had in common '(i) a perception that the basic legal framework was flawed and unfair (Step i), (ii) the belief that the Electoral Management Body was either partisan or incompetent (or both) – Step ii) and (iii) that polling was logistically flawed to such an extent that the results could not reflect the will of the people' (ibid.: 114). In these cases, minority parties felt that the playing field was very much against them, and that the whole legal framework was biased in favour of the incumbent regime. Bad electoral governance, then, can lead to polarization rather than inclusion, and may indirectly contribute to higher levels of conflict (Elklit, 2001).[13] Electoral governance is thus about choices regarding electoral institutions that have an important bearing on the general levels of accountability and reciprocity between a political system and its surroundings, and hence on the overall legitimacy of the public realm.

In sum, governance approaches in relation to regime transitions attempt to avoid the normative presumptions underlying existing approaches and, as in other sub-fields, they include the multiplicity of actors involved in the processes of institutional change. The strength of the governance approach is clearly that it is broader and less normative than other approaches. It is broader because it explicitly acknowledges the many different factors that may generate legitimacy for the public realm. In a democracy, the public sphere may be legitimate, but it may not be. In a non-democracy, the public realm may be legitimate if there are high degrees of inclusion or if decentralized governance allows citizens to participate in local affairs. Governance allows a more open discussion about the sources of legitimacy.

However, in the desire to define itself as a distinct approach to regime change, the governance approach tends to ignore other existing perceptions of governance. Hence, as we have seen in chapter 5, effective economic governance is also a source of legitimacy. Effective economic governance may even promote democratic governance by creating the predictability and stability necessary for democratization to take place. Hence, by focusing on how to separate governance and democracy, governance approaches tend to neglect other dimensions of governance that have an important bearing upon processes of regime change. Paradoxically, while the conceptual work combining governance in regime transition with other governance approaches still needs to be done, the practical work of measuring governance takes account of all the different aspects of governance, political as well as administrative and economic.

Measuring governance

Governance is not an easy concept to measure. When measuring, for instance, economic and social development, relatively solid data exist in the form of a nation's Gross Domestic Product, or the UNDPs Human Development Index. When measuring the degree of democracy, relatively clear indicators can be found, if a minimum liberal definition of democracy concerning civil and political liberties and regular elections is used. The information provided by Freedom House annual *Freedom in the World* indicators is a case in point. On the contrary, governance touches upon perceptions of reciprocity, trust, accountability and authority. These political issues are difficult to pin down, or indeed to talk about, by national experts who do not want to be associated with criticism of their own regimes.

In the World Bank's governance work, data was gathered from existing data that touched upon governance issues. In addition to Freedom House, these were, among others, *The Economist* Intelligence Unit's country risk service and the Heritage Foundation's economic freedom index (Kaufman et al., 1999). This attempt to bring information on governance issues together into a single set has resulted in six aggregate measures on governance aspects, including accountability, political instability, rule of law, government effectiveness and graft. However, it also expresses the need to collect more focused governance data.

The World Governance Survey (WGS), based at the UN University, is a response to that need and is the first attempt to generate a global database on perceptions of governance. Contrary to the efforts by staff in the World Bank, the WGS builds on new data gathered entirely for the purpose of measuring governance. The survey is based on a governance concept that is split into six sub-components:

1 Rules that shape the way citizens raise and become aware of public issues (civil society).
2 Rules that shape the way issues are combined into policy by political institutions (political society).
3 Rules that shape the way policies are made by government institutions (government).
4 Rules that shape the way policies are administered and implemented by public servants (bureaucracy).
5 Rules that shape the way state and market interact to promote development (economic society).
6 Rules that shape the setting for resolution of disputes and conflicts.

Each sub-component is measured by five questions in a comprehensive questionnaire. For example, an indicator of 'civil society' would be the question 'To what extent do citizens have the freedom of expression?' An indicator of 'political society' would be the question 'To what extent is the legislature representative of society?' The range of answers goes from 'very low' to 'very high'. The questionnaire is answered by thirty-five well-informed persons, who are asked to evaluate their country's performance on each dimension, both five years ago and at the present time. The governance survey thus aims to give a picture of the quality of governance in a country over a five-year period, and it also endeavours to construct a governance index that can be used to compare countries.[14]

The WGS is an impressive attempt to measure governance processes, but it raises some points of concern. The use of subjective indicators of governance process (local experts' judgements) has many advantages. For example, these indicators can capture people's perceptions of governance better than objective indicators. But using subjective indicators also makes each evaluation specific to that country, as the local country expert is likely to rank his country in relation to how it was five years ago. If governance processes have improved dramatically in five years he or she is likely to rank the country in the top category of very high, even if the processes, by comparison with some other countries, are of dubious quality and would be ranked moderately from an objective viewpoint. Hence, the use of subjective indicators raises concerns about cross-comparability of country results. Nonetheless, the WGS is an attempt to take the political pulse of systems without assuming that the overall direction is that towards liberal democracy.

Conclusion

Modernization approaches to democracy typically list the sociostructural features they consider necessary for democratic governance, and have been criticized for being overly deterministic. Transition scholars brought in a refreshing element of voluntarism, arguing that democracy can be decided at any level of socio-economic development. However, by assuming that countries in transition were en route to democracy, transition theory in a way fell into the same pitfall as early modernization theory: that there is only one direction of political development. Institutional approaches offer a middle ground between structures and actors, and examine not only how institutions circumscribe political agency, but also how political agents may in turn alter institutions. In this context, governance was introduced to study regime changes, without presuming that they were changes towards a democratic system. Governance is not equal to democracy. Democracy is one institutional set-up that may or may not be the outcome of processes of governance. Hence governance theory does not share the unidirectional underpinnings of transition theory. Governance is the conscious management of regime structures, and brings the focus on to how and why institutions change. Governance theory does not have transition theory's sharp focus on the political elite, but may involve government as well as non-governmental actors. In that sense, the conception of governance as more than government is shared with governance conceptions found in public administration and international relations. However, it could be more related to these other conceptions, since processes destroying or generating legitimacy for the public realm are arguably also affected by other types of governance.

7

Governance and the World Bank

The World Bank ignited a large debate on governance when it identified bad governance as a cause of economic crisis in many Third World countries. It called for greater transparency, efficiency and accountability in the countries to which it gave loans. However, scholars started applying these criteria to the World Bank itself: they asked whether the Bank as an international organization was accountable or followed transparent procedures. Thus, the issue of the governance of international organizations was added to the debate. Finally, the World Bank is also increasingly part of global governance processes as it takes part in redistribution from rich to poor and as it analyses the consequences of rich countries' trade policies to the poor countries. Three ways of how governance and the World Bank interrelate can thus be identified: 'good governance' as policy condition; governance of the World Bank as organization; and the World Bank as part of global governance. The World Bank programmes are an illustration of the difficulty of transferring particular models of governance to other countries. The World Bank as an organization illustrates how increased globalization and fragmentation has rendered accountability structures more complex. The World Bank is thus a case of the relevance of governance in contemporary global politics.

'Good governance' as policy condition

The World Bank contributed significantly to the emanation of the concept of governance in the 1990s. It introduced the concept of governance in a 1989 report pointing to corruption, bad policies and nepotism as severely hampering development. With the report, the World Bank sparked a debate in the international development community on what good governance was about, on how to promote good governance, and on whether exporting the Western systems of accountability and democracy is feasible or indeed realistic.

The World Bank does not operate with one single definition of governance. Rather, the usage varies according to the particular report at hand. For example, in the 1989 report, governance is defined as 'the manner in which power is exercised in the management of a country's economic and social resources for development' (World Bank, 1989: 60). In a later report, 'governance is the institutional capability of public organizations to provide the public and other goods demanded by a country's citizens or their representatives in an effective, transparent, impartial, and accountable manner, subject to resource constraints' (World Bank, 2000a: 48). In spite of the varying definitions, the core features of the Bank's operational notion of governance refer to reducing corruption and strengthening rule-bound behaviour.[1]

This understanding entails four components of good governance that the World Bank has adopted as policy guidelines in recipient countries. *Public sector management* entails civil service reform and privatization initiatives. *Legal framework for development* is about making and enforcing rules that can make a market work, such as private property rights. *Accountability* aims at strengthening institutions to hold the government accountable, as for example an ombudsman, the Auditor General or parliamentary public accounts committees. Finally, *transparency and information* are keywords for programmes that support a free media or help the government publicize statistics, such as publishing the public budget annually.

The World Bank's support for good governance was new in the sense that it was much more political than had so far been seen. Good governance programmes touched upon sensitive issues of distribution of power and resources, and some of them raised protests locally. For example, privatization programmes mean that the state sells off many of its enterprises and therefore loses an important avenue for gaining support through appointments to positions in these organizations. Additionally, civil service reform often involves laying off thousands of public employees. It also means removing essential functions to semi-autonomous bodies, which reduces the degree of control that the central government can exercise. Thus resistance to governance programmes is likely to emerge among groups who lose from the reforms, such as officials who were employed in state-owned enterprises or government staff in fear of losing their jobs (World Bank, 1997).

The record of these programmes was mixed. It became clear that supporting institutional reforms was much more difficult than supporting specific projects, such as building a road or a hospital (Israel, 1987). The rise of the governance agenda in the development community thus raised key questions of the dynamics at stake in processes of nation- and state-building. It was argued that the 'external factor' should be taken seriously in the study of domestic politics (Doornbos, 1995). Changes in regime structures, for example, did not take place in complete insulation from the outside world. They could be triggered by the demands from international financial institutions for economic austerity, leading to social protests that could then cause the government to introduce reforms (Sørensen, 1993a). Or the failure to comply with aid conditions could lead to a cut in aid, and hence undermine the patronage that had so far bought critical support for the regime (Grindle, 1996). It is widely agreed that drastic cuts in aid at the end of the cold war caused some regimes, for example the Somalian and the Zairean regimes, to collapse (Clapham, 1996). World Bank-supported programmes may also play a part in domestic politics in more subtle ways, such as strengthening some parts of the government (the ministries of finance) while weakening others (the ministries of planning). The adoption of governance programmes, then, promoted a more explicit recognition within academia of the role of external actors in processes of state-building.

In the early 2000s, the governance concept seems to have gradually lost importance in the World Bank. It has proved extremely difficult to monitor recipient country compliance with all the specific conditions attached to good governance programmes. A World Bank report in 1998 assessed the effectiveness of aid in a large number of countries, and its main conclusion was that aid worked best in countries with a good policy environment (World Bank, 1998b, van der Hoeven, 2001). So, from demanding good governance *ex ante*, there has been a movement towards *ex post* selectivity: good governance is now considered more a criterion against which to decide who qualifies for assistance (Doornbos, 2001). While good governance has not been abandoned by the World Bank, its usage has thus changed from being something to promote in developing countries to being a requirement before recipient countries are allowed loans in the first place. In sum, the practice of international institutions such as the World Bank triggered a debate in comparative politics about how external forces influence domestic politics, and whether it was at all possible to transfer models of 'good governance' built on Western ideas to non-Western settings (see chapters 5 and 6).

One factor is the World Bank's emphasis on good governance in creditor countries. Another is whether the Bank itself, as an organization, lives up to norms of good governance, such as accountability and transparent procedures. Whereas the World Bank's governance programmes have been subject of debate in comparative politics and in theories about the role of the state in development, this latter question of accountability relates more to the debate in international relations regarding ways in which international organizations can be held accountable.

Governance of the World Bank

Is the World Bank itself subject to the norms of accountability, responsiveness and transparency that it requires from recipient governments? That question is not easily answered. The World Bank is a multi-purpose organization, and therefore, it is difficult to identify *exactly to whom* the Bank should be accountable. The difficulty posed by this question justifies an outline of the Bank's history, its purposes, and the interests represented by the World Bank. Such a discussion shows that the World Bank must be accountable to its major shareholders but that it also has a global constituency consisting of, among others, an increasingly assertive group of international non-governmental organizations. This latter group will be discussed on pages 183–6 in the third section on global governance.

The International Bank for Development and Reconstruction (IBRD) was established in the late 1940s in the aftermath of the Second World War, which had left large parts of Europe and Japan in ruins. The Bank's purpose was to provide capital for development and reconstruction in capital-poor areas. By the beginning of the 1960s, Europe's reconstruction had proved a success, and, in principle, it was no longer a capital-poor area. In the meantime, however, more and more colonies in Africa and South Asia achieved independence from their colonial powers, and it was natural that the Bank started focusing on the emerging world. It typically financed large infrastructural projects, such as power plants or road networks. Often, these projects would not have been undertaken for private capital, since private investors would consider them too risky. In 1960, the International Development Agency (IDA) was established in order to give credit on very favourable terms, because it became difficult to find projects with returns big enough to satisfy IBRD conditions. IDA loans thus have a large grant element and they go to the very poorest countries.

The World Bank is thus first and foremost a bank. The core institution, the IBRD, borrows on private capital markets and lends at low rates to needing members. It can lend at quite favourable terms because its member states provide guarantees for the loans it takes. The Bank, like any bank, must be accountable towards its shareholders, which are its members. The United States is the largest shareholder, with 16.62 per cent of the shares. The next largest holder is Germany, with less than 5 per cent of the shares. The United States therefore has a lot of influence on Bank decisions, and has a veto power on constitutional issues. The US executive

The World Bank between the US and the world

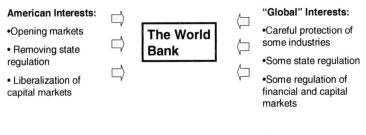

Figure 7.1 The World Bank between the US and the world

director is known to be extremely influential to the extent that any policy that displeases him or her will not be implemented (Woods, 2000, Wade, 2001). The United States also effectively chooses the World Bank's president, and it makes the single biggest contribution to IDA, which is funded by the surplus from IBRD and member-state contributions. So, like any bank, the IBRD must be accountable to its major shareholder, and IDA towards its major source of income. But, on the other hand, the World Bank derives much legitimacy from being a multi-lateral institution acting in an impartial manner. This legitimacy is crucial in order for the Bank to enjoy wide acceptance and cooperation.

Figure 7.1 illustrates how accountabilities are split between US and 'global' interests – US in order to get capital injections, and 'global' in order to gain legitimacy. Obviously, there is no such thing as 'global' interests, but the term is used here to illustrate that a number of states in the global community have had different experiences of economic development from those of the United States. The Scandinavian countries, for example, have long argued that the state could play a role in development and provide a safety-net for the poor in order for economic growth to become more balanced. Likewise, Japan and the East Asian tigers boosted industrial development by acting as investors when private agents found the risks too high. Also, they funded crucial research and development in new industries, and protected these new industries by imposing tariffs until they were considered viable enough to compete on world market terms (Evans, 1996; Weiss, 1998). These countries have had positive experiences with state regulation and are not, like the US and Britain, strong advocates of deregulation.[2] The term 'global' therefore reflects a more positive view of state intervention. Sometimes the global interests have influenced Bank processes more than others: Japan pushed for the publication of the 1993 report *The East Asian Miracle*, which acknowledged the important role of the state in the East Asian economic boom, but, in general, free-market ideology was never abandoned (Wade, 1996).

The World Bank and its presidency, then, have to maintain a difficult balancing act and, in this balancing act, accountabilities must be turned in more than one direction: to its major shareholder, the USA, and to the global community of states, and even, as we will see on pages 183–6, to an emerging global civil society. This difficult situation is reflected in many aspects of the Bank's work. Three examples are worth mentioning. The first illustration of how the Bank must please contradicting interests concerns its struggles to define the governance concept in an impartial manner.

According to the first World Bank report (1992) entirely devoted to governance, the concept has three important aspects:

1　The form of political regime.
2　The process by which authority is exercised in the management of a country's economic and social resources for development.
3　The capacity of government to design, formulate, and implement policies and discharge functions.

The report explains that it confines itself to the latter two, because its mandate forbids it to get involved in the domestic politics of creditor countries.³ The global community of states is not eager to let the Bank interfere with countries' internal affairs. The Bank has, however, been under pressure from the United States and other Western donors to broaden its agenda to include matters of human rights and democracy. Its recent adoption of human rights as an important part of development should be seen in this light (Hyden and Court, 2001; Kendal, 1995; World Bank, 1998a). When understanding governance as the 'exercise of power for development', as the Bank does, it is very difficult not to touch upon sensitive political issues. Indeed, it is often argued that politics is about power, about 'the capacity of social agents, agencies and institutions to maintain or transform their environment, social or physical' (Held, 1987: 275). As noted, World Bank governance programmes often affect domestic agents, and their relative capacities to transform their environment. In other words, the Bank does affect domestic political matters, whether it desires to or not. It does, however, continue to insist upon a neutral definition of governance, not involving aspects of the political regime, and, therefore, the Bank's work on governance reflects the tension between American and 'global' interests.

A second illustration of how interests collide in the Bank and render accountability more complex is the publication *Attacking Poverty* (World Bank, 2000a). The background to the publication was that in 1998 the Bank's chief economist, Joseph Stiglitz, publicly criticized the way the International Monetary Fund had tackled, and in some respects possibly triggered, the East Asian financial crisis in 1997. Pressure from the International Monetary Fund (IMF) had forced the East Asian countries to liberalize their financial and capital markets. The crisis emerged when investors pulled out of an unsustainable real estate boom, partly caused by IMF pressure to remove restrictions on bank lending on real estate (Stiglitz, 2001: 178). The IMF's response was to impose tight fiscal policies, but, since these countries already had budgetary surpluses starving the economy of much-needed investment in infrastructure and education, the result was to further deepen rather than end the crisis (Wade, 2001).⁴

Since the American Treasury had a strong interest in opening financial and capital markets, Stiglitz's critique of the

IMF was not well received. The US deputy secretary in the Treasury therefore asked the World Bank's president, James Wolfensohn, to persuade Stiglitz to stop his criticism. Wolfensohn reluctantly did so, and Joseph Stiglitz chose to resign. In the meantime, the publication on poverty was under way. The person in charge of the report-team was Ravi Kanpur, Stiglitz's appointee, who had been chief economist for the Bank's Africa section. At the time of Stiglitz's resignation, the draft poverty report was circulated for comments. According to Robert Wade (2001), the draft was in many ways anathema to Treasury thinking: It had a controversial section on empowerment of poor people, requiring the provision of social safety-nets, and therefore entailed a larger role of the state in social development. This section drew on completely new material that had been researched by the Bank in relation to its 'Voices of the Poor' project, in which tens of thousands of people were interviewed about their own life chances. In the draft report, providing safety-nets was therefore prioritized above free-market reforms. Also, there was a section on how to democratize and regulate capital and financial markets.

The US Treasury asked for major revisions of the report in a more neo-liberal direction, revisions that Kanpur felt it would be irresponsible to undertake, so he too resigned. The final report represented a compromise, with a larger neo-liberal element than the draft. It contained a new chapter on growth and poverty, and the chapter on markets and the poor no longer emphasized pre-establishment of safety-nets. The section on empowerment was moved to the latter half of the report, while the need for controlling capital and financial flows was substantially watered down. Wade's conclusion is that the US has too much control over the Bank. Of course, that is a normative view. But the case illustrates the delicate balancing act the Bank has to carry out between American and 'global' interests.

The third and final illustration to be mentioned here of how the Bank strikes a balance between a neo-liberal (American) approach and a 'global' view more benevolent to state direction is contained in a speech of 6 March 2002 by the president, James Wolfensohn, in which he talks about partnerships in development (table 7.1). Wolfensohn is known to be a strong president, who has been able to accommodate a lot of the criticism of the Bank and who has strengthened Bank autonomy vis-à-vis the US Treasury. His speeches, however, reflect both views.

In neo-liberalism, the goal is to maximize individual and social well-being through market-led economic growth. Therefore, the main actors are individual entrepreneurs and private firms. Economic relations are seen as a positive-sum game in which cooperation is to the benefit of all (Jackson and Sørensen, 1999). State regulation or intervention in the economy is seen as a potential threat to growth because it distorts prices and incentives. It should therefore be minimized whenever possible. A 'global' view, as used here, reflects a more positive view on the role of the state; although basically agreeing with the dominance of the market, it acknowledges that some protection of infant industries may be in order. It also sees economic relations as potentially conflictual and zero-sum, because some individuals or groups may get richer at the expense of others. The main actors, therefore, are not only individuals and private firms but also classes and states.

The quotes listed in table 7.1 represent both views. In the left-hand column, quotes reflecting the benefit of the market are listed, while the right-hand column quotes reflect the view that capitalism can create inequality and that redistribution on a global scale is necessary. The duality that the speech expresses is a cause of wide-ranging criticisms of the Bank. The left has criticized the Bank for being an imperialist institution with a bad record on poverty reduction and social issues. The right has argued that the Bank should be shut down because it is overly interventionist, destroys free market operation and is overly political (Gilbert and Vines, 2000).

Some (such as Wade) argue that the World Bank is much too dominated by the United States' neo-liberal views, while others, such as Ngaire Woods, acknowledge a large US influence but also emphasize the varying ability of different World Bank presidents to assert their autonomy (Woods, 2000). It seems that, even if the Bank has become more nuanced and is not merely a neo-liberal institution, there is a difference between rhetoric and practice. At the practical level, many recommendations and programmes reflect a neo-liberal bend.

Table 7.1 Neo-liberal and 'global' views in a Wolfensohn speech

Quotes reflecting neo-liberal views	Quotes reflecting 'global' views
• All peoples are partners in making the world a safe place • There is no wall. We are linked by trade, investment, finance, by travel and communications • Over the past 40 years, life expectancy at birth in developing countries has increased by 20 years – about as much as was achieved in all of human history prior to the middle of the twentieth century • [Good governance policies] have generated growth led by the private sector . . . By building a more favourable environment for productivity and development, they are creating jobs, encouraging growth in domestic savings and investment, while also spurring increases in foreign direct investment flows • [Western leaders] must move forward on the issue of trade openness, recognizing that without market access poor countries cannot fulfil their potential no matter how well their policies • Rich nations must also take action to cut agricultural subsidies • We have learned that we must focus on the conditions for investment and entrepreneurship, particularly for smaller enterprises and farms.	• Poverty can lead to exclusion, anger, even conflict • Belief in that wall has for too long allowed us to view as normal a world where less than 20 per cent of the population . . . dominates the world's wealth . . . and takes 80 per cent of its dollar income • Belief in that wall has allowed us for too long to view the violence, disenfranchisement, and inequality in the world as the problem of poor, weak countries and not our own • Too much inequity . . . , too much exclusion, too many wars . . . and now AIDS threatening to reverse many of the gains made over the last 40 years • We know that there are conditions which foster successful development: Education and health programs to build the human capacity of the country . . . • We have learned that debt-reduction for the most highly indebted poor countries is necessary • Rich countries must recognize that even with action on trade . . . there is still a fundamental need to boost resources for developing countries . . . to roughly 0.5 per cent of GNP • . . . But that is not enough for pro-poor growth: we must also promote investment in people, empowering them to make their own choices

Source: 'A Partnership for Development and Peace', speech delivered at the Woodrow Wilson International Center by James D. Wolfensohn, president of the World Bank Group, Washington DC, 6 March 2002; available at: www.worldbank.org/News/Speeches

Structural Adjustment Loans during the 1990s have entailed expenditure cuts and deregulation. There is a tendency, then, for Bank rhetoric to be more ideological and 'global', while Bank practice tends to be more in line with neo-liberal ideas.

To sum up, the World Bank must be accountable towards its major shareholder, which is the United States. If it fails to represent US interests, the American Congress may reassert control over development assistance and reduce funding to the Bank. On the other hand, it is essential to represent all member states if the Bank is to be a legitimate institution. Thus, World Bank accountability is directed towards more than one actor.

With globalization, a new type of global actor has emerged: the international non-governmental organization (NGO). In addition to the cross-pressure from the USA and the other member states, international NGOs are increasingly pressurizing the World Bank to take their interests into consideration. This brings us to the third aspect of the World Bank and governance: the World Bank's participation in a process of global governance that requires it to take an emerging global civil society seriously.

The World Bank and global civil society

In a period of globalization, an increasing amount of public policy problems that arise are of a global nature: terrorism, drug-trafficking, environmental problems, trade standards, financial markets and migration are just a few examples. These problems call for solutions, and the World Bank has become involved in the search for such solutions.

Globalization can be defined as networks of interdependence at worldwide distances (Nye, 2001). It is not only the economy and markets that have tied people together across nations: globalization also has a political, cultural, social and environmental dimension. This has created a political backlash, where people who experience globalization forces as too powerful initiate protests against it. Large international organizations can no longer hold big meetings without the possibility of massive protests and demonstrations. The protesters come mainly from rich countries. Some of them represent Northern non-governmental organizations. And some of these NGOs collaborate with sister organizations in the South, who may represent smaller grassroots movements of people directly affected by World Bank-supported projects.

Local–global civil-society advocacy networks have pressured for the World Bank to apply good governance norms to its own organization in order to become more transparent and accountable in relation to, for example, human rights and environmental issues. A central actor in the 'anti-globalization' movement is the 'People's Global Action' group, who criticizes the World Bank for, among other things, maintaining its privatization policies and the demand for expenditure cuts in Third World countries. An Eastern European-based international NGO, 'Bankwatch', monitors the operations of the World Bank and IMF to prevent environmentally and socially harmful impacts of development finance.[5]

The emergence of this kind of global civil society could not be ignored by the World Bank, which has not been entirely unresponsive to the demands for change. Pressure from civil-society groups has contributed to institutional measures to increase the Bank's accountability towards groups affected by its programmes. For example, in environmental policies, during the 1980s there was a growing awareness of rainforest destruction and indigenous peoples' rights. NGOs began highlighting cases of World Bank-sponsored projects, in which rainforests had been destroyed or indigenous peoples had been adversely affected (Fox and Brown, 1998). These campaigns, together with internal critique in the Bank, resulted in the creation of an environmental department as part of a reorganization in 1987.

A controversial case in which indigenous people were affected was Nepal's Arun III Hydroelectric Dam. There had been much protest against the project because it involved the resettlement of tens of thousands of people. The new president of the Bank, James Wolfensohn, decided to cancel Bank support of the project, thus responding to NGO demands, overruling his own senior management in this regard, and shocking both critics and supporters (Fox and Brown, 1998: 3).

The Arun controversy indirectly triggered the establishment of a new accountability mechanism: the Bank's Inspection Panel in 1994. Through the Inspection Panel, citizens of developing countries can directly communicate grievances regarding the environmental and social costs of World Bank projects. The Panel, which is independent and does not employ World Bank staff, then investigates whether the Bank has lived up to its own environmental and social standards in a specific project. It is widely agreed that the Inspection Panel was created in response to sustained advocacy campaigns by coalitions of non-governmental organizations in the North, with grassroots in the South (Fox, 2000). In the US, NGOs collaborated with members of Congress to pressure for reforms in the Bank. Since Congress can control funding of the IDA, it was a powerful channel of influence. Jonathan Fox and L. David Brown quote a Bank official:

> I was in charge of trying to . . . help . . . to raise money for IDA and you all know it's gotten very difficult to do so. One thing I learned very quickly is that we need the support of NGOs in the North in order to do that. It also became very clear very quickly that the NGOs in the North are very closely related to their work and experience with the NGOs in the South. And so it became very quickly clear that we had to build better bridges to the NGOs in the South.[6]

The establishment of the Inspection Panel is one indicator that the World Bank has become more responsive towards its surroundings. An indicator of increased transparency is the publication of a huge number of documents on the Internet. Bank procedures and Bank collected data, as well as country reports, are publicly accessible. In addition, the World Bank tries to respond to NGO criticism by setting up space for debate on the Internet. For example, in connection with the 2002 Oslo conference on development economics, the Bank responds on its website to claims by NGOs (represented by the Oslo 2002 movement).[7] The Poverty Reduction Strategy Papers that the Bank now requires recipient governments to implement, in collaboration with stakeholders and civil-society groups, may be seen as another example of how the Bank has focused on openness and responsiveness.

In sum, the World Bank has become more accountable to a global constituency represented by international NGOs – a constituency that the World Bank considers to have a legitimate interest in its policies. However, the question is whether the Bank has become more accountable in practice or merely in policy. Jonathan Fox has analysed the cases taken up by the Inspection Panel since it was established, and he points out that member governments often block further investigation. In the case of Brazil's Itaparica Dam, for example, the Brazilian government promised irrigation to displaced farmers in order to get the Bank's board to reject the claim. In doing so, it avoided further and more serious investigation of how people were adversely affected by the project. Fox (2000) thus argues that the extent of real change as a result of the establishment of the panel is quite small.

Conclusion

The World Bank and governance interrelate in three ways. The first has been a matter of debate in comparative politics because it is about the conditions the Bank attaches to loans to poor countries, and therefore affects the discussion regarding the best model of economic governance and how Bank conditions affect state and politics in general. In the 1990s, the Bank supported good governance programmes, but since the turn of the twenty-first century it has become more selective, tending to prefer to give loans to countries that already have good governance.

The second way in which governance and the Bank interrelate has more to do with the debate in international relations regarding how to hold large international organizations to account. In this respect, the World Bank is accountable towards its largest shareholder, the United States. But it must also be accountable towards the rest of its member states in order to be accepted as a legitimate institution. Because of globalization, global civil society pressures international organizations such as the World Bank to apply good governance principles to their own organization. The third way the Bank and governance interrelate is that it is a part of global governance, and, therefore, the Bank increasingly becomes accountable to a global public in addition to being accountable towards its members and shareholders. The World Bank, particularly under the Wolfensohn presidency, has taken some steps to improve accountability and transparency. The extent to which these efforts will change Bank practice remains to be seen. But since the United States is the largest shareholder, future changes are not likely to be entirely anathema to the interests of the American government. Governance of the World Bank must still strike a balance between diverging constituencies. The World Bank is thus a case of complex accountability structures and blurred boundaries between domestic and international in a more globalized world.

8
Conclusion

> The army of governance theorists is so disparate that one is
> led to think that the word, governance, itself is like a label
> placed on a whole batch of bottles which are then distributed
> among diverse producers each of whom fills them with the
> drink of his choice. The consumer has to look carefully.
>
> Baudin, 1942:4–5[1]

The statement above was written about the concept of corporatism, but the very same could be said about governance.
As the introduction to this book makes clear, governance is
used in many different contexts and has many different definitions. For example, in public administration and public
policy, one usage of governance relates it to network steering
while a broader perception of the concept refers to the
management of all kinds of rules and practices affecting
policy-making, be they of a hierarchic, market- or network-
dominated character. And in European studies, governance is
used both as referring to multi-level policy-making and as
referring to something broader, as more than government but
not necessarily of a multi-level type.

However, it is possible to discern a core of governance
which is common to the different usages. This core has to do
with the conception of governance as referring to something

more than government. Governance processes include state as well as non-state actors who are bound together in a plurality of networks. Governance theories share a broad institutional background, and they are all reactions to perceived inadequacies of existing approaches within their sub-fields. Governance, therefore, is not just old wine in new bottles, but denotes a new approach to the study of politics.

By summarizing the preceding chapters about governance in public administration and public policy, in international relations and in comparative politics, this concluding section outlines the common features of governance as used in the three sub-fields of political science. It then discusses the consequences of insights from governance theory for the boundaries of the sub-fields and explores the different usages of governance between the sub-fields. It returns to the issues of democracy and accountability, ending with a discussion of common problems that occur with a governance approach.

Summarizing the chapters

In the introductory chapter, governance was defined in terms of rules, where rules include norms and formal and informal codes of behaviour. Governance refers to the *setting*, *application*, and *enforcement of rules*. In governance theory, concern with both the *input-side* (democratic procedures) and the *output-side* (efficient and effective institutions) can be discerned, although the latter has clearly been debated most. There is also a common concern with rules of the game, but the focus varies between setting, application or enforcement.

In chapter 2, the debate on governance in *public administration* and *public policy* was sketched. Governance was introduced as a consequence of changes in the public sector during the 1980s, which had been characterized by a wave of new public management reforms. In the aftermath of the reforms, an increasing number of policy networks have emerged. These often prove to be efficient deliverers of service, but they may also lead to fragmentation, and they certainly provide a challenge to overall coordination.

Table 8.1 Summarizing governance theory

	Public administration and public policy	International relations	European governance	Comparative politics I	Comparative politics II
Legitimacy	Output	Output (and input)	Output	Output	Input
Focus	Efficiency	Efficiency (and democracy)	Efficiency	Efficiency	Democracy
Policy sector	Institutions of service delivery	Institutions of international cooperation	Institutions of structural policy (and regulatory policy)	Institutions of economic development (mainly industrial policy)	Institutions of the political regime
Main concepts	Policy networks, steering	International and transnational networks, globalization	Networks, multi-level governance	Networks, state–society synergy	Networks, trust, reciprocity, public realm

Government is only one of many actors in the delivery of services and, as a consequence, it needs to strengthen its coordinating role. Scholars thus argue that governments must accept they can no longer steer directly, but must learn how to manage networks in an indirect way to enable an efficient service delivery, for example by including important groups in negotiations about policy decisions.

There are two major conceptions of governance in public administration and public policy. One is narrow, relating governance to the management of networks, the other broad, referring to the process whereby rules of public policy-making and implementation are set, applied and enforced. These rules (or institutions) can stress a hierarchic, network-oriented or market-oriented organization. While the primary concern in the literature has been with service delivery, it remains an open question whether networks play a large role in all policy sectors. In other words, the role of the state in governance varies according to sector.

The focus in governance theory has been on the efficiency of public policy-making and implementation. Legitimacy is thus mainly seen to derive from the output-side: from effective performance. However, some scholars have additionally raised the issue of input-oriented legitimacy: in a situation where much policy-making and implementation takes place within relatively closed networks, the question of how democratic accountability is ensured becomes urgent. Legitimacy and accountability may be increased by including all stakeholders in the policy network; however, the need to make sure that policies are in the interest of all in an aggregated sense, rather than dominated by particularistic interests, calls for the establishment of procedural rules, such as deliberative forums.

In *international relations*, the concern with governance emerged as a result of evidence that complex interdependence had accelerated. Globalization, with intensified global interactions, implies that there is an identified need for regulation at the global level. New international institutions for global problem-solving have emerged, while existing global institutions have taken on new tasks. These changes have led to other actors than the state playing an important role on the global scene. For example, global transnational networks have emerged around issues such as the environment, human rights or landmines.

The concern with governance by IR scholars has been concentrated mainly among liberalists and solidarists within the English School. Realists and pluralists do not consider the construction of institutions for global governance to be feasible. A common definition of global governance is provided by James Rosenau, referring to systems of rule at all levels of human activity – from the family to the international organization – in which the pursuit of goals through the exercise of control has transnational repercussions. Chapter 3 defines global governance along the same lines, as referring to the process whereby rules of global public policy-making are set, applied and enforced.

An important question for IR scholars is the effectiveness of international institutions and whether nation-states can be bound at all by international rules. Realists argue that rules can only bind states as long as the rules are in accordance with the interests of that state. Pluralists argue that the rules of sovereignty and non-intervention indeed serve to maintain order most of the time. Liberalists (such as Keohane) often argue that more international rules should be established in order to provide efficient global policy-making. Strong liberalists (such as Rosenau) go further by arguing that the main question is not only whether *states* will be bound by rules, but is also about recognizing the myriad of actors already engaged in affecting norms and rules in global politics. IR scholars should therefore abandon the presumption that states should always and necessarily be the basic analytical unit.

The concern in IR theory has mainly been on the output-side and with the need to strengthen the effectiveness of global institutions. However, there is also an increasing concern with the democratic accountability of such institutions, and thus about the input-side as well: there is a lively debate whether it is possible to establish procedures on the global level to ensure more democracy, or whether it is more realistic to concentrate on existing institutions and, if so, how their accountability could be increased.

Studying the *European Community* was for a long period mainly a concern of international relations scholars, as described in chapter 4. The governance approach has the virtue of moving European Studies beyond the debate about integration as a supra-national or intergovernmental affair. Instead, the governance approach takes our attention to what happens, not only at the intergovernmental conferences where treaties are signed, but in the European polity. Rather than asking the IR question about the extent of integration (how far has it proceeded?), the governance approach identifies the actors involved in the EU policy process and analyses the impact on national policy-making (what are its consequences?).

Some EU scholars identify multi-level governance (MLG) with a specific institutional set-up, involving networks of actors at three levels: the regional, the state and the EU level. Others have a broader conception of governance as the setting, application and enforcement of rules for European policy-making, be they networks, markets or hierarchies. The specific institutional set-up varies according to policy sector: Cohesion policy, for example, is characterized by networks of supra-national and national actors, as well as sub-national actors, whereas in regulatory policies, both hierarchic and network steering are commonplace.

Studies of governance in the EU have mainly been concerned with the efficiency of European policy-making, for example, the methods of securing compliance by member states. The EU's legitimacy is thus seen to derive mainly from the output-side. But the democratic deficit of the EU has also been raised by governance scholars. They provide the insights that, precisely because many actors and levels are involved in European processes of governance, efforts to increase democratic legitimacy have to be directed at multiple arenas.

Chapters 5 and 6 outlined governance in relation to two prominent debates in *comparative politics*: one about the role of the state in development, the other about democratization. The first is perhaps most appropriately termed comparative political economy, and overlaps slightly with some of the issues touched upon in chapter 2, because economic policy obviously is also of interest to scholars in comparative public policy.

Theories about the state and economic development discuss the optimal model for development. The classical liberal model emphasized market-led development; the Keynesian model a more regulated market-capitalism; and the neo-liberal model has argued for deregulation and a dismantling of the state. The dichotomy between market and state in these models tends to ignore other ways in which the economy can be governed. Self-governing networks are important in this context, because they span across the public–private divide. Governance refers to how institutions for economic policy-making and implementation are set up, and what their consequences are. Governance does not refer to one particular model of development, but many scholars used insights from studying developmental states in East Asia to criticize the particular governance model applied by Western donors. The main concern of students of governance and development has not been democratic-input procedures. It has been implicitly assumed that institutions generate legitimacy through effective outputs. To the extent that democracy has been debated, it has been part of an argument that democracy is not a necessary prerequisite for the developmental state, as the East Asian experience demonstrates. However, democratic procedures may be an intrinsic part of the developmental states elsewhere, which is illustrated by the examples of Botswana and Mauritius.

Democratization theories were initially dominated by the modernization approach that searched for the structural prerequisites of democracy. Transition theories, on the contrary, studied actors in transition processes, and assumed they would carry through a transition process that eventually led to democracy. Governance treads a middle ground and acknowledges institutional constraints on individual behaviour, yet, at the same time, when institutions are in flux, individuals and groups have a potentially large influence on defining new rules. Governance is about the setting, application and enforcement of regime rules, but the focus is on the *setting* of rules, precisely because a transition implies a move away from one institutional set-up towards another. Governance in democratization theory is thus, in a sense, meta-policy-making: it refers to the setting of rules that guide rule-making. Contrary to transition theory, governance does not assume that transitions will result in democracy; rather, democracy may be one outcome of governance processes.

Governance is less loaded than democracy and is therefore capable of covering broader processes of change.

In all, governance in comparative politics involves the study of different institutional models and processes that are relevant to economic development and regime change. The difference between the two is on the type of rules in focus: theories about the state in development focus on setting an institutional framework for economic policy-making, while democratization theories focus on setting an institutional framework for the political regime – a constitution. Both study the conditions of governance and debate how some economies and societies are less governable than others. Because governability varies, one unique model of governance cannot be applied universally, and this is true for political as well as economic constitutions. States take up the challenges posed by globalization in different ways. Weaker states tend to depend heavily on the international financial institutions and therefore carry out neo-liberal programmes that may not be suitable to their economic and political situation. International trade rules do not allow weak states to follow the same rather protectionist strategies that the developed countries followed before them. Stronger states, such as the developmental states in East Asia, tend to be more autonomous towards external actors and have experimented with their own, more state-directed, models. Thus, although globalization may involve a fragmentation or dislocation of power away from the nation-state, state institutions remain important filters for global processes, resulting in different outcomes for different national settings. The two traditions in comparative politics have remained distinct. While there is a literature on how democratization affects economic reform, there is still a need for research about how processes of regime governance and economic governance interact.

Finally, chapter 7 demonstrated how studying an international organization such as the World Bank can involve drawing upon more than one way to use the concept of governance; in this case governance in relation to development models, but also as a framework for analysing regime transitions. Also, governance as a global process is relevant, because the Bank is an important part of global decision-making structures regarding economic redistribution, environmental issues and, also, the promotion of 'good governance'. Finally, the World Bank is an institution that illustrates the complex accountability structures that characterize global politics today.

Disciplinary boundaries

Governance theories have developed out of different theoretical debates, and they remain quite insulated. With a few exceptions (especially between Rosenau and Rhodes), there are not many cross-references between the governance literature in different sub-fields. Yet the very focus of governance theory, i.e. to investigate the political implications of – and responses to – social and economic change, indicates that sharp boundaries between political science sub-fields cannot be upheld.

Borders between nation-states were never watertight. Indeed, a long-standing tradition in political sociology, represented by authors such as Anthony Giddens and Michael Mann, maintains that the nation-state was never entirely a domestic creation. The spread of the modern nation-state across the globe is seen by these authors as a defining feature of globalization. Globalization entailed the consolidation of, rather than the erosion of, states.

With accelerated globalization since the 1980s caused by, among other things, the deregulation of capital flows and a new electronic communication infrastructure, social relations extend even more across borders. The only possible exceptions to the global reach of markets are some parts of Africa and South Asia. If we recognize that *loci* of authority extend beyond the nation-state, the study of politics has to let go of artificial boundaries between comparative politics and international relations, or between comparative political economy and international political economy. In this book, these boundaries are upheld to maintain structure and clarity, but another important reason is that the debates have largely remained with the distinct sub-fields. If the purpose, as in this volume, is to relate governance to existing debates, the distinction between sub-fields is therefore maintained. Reading through the chapters should make clear that there is a great need for sub-disciplinary interchange (although there are some exceptions regarding this distinction between sub-fields in recent publications, for example, Pierre, 2000). Since there are many common concerns in governance theory, there are also common problems, an issue we shall turn to now. More cross-disciplinary collaboration among governance theorists could mean that such problems would be more adequately addressed.

Key discussions and common problems in governance theory

In conclusion, we shall turn to the key features currently occupying all governance theorists regardless of sub-field. These are networks, reciprocity, accountability and democracy. They are discussed from different angles and with varying attention, but they remain vital concerns. This final section also addresses some problems in governance theory, mainly concerning the lack of attention to issues such as power, interests and conflict.

Networks and reciprocity

To a certain extent, all governance scholars study relations of reciprocity, whether inside networks or across networks. To illustrate, governance in relation to democratization theory deals with the fundamental issue of generating legitimacy for the public realm by establishing democratic procedures. These procedures involve reciprocal action by state as well as societal actors. Theories about economic governance stress the reciprocal interaction between state and economic agents in networks that increase the efficiency and implementation of economic policy. The theory about European governance stresses the involvement in policy-making of networks of national representatives, commission officials and non-state actors. Governance in public administration and public policy developed out of the debate on policy networks, in which horizontal reciprocity among the members of a network is seen as essential. Governance in international relations is also occupied with how to govern international networks. Many IR scholars believe that reciprocity and trust, spanning across nations, is crucial for the establishment of international institutions of governance.

There is a difference with regard to scale, of course. Whereas units of the networks may be individuals in local governance, they are most often organizations, or individuals representing organizations, at the national level. At the global level, the units are states and NGOs. The larger the network and the wider it expands, the more likelihood there is of difficulty in locating the core of authority. In the case of a policy process in a medium-sized town, networks may render the identification of authority more difficult, but, in a network comprising many international NGOs and other actors, it can be almost impossible to identify who is responsible for a certain action. The difference of scale thus gives rise to different consequences for accountability and democracy, as we shall see on the following pages.

There is also a difference with regard to whether networks are viewed in positive or negative terms. In public policy, for example, networks are usually viewed in a positive manner, because they increase policy-making efficiency. They can generate information and ease implementation immensely. However, some also highlight the negative implications: networks can function as barriers that impede effective implementation. In theories of development and democratization, networks are seen to have more ambiguous consequences. On the one hand, horizontal networks help to generate trust and reciprocity across regions and ethnic groups. On the other, vertical networks may reinforce cleavages and inter-group conflict. In international relations, the democratic potential of networks as pressure groups on governments is recognized, but their unaccountability is viewed as a serious problem.

Finally, although negative as well as positive implications are discussed, there is still very little emphasis on conflict within or among networks. Self-governing networks are based on reciprocity and consensus. Yet there has been very little discussion (with a few important exceptions) of a failure to reach consensus. What happens when conflicting interests within the network cannot be reconciled? In much governance theory, relations seem to run smoothly and there are few frictions. However, the essence of politics concerns the determination and allocation of values, and decision-making cannot escape conflicting interests with regard to how values are allocated. The democratic state (as pointed out by Paul Hirst (2000)) was designed to contain conflict; networks were not. It seems, then, that states will still have an important role as providers of the stability which is a pre-condition for effective decision-making in the first place.

Accountability

The common concern with networks additionally implies a preoccupation with accountability. Governance has been identified both narrowly with network management and more broadly as referring to the management of rules. In both senses, there is recognition that policy-making is no longer strictly confined to the nation-state. The search for accountability characterizes most sub-fields, although in varying ways. In public administration and policy, the main focus of the debate on the question of accountability has been not so much with regard to democratic control, but rather as it pertains to bureaucratic or hierarchic control. The expansion of self-organizing, self-regulating networks in service delivery implies a loss of direct control. If public care for the elderly, for example, is contracted out to a private organization that again contracts out specific service functions to yet another set of private contractors, the accountability chain may break. The control over the use of money may be weakened, because the degree of separation between the government and the services it funds become larger. The preoccupation with accountability, in other words, has related more to a concern with how to control the use of resources in order to perform efficiently rather than democratically. This is true for international relations, too, in the sense that the rise of international regimes, NGOs and other multinational actors means a fragmentation of policy-making authority. States no longer have (if they ever had) full control over regulation and decision-making. Above the state there is no authoritative body, nor likelihood of one, which can ensure that the multiple actors in global politics can be responsible for their actions. In addition, the case of the World Bank clearly illustrates how accountability has become more complex and multi-directional. The main debates have concerned ways to ensure efficiency and transparency, and thereby ameliorate corruption problems.

When discussing the role of the state in economic development, the emphasis on performance accountability can be discerned as well. The developmental state was accountable in many ways, despite the fact that it was not a democracy in the liberal sense. Financial and outcome responsibility was high, and the public authorities were often part of networks to promote technological innovation. Hence, networks were accountable in the sense that they were responsible for producing results.

When discussing governance and regime transitions, accountability becomes central not only in terms of performance but also in terms of fairness and equality. Network management is a strategy to build trust and reciprocity, i.e. social capital, because inclusion will promote interaction across regional or ethnically based groups. Accountability is a crucial part of such a strategy because, without it, social capital may be destroyed. In governance theory in comparative politics, it is therefore assumed that accountability increases with increased reciprocity between state and societal actors. This will help build democracy and, essentially, it will strengthen the state's ability to formulate and implement policies that promote economic and social development.

Although international relations and public administration scholars see the rise of networks as enhancing flexibility and as potentially enhancing efficiency, they also see them as threatening accountability because they are out of reach of the state. This is not always the case in theories of governance in comparative politics, where the state may derive its strength from formal or informal policy networks. In economic governance, the state may gain from inducing networks of economic agents to self-governance. The questions of state control and state strength are not looked upon in the same light within the different sub-fields and a further exploration of these issues is arguably needed.

In sum, the type of accountability most in focus in governance theory has been bureaucratic, or performance-related accountability, with the exception of the literature on democratization. In all sub-fields, however, there is an increasing concern with democratic accountability, which has important, though different, implications at different levels of governance.

Democratic governance at different levels

At the local level, the rise of community networks and voluntary organizations in service delivery has had positive as well as negative implications. On the positive side, there is more flexibility, and service deliverers have been observed to be more responsive towards clients' needs. In addition, participation has broadened and individual members of networks have been empowered. On the negative side, there is more fragmentation, less control, and the risked exclusion. Remedies to these problems have been put forward, one suggestion being that local councillors could be more involved in the networks. However, the role of local councillors should also be to ensure the aggregate interest of the whole community, so there is a danger that local councillors might identify excessively with the interest of one particular network. Hence, a procedural solution could be the establishment of deliberative forums in which decisions are discussed with a representative group of citizens.

At the national level, it has been argued that the emergence of networks, with the increased complexity and globalization of economy and society, narrows both the reach and the degree of control left in the nation-state. Although we have argued that abandoning the state as an important *locus* of authority and power is premature, it can be maintained that the conditions under which democracy is exercised have changed. When the state administration loses its reach, national parliaments can no longer hold it to account. However, even in such a situation, national parliaments may still play a role as democratic inputs to supra-national organs, as has been debated in the case of the EU. The implications of globalization and network society for democratic governance thus need to be examined further. Some democratization theorists have not yet taken globalization and the challenges it poses for democracy into account, but others, such as Andrew McGrew, David Held (cosmopolitan democracy) and Paul Hirst (associational democracy), argue for the necessity of experimenting with democratic models more fitting to the complex and fluid power structures that characterize modern politics. Although different, both models support democratization at many levels and they argue for the importance of democratizing self-governing organizations at the lowest levels. Functions that can be carried out by such organizations should be decentralized, although national parliaments would still be important as watchdogs and forums, in which decisions regarding the allocation of public funding could be taken.

On the regional level, the European Union is an example of a supra-national organization that in many ways resembles national political systems, and governance theory studies it as such. Multi-level and transgovernmental policy networks increase efficiency in many areas, but they also render accountability mechanisms more complicated. Negotiations take place in these networks which are beyond the control of national parliaments. The European Parliament could play a role, but its influence remains limited. In some sense, then, policy-making in the EU is beyond the control of European citizens, and it is possible to talk about a democratic deficit in the EU. The insights from governance theory are that the multiple *loci* of policy-making and implementation imply that democratization cannot be introduced at one level only; it involves greater openness and transparency at multiple levels.

At the global level, the implications of globalization, networks and complexity for democratic accountability are more difficult to discuss. At the local level, the democratic problem posed by networks seems easier to solve than the democratic challenge provided by networks and regimes at the international level. There is no global government and it is naive to assume such government could be designed in the near future. The best we can do is to improve the accountability of existing institutions, and a number of actors are making efforts in that respect. As chapter 7 on the World

Bank made clear, international NGOs have started to demand more accountability from international organizations. In addition, some boycotts of big multinationals have actually led to changes in the way companies act. McDonald's or Nike are among examples of large corporations that have been targeted by such actions. Such cases make James Rosenau (2000: 195) argue that 'nascent forms of democratic governance can be discerned in the labyrinth of globalized space'. However, a global democracy based on the same principles as national democracy is not feasible, for the simple reason that power is diffused and exercised in a myriad of *loci*. In addition, making international institutions more accountable to NGOs will not suffice because, typically, the NGOs themselves are not accountable to any well-defined constituency. Therefore, further exploration of existing or possible accountability mechanisms at the global level is needed.

The insights from governance theory thus have different implications for democratic governance at the various levels. At the local, national, and possibly even at the regional level, measures to strengthen accountability are more realistic than at the global level, where there is no recognized elected forum for decision-making.

Continued importance of state and hierarchy?

The emphasis on networks in governance theory has a flip side. It tends to ignore the continued importance of hierarchy. And it tends to ignore the interplay between hierarchy and networks. As outlined in chapter 2, network governance may take place in the shadow of hierarchy. Networks may have representatives from different state-organizations. If interactions within the network become more frequent than interaction with the mother-organization, hierarchical accountability may suffer. This is what often occurs in weak states, where public officials are generally more loyal to their own ethnic group than to their employer. Further consideration of the interaction between hierarchies and networks is clearly needed, together with an examination of the conditions under which hierarchical solutions would be preferable to networks. Our discussion suggested that when benefactors from a policy are highly concentrated, interests may be skewed in one direction, with the result that a network could be dominated by these interests. Hierarchy would be needed to ensure that the outcome was in the interest of the majority.

In public administration and public policy, and to some extent in the governance literature in IR, there is a tendency to argue that governance now takes place *without* government. However, as discussed, the state arguably remains important, both in a number of policy sectors and on the international scene. States are key filters through which global processes are moulded. As channels of democratic input to supra-national organizations, states remain sources of legitimacy in modern governance.[2] States are better placed to contain conflict than networks. And, although states may lose sovereignty to supra-national organizations, they also gain strength from them – for example, EU member states sometimes attribute blame to the EU when implementing unpopular policies.

In comparative politics, the concern with the state is still prominent. This is probably because the attention is often on weak states in the developing world that are in the midst of state-building. Governance therefore implies the setting of meta-rules, i.e. rules about establishing a political order. In such settings, it is not the hollowing out of the state that is relevant, but rather how to strengthen a state that is under pressure from both the global economy and Western donors, as well as from societies that are very difficult to govern.

In all, governance does not take place without government, and governance theory should leave the role of the state open to empirical investigation rather than simply assume that the role is declining.

Under-emphasis on power

Finally, the attention on networks in governance theory tends to ignore a fundamental aspect of power: networks typically have limited membership. Although they span across the state–society divide, they include some actors and exclude others. For example, weak states are typically characterized by closed ethnic networks, in which case governance is concerned with setting rules that avoid conflict between them. Power often has a winner-takes-all character, because the ethnic group in power may favour its own members at the cost of other ethnic groups. This problem of network management is not as serious in stronger states, but it clearly illustrates the danger of letting particularistic interests dominate policy-making.

The focus on state–society synergy and on a win–win situation tends to underemphasize the cases in which the state is overly repressive or in which society needs to assert its autonomy against the state. Focusing on win–win situations is important, but there is a tendency to ignore who loses and how losers could be compensated. In international relations, too, the realist insight that state power and national interests may dominate institutions for global problem-solving provides a sobering angle on global governance enthusiasts. It could also be appropriate to further develop themes of neo-Marxist arguments regarding corporate power.

Hence, practically all usages of governance lack a discussion of power and interests. By analysing cases of state–society synergy and win–win situations, governance theory offers a new angle on the rules of policy-making, whether on a sub-national, national, transnational or supra-national scale. However, this should not allow us to ignore the fact that some actors have more power and may therefore dominate the allocation of values.

Despite these problems, governance is a concept that is here to stay in political science. Its reference to a process involving more than government indicates far more than a reworking of old ideas. It concerns the political implications of social change, applying a fresh focus on political institutions in a changing world.

Notes

Chapter 1 Introduction: The Meanings of Governance

1 The description of the frescos draws upon Koch (2002).
2 See also Kickert, Klijn and Koppenjan (1999: 3), who 'disagree with the ideas of the new public management'.
3 The reason why a separate chapter on the EU is warranted is that there is a separate theoretical debate about the EU. The rise of local and transnational networks and the concern with governance do imply that the EU is not a unique case but is a part of the changes taking place globally.

Chapter 2 Governance in Public Administration and Public Policy: Steering Inter-Organizational Networks

1 In Norwegian: *Den parlamentariske styrings-kjede.*
2 See 'Blacks vs teachers', *The Economist*, 8 March 2001.
3 It is debatable whether decentralization or citizens' empowerment is part of NPM. For example, New Zealand's reforms, which have been among the most comprehensive NPM reforms, have been characterized as having 'a preference for retaining key governmental powers and responsibilities at the central government level with only limited devolution to subnational government' (Turner and Hulme, 1997: 232). Also, Thatcher's reforms in many ways meant a reassertion of central

authority (Rhodes, 1997a). However, decentralization was a big issue in relation to NPM and, in many instances, decentralization happened alongside a strengthening of central government over other areas – as Rhodes puts it, 'more control over less'.

4 See also Marsh and Rhodes (1992).

5 Teubner and Willke, quoted in Mayntz (1993: 17).

6 When looking through Rod Rhodes's work, it is not possible to find a straightforward definition of governance. In some contexts, governance refers to a particular type of networks (Rhodes, 1996: 660). Governance equals what Rhodes has called the differentiated polity, consisting of intergovernmental relations and networks, while government equals the traditional Westminister model. When understanding governance as structure, formulations like the following become possible: 'Indirect management is the central challenge posed *by governance* for the operating code of central elites' (Rhodes, 1997a: 5, emphasis added). In other words, governance as a complicated structure poses new challenges for policy-making. In other contexts, governance is used more as process, as the steering of networks, and it is this meaning which is relevant in this section, where the implications for the strategies of political actors are discussed.

7 See also chapter 5 on the role of the state in economic development.

8 Pierre and Peters likewise argue that there is a tendency to equate traditional modes of governance with the old public administration, reserving the concept of governance for the new or emerging forms. However, governance is an old concept, what is new is the complexity of changing systems that governance must confront (Pierre and Peters, 2000: 17–18).

9 The study was carried out by Eva Sørensen and Jacob Torfing in relation to a larger research project on 'democracy from below', under the direction of Jørgen Goul Andersen, Aalborg University, and Jens Hoff, Copenhagen University.

Chapter 3 Governance in International Relations: Governing in a Global Era

1 Classical realism as described by Morgenthau or Carr is significantly less deterministic than Waltz's neo-realism. Neo-realism is used here because it is in opposition to interdependence theory and thus provides a model against which

to explain interdependence theory. The account here does not do justice to the entire realist paradigm. In addition, Waltz's theory was put forward in response to Keohane and Nye's interdependence theory. Keohane and Nye's *Power and Interdependence* preceded Waltz's *Theory of International Politics* by two years (1977 and 1979, respectively). However, realist assumptions are generally described as preceding those of liberalism.

2 This argument can mainly be attributed to Kenneth Waltz, who is a neo-realist. Traditional realists, such as Hans Morgenthau, found that the causes of war were anchored in human nature.

3 The account of liberalism draws mainly on Keohane and Nye (2001); Viotti and Kauppi (1987); and Jackson and Sørensen (1999). There are many different strands of liberalism: for instance, Jackson and Sørensen identify sociological liberalism, institutional liberalism, republican liberalism, interdependence liberalism, weak and strong liberalism. This chapter will not go into the details of the different strands.

4 It may also, according to some liberalists, be the result of the fact that democracies do not fight each other. Democracy encourages peaceful international relations because democratic governments are controlled by their citizens, who will not support wars with other democracies, and because such political systems tend to have common moral foundations (Jackson and Sørensen, 1999: 124). Another claim against the realist assumption that the balance of power is the main source of peace is that, for some states, it is simply too costly to fight each other. This is the case on the African continent where territories are vast, population densities low, and borders usually fluid and hard to control. The African states are often busy trying to maintain internal peace, and, if these states were to fight, they would spend valuable and scarce resources mobilizing armies that would have to travel large distances before a confrontation. War and conflict in Africa, therefore, tend to be intra-state civil wars rather than inter-state wars (Herbst, 2000). The image of international anarchy and domestic peace could in fact be turned on its head with regard to Africa, which can be characterized better by domestic anarchy (in some countries) and international peace.

5 Anthony Giddens's concept of modernity involves four institutional dimensions: surveillance, which is closely associated with the nation-state and its ability to control information and supervision of citizens; military power, which is also associated with the nation-state and its control of the means of violence

characteristic of the modern period; capitalism, which has been intertwined with the development of the modern nation-state because it has brought about surplus production that can be taxed, and has accumulated capital in competitive markets which the state has protected; and, finally, industrialism, which is about a transformation of nature, the development of a 'created environment' (Giddens, 1990: 59).

6 Anderson and Norheim (1993). 'Is World Trade becoming more regionalized?', *Review of International Economics*, 1, referred to in Held et al. (1999).

7 M. Wilkins. 'Comparative Hosts', *Business History*, 36, cited in Held, et al. (1999: 237).

8 http://www.lse.ac.uk/Depts/global/

9 See www.icbl.org and Rutherford (2000).

10 Solidarism belongs, together with pluralism, within the English School of international relations. It is described here along with liberalism, because solidarism, unlike pluralism, has a normative vision of a reformed system of global governance.

Chapter 4 European Governance: Between International Relations and Public Policy

1 David Mitrany, *A Working Peace System*, p. 51, cited in Haas (1964: 10).

2 The first pillar consists of the three 'old communities' together: the Coal and Steel Community, the Atomic Energy Community (Euratom) and the Economic Community (the common market).

3 The debate on a European Constitution was introduced by German Foreign Minister Joschka Fischer in May 1999. In a speech in Berlin he argued for the necessity of going beyond intergovernmentalism and increasing democratic legitimacy by a kind of new Philadelphia (a parallel to the US constitution-making process). The speech can be found at the German foreign office's website: www.auswaertiges-amt.de

4 *International Herald Tribune*, 31 January 2003: 'A Union (European) now divided'; and 14 February 2003: 'Blair demands EU back war in Iraq'.

5 See more about the youth meeting at http://www.acc. eu.org/uploads/YOUTH_Pressrelease.pdf

6 As Martin Kohler argues, the term 'the public sphere' denotes '... an organizing principle for the legitimacy of political order' (Kohler, 1998: 236).

Chapter 5   Governance in Comparative Politics I: The State and Economic Development

1 See also chapter 2 on the New Public Management.
2 The so-called Tobin Tax. See http://www.ceedweb.org/iirp/factsheet.htm
3 For critique of structural adjustment programmes, see, for example, Gibbon and Raikes (1996); Mkandawire and Olukoshi (1995); Mkandawire and Soludo (1999); or Olowu (1999).
4 Unfortunately, the Harambee were later destroyed by Kenyatta's more authoritarian successor, Daniel Arap-Moi.

Chapter 6   Governance in Comparative Politics II: Theories of Democratization

1 Huntington (1965: 392). See Remmer (1997) for a discussion of Huntington's article.
2 See also Hollis (1994) for an outline of the structure–actor debate.
3 For example, defining polyarchy as a relatively democratized regime, a regime that is 'highly inclusive and extensively open to public contestation', Robert Dahl (1971: 8, 65) notes that 'the higher the socioeconomic level of a country, the more likely that its regime is an inclusive or near-polyarchy'. He is thus careful not to point to a direct causal link between the level of development and democracy. Even Lipset takes care not to speak of *pre*requisites, but merely talks of 'some social requisites' of democracy. He thus notes a correlation but does not claim a direct causation. However, in his article he often slips into the language of causation rather than correlation, which is why his theory is often interpreted as deterministic (Rustow, 1970: 342).
4 Vanhanen constructed a political Index of Democratization (ID) and another socio-economic Index of Power Resources (IPR). His major hypothesis is that all countries above his threshold level of 6.5 on the IPR should be democracies, and all countries below his minimum level, 3.5 index points, should be non-democracies or semi-democracies (Vanhanen, 1990). Vanhanen's findings broadly confirm his hypothesis in that 73.6 per cent of the countries that were above 6.5 in his IPR qualified as democratic. Vanhanen (1997) reconfirmed his

hypothesis, based on an analysis of 172 rather than 147 states, and over a longer time period.

5 See Levi (1988) for a study of bargaining and tax systems in a variety of cases, from France and England in the Middle Ages to modern Australia. Although she focuses on the choices of rulers, she nevertheless emphasizes that the institutions shaping those choices derive from the underlying economic structure, the geography and geo-politics.

6 See also Moore (1997) for a more elaborate argument on why the type of income determines not only the degree of democracy, but also the extent to which the state is able to carry out essential functions, such as resource mobilization.

7 Bratton and van de Walle argue along the same lines: 'The foundational features are too deeply embedded in the society and economy to explain much on their own. Structural approaches are less appropriate when discussing changes within a short time span' (1997: 22).

8 Rustow makes clear that 'no minimal level of economic development or social differentiation is necessary as a prerequisite for democracy' (1970: 352).

9 See also Weingast (1997). Przeworski's approach may be seen as institutionalist because he assumes that institutions affect actors' interests; however, he may also be placed within transition theory, in that he maintains that democracy can be decided at any moment (Johannsen, 2000: 53).

10 See also Lijphart (1991) for a discussion on proportional representation, plurality, parliamentary or presidential systems.

11 See Brautigam (1992) or Moore (1997).

12 The notion of the third wave comes from Samuel Huntington (1990). The first wave of democratization, according to Huntington (1990), was in the nineteenth century when the United States, followed by France, Great Britain and some smaller European countries, democratized. The second wave was in the immediate post-Second World War period, in which West Germany, Japan, Italy and Korea shifted to democracy; Turkey and six Latin American countries: Brazil, Costa Rica, Argentina, Columbia, Peru and Venezuela took moves towards democracy as well. The third wave, according to Huntington, began with the end of the Portuguese dictatorship in 1974, followed shortly after by the end of the dictatorships in Greece and Spain. Throughout the late 1970s and the 1980s, democratic transitions occurred in a number of Latin American and

Asian countries. Then, after 1989, came the democratization of a large number of post-Communist countries in Eastern Europe, and Africa followed suit in the 1990s, with thirty-eight of the forty-seven countries in sub-Saharan Africa holding competitive multiparty elections by the end of 1994 (Bratton and van de Walle, 1997).

13   Inclusiveness, i.e. that everyone has the right to take part in the government of his or her country, is a right stipulated in the Universal Declaration of Human Rights, particularly in Article 21 (3), which puts special emphasis on inclusiveness by stipulating that elections shall be by universal suffrage. See Suksi (2002) for a rights-based analysis of good governance in the electoral process.

14   Read about the WGS at http://www.unu.edu/p&g/wgs/.

Chapter 7   Governance and the World Bank

1   The World Bank does a lot of work on governance, and its ongoing research on the issue can be found at http://www.worldbank.org/wbi/governance/ and http://www1.worldbank.org/publicsector/

2   Paradoxically, even the British and American governments pursued protectionist policies during earlier periods of economic development (Chang, 2003).

3   The mandate is listed in the Articles of Agreement of the World Bank (Article IV, section 10), and has been decided upon by all the member states.

4   See also Stiglitz's own account of the role of the international financial institutions in the East Asian crisis in Stiglitz (2000), and see Chang (2001) for selected speeches by Stiglitz.

5   http://www.bankwatch.org/ and http://www.nadir.org/nadir/initiativ/agp/free/imf/index.htm

6   Johannes Linn, cited in 'The World Bank Participation Sourcebook Launch' panel discussion, 26 February 1996, official transcript, pp. 66–7, quoted in Fox and Brown (1998:7).

7   See http://wbln0018.worldbank.org/EURVP/web.nsf/Pages/ABCDE+Home+Page. One of the claims, for example, is that 'The World Bank is an undemocratic institution utilized by wealthy nations to increase their control over poorer nations'. To this, the Bank responds – among other things – that it represents all its member states and that it engages in dialogue with many civil-society groups.

Chapter 8 Conclusion

1 Louis Baudin (1942), *Le Corporatisme. Italie, Portugal, Allemagne, Espagne, France*, Paris, pp. 4–5, quoted in Schmitter (1974: 88), world corporatism substituted by governance.
2 As also argued by Hirst and Thompson (1995) and Hirst (2000).

References

Almond, Gabriel A. and Verba, Sidney (1963). *The Civic Culture. Political Attitudes and Democracy in Five Nations*, Princeton: Princeton University Press.

Almond, Gabriel A. et al. (2000). *Comparative Politics: A Theoretical Framework*, New York: Longman.

Amsden, Alice (1989). *Asia's Next Giant: South Korea and Late Industrialization*, Oxford: Oxford University Press.

Andersen, Vibeke Normann and Hansen, Kasper Møller (2002). 'Deliberativt demokrati og den nationale folkehøring om euroen', *Politica*, vol. 34, no. 1, 78–97.

Annan, Kofi (1998). 'The Quiet Revolution', *Global Governance*, vol. 4, no. 1, 123–38.

Archibugi, Daniele (1998). 'Principles of Cosmopolitan Democracy', in Daniele Archibugi, David Held and Martin Kohler (eds).

Archibugi, Daniele, Held, David and Kohler, Martin (eds) (1998). *Re-imagining Political Community*, Cambridge: Polity.

Ayoob, Mohammed (2001). 'Humanitarian Intervention and International Society', *Global Governance*, vol. 7, no. 3, 225–32.

Bachrach, Peter and Baratz, Morton S. (1962). 'Two Faces of Power', *The American Political Science Review*, vol. 56, no. 4, 947–52.

Barkan, Joel D. (1992). 'The Rise and Fall of a Governance Realm in Kenya', in Michael Bratton and Goran Hyden (eds).

Barkey, Karen and Parikh, Sunita (1991). 'Comparative Perspectives on The State', *Annual Review of Sociology*, vol. 17, no. 1, 523–49.

Bates, Robert H. (1981). *Markets and States in Tropical Africa: The Political Basis of Agricultural Policies*, Berkeley, CA: University of California Press.

Bates, Robert (1997). 'Comparative Politics and Rational Choice: A Review Essay', *American Political Science Review*, vol. 91, no. 3, 699–704.

Bates, Robert H. (1999). 'The Economic Basis of Democratization', in Richard Joseph (ed.), *State, Conflict and Democracy in Africa*, Boulder, CO: Lynne Rienner.

Beblawi, Hazem and Luciani, Giacomo (eds) (1987). *The Rentier State*, London: Croom Helm.

Benyon, John and Edwards, Adam (1999). 'Community Governance of Crime Control', in Gerry Stoker (ed.).

Bienen, Henry and Herbst, Jeffrey (1996). 'The Relationship between Political and Economic Reform in Africa', *Comparative Politics*, vol. 29, no. 1, 23–42.

Binder, Leonard et al. (1971). *Crises and Sequences in Political Development*, Princeton: Princeton University Press.

Blom-Hansen, Jens (1997). 'A New Institutional Perspective on Policy Networks', *Public Administration*, vol. 75, no. 4, 669–93.

Bratton, Michael and Hyden, Goran (eds) (1992). *Governance and Politics in Africa*, Boulder, CO: Lynne Rienner.

Bratton, Michael and van de Walle, Nicolas (1992). 'Toward Governance in Africa: Popular Demands and State Responses', in Michael Bratton and Goran Hyden (eds).

Bratton, Michael and van de Walle, Nicolas (1997). *Democratic Experiments in Africa, Regime Transitions in Comparative Perspective*, Cambridge: Cambridge University Press.

Brautigam, Deborah (1992). 'Governance, Economy, and Foreign Aid', *Studies in Comparative International Development*, vol. 27, no. 3, 3–25.

Brautigam, Deborah (1996). 'State Capacity and Effective Governance', in Benno Ndulu and Nicolas van de Walle (eds), *Agenda for Africa's Economic Renewal*, Oxford: Transaction Publishers.

Brautigam, Deborah (1999). ' "The Mauritius Miracle": Democracy, Institutions, and Economic Policy', in Richard Joseph (ed.), *State, Conflict, and Democracy in Africa*, Boulder, CO: Lynne Rienner.

Brown, Lester R. and Flavin, Christpoher (1999). 'A New Economy for a New Century', in World Watch Institute, *State of the World*, New York: W.W. Norton & Company.

Burley, Anne-Marie and Mattli, Walter (1993). 'Europe before the Court: A Political Theory of Legal Integration', *International Organization*, vol. 47, no. 1, 41–76.

Buzan, Barry (1991). *People, States, and Fear*, London: Harvester Wheatsheaf.

Carothers, Thomas (2002). 'The End of the Transition Paradigm', *Journal of Democracy*, vol. 13, no. 1, 5–21.

Chabal, Patrick and Daloz, Jean-Pascal (1999). *Africa Works. Disorder as Political Instrument*, The International African Institute and Oxford: James Currey.

Chang, Ha-Joon (2001) (ed.). *Joseph Stiglitz and the World Bank. The Rebel Within*, London: Anthem Press.

Chang, Ha-Joon (2003). 'Kicking Away the Ladder: Neoliberals Rewrite History', *Monthly Review*, vol. 54, no. 8, 10–15.

Clapham, Christopher (1996). *Africa and the International System. The Politics of State Survival*, Cambridge: Cambridge University Press.

Collier, Ruth Berins (1999). *Paths Toward Democracy. The Working Class and Elites in Western Europe and South America*, Cambridge: Cambridge University Press.

Commission on Global Governance (1995). *Our Global Neighborhood*, Oxford: Oxford University Press.

Cornett, Linda and Caporaso, James A. (1992). ' "And Still It Moves!" State Interests and Social Forces in the European Community', in Rosenau and Czempiel (eds).

Cox, Robert W. (1996). With Timothy J. Sinclair. *Approaches to World Order*, Cambridge: Cambridge University Press.

Dahl, Robert A. (1961). *Who Governs? Democracy and Power in an American City*, New Haven and London: Yale Studies in Political Science.

Dahl, Robert A. (1971). *Polyarchy. Participation and Opposition*, New Haven and London: Yale University Press.

Dahl, Robert A. (1989). *Democracy and its Critics*, New Haven and London: Yale University Press.

Daugbjerg, Carsten (1998). 'Linking Policy Networks and Environmental Policies: Nitrate Policy Making in Denmark and Sweden 1970–1995', *Public Administration*, vol. 76, no. 2, 275–94.

Day, Patricia and Klein, Rudolf (1987). *Accountabilities: Five Public Services*, London: Tavistock Publications.

Diamond, Larry (1999). *Developing Democracy. Toward Consolidation*, Baltimore: The Johns Hopkins University Press.

Doornbos, Martin, (1995). 'State Formation under External Supervision: Reflections on "Good Governance" ', in Olav Stokke (ed.), *Aid and Political Conditionality*, EADI Book Series 16, pp. 377–91.

Doornbos, Martin (2001): ' "Good Governance": The Rise and Decline of a Policy Metaphor?', *The Journal of Development Studies*, vol. 37, no. 6, 93–117.

Easton, David (1965). *A Framework for Political Analysis*, New Jersey: Prentice-Hall.

Eckstein, Harry (1998). 'Unfinished Business Reflections on the Scope of Comparative Politics', *Comparative Political Studies*, vol. 31, no. 4, 505–34.

Elklit, Jørgen (2001). 'Elections: Politics of Polarisation or Inclusion? Inconclusive Reflections Based on Experiences from Three Sub-Saharan African Countries, Lesotho, South Africa, and Tanzania', paper prepared for the Bergen Seminar on Development, Solstrand Fjord Hotel, Norway, June.

Elklit, Jørgen and Reynolds, Andrew (2002). 'The Impact of Election Administration on the Legitimacy of Emerging Democracies: A New Comparative Politics Research Agenda', *Commonwealth and Comparative Politics*, vol. 40, no. 2, 86–119.

Enemuo, Francis (2000). 'Problems and Prospects of Local Governance', in Goran Hyden et al. (eds), *African Perspectives on Governance*, Trenton: Africa World Press, Inc.

Eriksen, Erik Oddvar (2001). 'Nye Deltakelsesformer og deliberativt demokrati', in Erik Eriksen and Marit Skivenes (eds).

Eriksen, Erik Oddvar and Skivenes, Marit (eds) (2001). *Deliberasjon og demokrati*, Bergen: LOS-Senteret.

European Commission (2002). *Report of the High Level Group on Industrial Relations and Change in the European Union*, Directorate-General for Employment and Social Affairs, January.

Evans, Peter (1995). *Embedded Autonomy. States and Industrial Transformation*, Princeton: Princeton University Press.

Evans, Peter (1996). 'Government Action, Social Capital and Development: Reviewing the Evidence on Synergy', *World Development*, vol. 24, no. 6, 1119–32.

Evans, Peter, Rueschemeyer, Dietrich and Skocpol, Theda (eds) (1985). *Bringing the State Back In*, New York: Cambridge University Press.

Falk, Richard (1995). *On Humane Governance: Toward a New Global Politics*, Philadelphia: Pennsylvania University Press.

Falk, Richard (1999). *Predatory Globalization. A Critique*, Cambridge: Polity.

Feeny, David (1993). 'The Demand for and Supply of Institutional Arrangements', in Vincent Ostrom et al. (eds), *Rethinking Institutional Analysis and Development: Issues, Alternatives and Choices*, San Francisco: ICS Press.

Finlayson, Jack A. and Zacher, Mark W. (1983). 'The GATT and the Regulation of Trade Barriers: Regime Dynamics and Functions', in Krasner (ed.).

Fox, Jonathan A. (2000). 'The World Bank Inspection Panel: Lessons from the First Five Years', *Global Governance*, vol. 6, no. 3, 279–319.

Fox, Jonathan A. and Brown, L. David (1998). *The Struggle for Accountability. The World Bank, NGOs, and Grassroots Movements*, Cambridge, Mass.: The MIT Press.

Friis, Lykke (2001). *Den Europæiske Byggeplads. Fra fælles mønt til europæisk forfatning*, Centrum: Haslev.

Frølund Thomsen, Jens Peter (2000). *Magt og Indflydelse*, Aarhus: Magtudredningen.

Gamble, Andrew (2000). 'Economic Governance', in Jon Pierre (ed.).

Gibbon, Peter and Raikes, Phil (1996). 'Tanzania', in Poul Engberg-Pedersen et al. (eds), *Limits of Adjustment in Africa*, Oxford: James Currey.

Giddens, Anthony (1985). *The Nation-State and Violence*, Cambridge: Polity.

Giddens, Anthony (1990). *The Consequences of Modernity*, Cambridge: Polity.

Gilbert, Christopher L. and Vines, David (2000). 'The World Bank: An Overview of the Major Issues', in Christopher L. Gilbert and David Vines (eds), *The World Bank. Structure and Policies*, Cambridge: Cambridge University Press.

Global Witness (1998). *A Rough Trade. Angola*, Global Witness Report, December.

Goodman, James (1997). 'The European Union: Reconstituting Democracy beyond the Nation-State', in Anthony McGrew (ed.), *The Transformation of Democracy*, Cambridge: Polity.

Grindle, Merilee S. (1996). *Challenging the State: Crisis and Innovation in Latin America and Africa*, Cambridge: Cambridge University Press.

Haas, Ernst B. (1958). *The Uniting of Europe. Political, Social and Economic Forces, 1950–1957*, London: Stevens and Sons Limited.

Haas, Ernst B. (1964). *Beyond the Nation-State. Functionalism and International Organization*, Stanford: Stanford University Press.

Haggard Stephan and Kaufman, Robert R. (eds) (1992). *The Politics of Economic Adjustment*, Princeton: Princeton University Press.

Haggard Stephan and Kaufman, Robert R. (1995). *The Political Economy of Democratic Transitions*, Princeton: Princeton University Press.

Hall, Peter A. (1993). 'Policy Paradigms, Social Learning and the State: The Case of Economic Policy-Making in Britain', *Comparative Politics*, vol. 25, no. 3, 275–96.

Hall, Peter A. and Taylor, Rosemary C. R. (1996). 'Political Science and the Three Institutionalisms', *Political Studies*, vol. 44, no. 5, 936–57.

Hall, Peter A. and Soskice, David (eds) (2001). *Varieties of Capitalism. The Institutional Foundations of Comparative Advantage*, Oxford: Oxford University Press.

Hansen, Karin (2001). 'Local Councillors: Between Local Government and Local Governance', *Public Administration*, vol. 79, no. 1, 105–23.

Held, David (1987). *Models of Democracy*, Cambridge: Polity.

Held, David (1993). 'Democracy: From City-States to a Cosmopolitan Order', in David Held (ed.). *Prospects for Democracy. North, South, East, West*, Cambridge: Polity.

Held, David (1998). 'Democracy and Globalization', in Daniele Archibugi, David Held and Martin Kohler (eds).

Held, David (et al.) (1999). *Global Transformations. Politics, Economics and Culture*, Stanford: Stanford University Press.

Held, David and McGrew, Anthony (2000). 'The Great Globalization Debate', in David Held and Anthony McGrew (eds), *The Global Transformations Reader. An Introduction to the Globalization Debate*, Cambridge: Polity.

Helleiner, Gerald K. (2001). 'Markets, Politics and Globalization: Can the Global Economy be Civilized?', *Global Governance*, vol. 7, no. 3, 243–64.

Herbst, Jeffrey (2000). *States and Power in Africa, Comparative Lessons in Authority and Control*, Princeton: Princeton University Press.

Hirschman, Albert O. (1970). *Exit, Voice and Loyalty: Responses to Decline in Firms, Organizations, and States*, Cambridge: Harvard University Press.

Hirst, Paul (1994). *Associative Democracy. New Forms of Economic and Social Governance*, Cambridge: Polity.

Hirst, Paul (2000) 'Democracy and Governance', in Jon Pierre (ed.).

Hirst, Paul and Thompson, Grahame (1995). 'Globalization and the Future of the Nation State', *Economy and Society*, vol. 24, no. 3, 408–42.

Hirst, Paul and Thompson, Grahame (1996). *Globalization in Question: The International Economy and the Possibilities of Governance*, Cambridge: Polity.

Hix, Simon (1998). 'The Study of the European Union II: The "New Governance" Agenda and its Rival', *Journal of European Public Policy*, vol. 5, no. 1, 38–65.

Hodges, Tony (2001). *Angola from Afro-Stalinism to Petro-Diamond Capitalism*, Oxford: James Currey.

Hodson, Dermot and Maher, Imelda (2001). 'The Open Method as a New Mode of Governance: The Case of Soft Economic Policy Co-ordination', *Journal of Common Market Studies*, vol. 39, no. 4, 719–46.

Hoffman, Stanley (1966). 'Obstinate or Obsolete? The Fate of the Nation-State and the Case of Western Europe', *Daedalus*, no. 95, 892–908.

Hoffman, Stanley (1982). 'Reflections on the Nation-State in Western Europe Today', *Journal of Common Market Studies*, vol. 21, 21–37.

Hofhansel, Claus (1999). 'The Harmonization of EU Export Control Policies', *Comparative Political Studies*, vol. 32, no. 2, 229–56.

Hollis, Martin (1994). *The Philosophy of Social Science. An Introduction*, Cambridge: Cambridge University Press.

Holm, John and Molutsi, Patrick (1990). 'Developing Democracy when Civil Society is Weak', *African Affairs*, vol. 89, no. 356. 323–40.

Holm, John D. and Molutsi, Patrick P. (1992). 'State–Society Relations in Botswana: Beginning Liberalization', in Michael Bratton and Goran Hyden (eds).

Hooghe, Liesbet (1996). 'Introduction: Reconciling EU-wide Policy and National Diversity', in Liesbet Hooghe (ed.), *Cohesion Policy and European Integration: Building Multi-Level Governance*, Oxford: Oxford University Press.

Huntington, Samuel P. (1965). 'Political Development and Political Decay', *World Politics*, vol. 17, no. 3, 386–430.

Huntington, Samuel P. (1991). *The Third Wave: Democratization in the Late Twentieth Century*, Norman: University of Oklohoma Press.

Huntington, Samuel P. (1997). *The Clash of Civilizations and the Re-making of World Order*, New York: Simon and Schuster.

Hyden, Goran (1983). *No Shortcuts to Progress, African Development Management in Perspective*, London: Heinemann Educational Books Ltd.

Hyden, Goran (1992). 'Governance and the Study of Politics', in Bratton, Michael and Goran Hyden (eds), *Governance and Politics in Africa*, Boulder, CO: Lynne Rienner.

Hyden, Goran (1999). 'Governance and the Reconstitution of Political Order', in Richard Joseph (ed.), *State, Conflict, and Democracy in Africa*, Boulder, CO: Lynne Rienner.

Hyden, Goran (2000). 'The Governance Challenge in Africa', in Goran Hyden, Dele Olowu and Okoth Ogendo (eds), *African Perspectives on Governance*, Trenton/Asmara: Africa World Press, Inc.

Hyden, Goran (2002). 'Why Africa Finds it so Hard to Develop', paper presented at the Conference on 'Culture, Democracy, and Development: Cultural and Political Foundations of Socio-

Economic Development in Africa and Asia', Monte Verita, Ascona, Switzerland, 6–11 October.

Hyden, Goran and Court, Julius (2001). 'Governance and Development: Trying to Sort Out the Basics', UNUwider, unpublished working paper.

Israel, Arturo (1987). *Institutional Development. Incentives to Performance*, Baltimore and London: World Bank and Johns Hopkins University Press.

Jachtenfuchs, Markus (1997). 'Conceptualizing European Governance', in Knud Erik Jørgensen (ed.). *Reflective Approaches to European Governance*, London: Macmillan.

Jachtenfuchs, Markus (2001). 'The Governance Approach to European Integration', *Journal of Common Market Studies*, vol. 39, no. 2, 245–64.

Jackson, Robert H. (1990). *Quasi-states: Sovereignty, International Relations and the Third World*, Cambridge: Cambridge University Press.

Jackson, Robert (2000). *The Global Covenant. Human Conduct in a World of States*, Oxford: Oxford University Press.

Jackson, Robert H. and Rosberg, Carl G. (1982). *Personal Rule in Black Africa: Prince, Autocrat, Prophet, Tyrant*, Berkeley, CA: University of California Press.

Jackson, Robert and Georg Sørensen (1999). *Introduction to International Relations*, Oxford: Oxford University Press.

Jessop, Bob (1995). 'The Regulation Approach and Post-Fordism: Alternative Perspectives on Economic and Political Change?' *Economy and Society*, vol. 24, no. 3, 307–33.

Jessop, Bob (1998). 'The Rise of Governance and the Risk of Failure: The Case of Economic Development', *International Social Science Journal*, vol. 50, no. 155, 29–46.

Jessop, Bob (2000). 'Governance Failure', in Gerry Stoker (ed.).

Jessop, Bob (2002a). 'Governance and Meta-governance: On Reflexivity, Requisite Variety, and Requisite Irony', The Department of Sociology, Lancaster University at www.comp.lancs.ac.uk/sociology/soc108rj.htm

Jessop, Bob (2002b). *The Future of the Capitalist State*, Cambridge: Polity.

Johannsen, Lars (2000). *The Constitution and Democracy: The Choice and Consequence of the Constitution in Post-Communist Countries*, Aarhus: Politica.

Johannsen, Lars (2002). 'Demokratiseringsteori. Klynger af Forklaringer', *Politica*, vol. 32, no. 2.

Johnson, Chalmers (1982). *MITI and the Japanese Miracle. The Growth of Industrial Policy, 1925–1975*, Stanford: Stanford University Press.

Jørgensen, Knud Erik (1997). 'PoCo: The Diplomatic Republic of Europe', in Knud Erik Jørgensen (ed.), *Reflective Approaches to European Governance*, London: Macmillan.

Kahler, Miles (1992). 'External Influence, Conditionality, and the Politics of Adjustment', in Stephan Haggard and Robert R. Kaufman (eds).

Karl, Terry Lynn (1990). 'Dilemmas of Democratization in Latin America', *Comparative Politics*, vol. 23, no. 1, 1–23.

Karl, Terry Lynn and Schmitter, Phillipe C. (1991). 'Modes of Transition in Latin America, Southern and Eastern Europe', *International Social Science Journal*, vol. 43, no. 2, 269–84.

Kaspersen, Lars Bo (2001). 'How Denmark became Democratic – The Impact of Warfare and Military Reforms', working paper, Department of Sociology, University of Copenhagen.

Kaufman, Daniel, Kraay, Aart, and Zoide-Lobatón, Pablo (1999). 'Governance Matters', Policy Research Working Paper 2196, The World Bank, October.

Keck, Margaret E. and Sikkink, Kathryn (1998). *Activists Beyond Borders: Advocacy Networks in International Politics*, Ithaca, NY: Cornell University Press.

Kendal, David Michael (1995). 'Human Rights in the World Bank's Work', in David Michael Kendal and Anders Krag-Johansen, *Human Rights and International Development Cooperation*, Copenhagen: Danish Centre for Human Rights.

Keohane, Robert (1999). 'Hobbes' Dilemma and Institutional Change in World Politics: Sovereignty in International Society', in Hans Henrik Holm and Georg Sørensen (eds), *Whose World Order? Uneven Globalization and the end of the Cold War*, Boulder, CO: Westview Press.

Keohane, Robert O. (2001). 'Governance in a partially globalized world', presidential address, American Political Science Association, 2000, *The American Political Science Review*, vol. 95, no. 1, 1–13.

Keohane, Robert and Nye, Joseph (2000). 'Introduction', in Joseph Nye and John D. Donahue (eds). *Governance in a Globalizing World*, Washington DC: Brookings Institution Press.

Keohane, Robert and Nye, Joseph (2001). *Power and Interdependence*, 3rd edn, New York: Longman.

Kickert, Walter J. M, Klijn, Erik-Hans and Koppenjan, Joop F. M. (1999). *Managing Complex Networks. Strategies for the Public Sector*, London: Sage Publications.

Kickert, W. J. M and Koppenjan, J. F. M (1999). 'Public Management and Network Management: An Overview', in Kickert et al. (eds).

Kjær, Mette (2002). *The Politics of Civil Service Reform. A Com-*

parative Analysis of Uganda and Tanzania in the 1990s, Aarhus: Politica.

Kjær, Mette and Kinnerup, Klaus (2002). 'Good governance – How Does It Relate to Human Rights?', in Hans-Otto Sano and Gudmundur Alfredsson (eds), *Human Rights and Good Governance*, The Hague: Martinus Nijhoff Publishers.

Klijn, Erik-Hans, Koppenjan, Joop and Termeer, Katrien (1995). 'Managing Networks in the Public Sector: A Theoretical Study of Management Strategies in Policy Networks', *Public Administration*, vol. 73, no. 3, 437–54.

Klitgaard, Robert (1997). 'Cleaning Up and Invigorating the Civil Service', report prepared for the Operations Evaluation Department, The World Bank.

Knudsen, Tonny Brems (2001). 'Contemporary Visions of Global Governance', paper for the International Studies Association Convention, Hong Kong, July.

Koch, Ida Elisabeth (2002). 'Good Governance and the Implementation of Economic, Social and Cultural Rights', in Hans-Otto Sano and Gudmundur Alfredsson (eds), *Human Rights and Good Governance. Building Bridges*, The Hague: Martinus Nijhoff Publishers.

Kohler, Martin (1998). 'From the National to the Cosmopolitan Public Sphere', in Daniele Archibugi, David Held and Martin Kohler (eds).

Kooiman, Jan (1993). 'Social-Political Governance: Introduction', in Jan Kooiman (ed.), *Modern Governance: New Government-Society Interactions*, London: Sage Publications.

Koremenos, Barbara, Lipson, Charles and Snidal, Duncan (2001). 'The Rational Design of International Institutions', *International Organization*, vol. 55, no. 4, 761–99.

Krasner, Stephen D. (1982). 'Structural Causes and Regime Consequences: Regimes as Intervening Variables', *International Organization*, vol. 36, no. 2, 185–205.

Krasner, Stephen D. (ed.) (1983). *International Regimes*, Ithaca, NY: Cornell University Press.

Krasner, Stephen D. (1999). *Sovereignty. Organized Hypocrisy*, Princeton: Princeton University Press.

Lauridsen, Laurids S. (1997) 'Et skridt frem og to tilbage: Kapitalens internationalisering eller økonomiens globalisering', *Den Ny Verden*, vol. 3, no. 3, 84–102.

Leftwich, Adrian (1993). 'Governance, Democracy and Development in the Third World', *Third World Quarterly*, vol. 14, no. 3, 605–26.

Leftwich, Adrian (2000). *States of Development. On the Primacy of Politics in Development*, Cambridge: Polity.

Levi, Margaret (1988). *Of Rule and Revenue*, Berkeley, CA: University of California Press.

Lijphart, Arend (1977). *Democracy in Plural Societies. A Comparative Exploration*, New Haven and London: Yale University Press.

Lijphart, Arend (1991). 'Constitutional Choices for New Democracies', *Journal of Democracy*, vol. 2, no. 1, 72–84.

Linklater, Andrew (1998). 'Citizenship and Sovereignty in the Post-Westphalian European State', in Daniele Archibugi, David Held and Martin Kohler (eds).

Linz, Juan J. (1990a). 'The Perils of Presidentialism', *Journal of Democracy*, vol. 1, no. 1, 51–69.

Linz, Juan J. (1990b). 'The Virtues of Parliamentarism', *Journal of Democracy*, vol. 1, no. 4, 84–91.

Lipset, Seymor Martin (1959). 'Some Social Requisites of Democracy: Economic Development and Political Legitimacy', *The American Political Science Review*, vol. 53, no. 1, 69–105.

Lipsky, M. (1980). *Street Level Bureaucracy*, New York: Russel Sage Foundation.

Loftager, Jørn (2001). 'Hvordan undersøge den politiske offentligheds tilstand?', in Erik Eriksen and Marit Skivenes (eds).

Lomborg, Bjørn (2001). *The Skeptical Environmentalist. Measuring the Real State of the World*, Cambridge: Cambridge University Press.

Lukes, Steven (1974). *Power – A Radical View*, Basingstoke: Macmillan.

McGrew, Anthony (1997). 'Democracy Beyond Borders?: Globalization and the Reconstruction of Democratic Theory and Politics', in Anthony McGrew (ed.). *The Transformation of Democracy?*, Cambridge: Polity.

McGrew, Anthony (2002). 'Between Two Worlds: Europe in a Globalizing Era', *Government and Opposition*, vol. 37, no. 3, 343–58.

Mair, Peter (1996). 'Comparative Politics: An Overview', in Robert E. Goodin and Hans-Dieter Klingemann (eds), *A New Handbook of Political Science*, Oxford: Oxford University Press.

Majone, Giandomenico (1992). 'Regulatory Federalism in the European Community', *Environment and Planning C: Government and Policy*, vol. 10, 299–316.

Mann, Michael (1988). 'The Autonomous Power of the State: Its Origins, Mechanisms and Results', in Michael Mann, *States, War and History*, Oxford: Blackwell.

March, James G. and Olsen, Johan P. (1989). *Rediscovering Institutions: The Organizational Basis of Politics*, New York: The Free Press.

March, James G. and Olsen, Johan P. (1995). *Democratic Governance*, New York: The Free Press.

Marks, Gary (1996). 'Exploring and Explaining Variation in EU Cohesion Policy', in Liesbet Hooghe (ed.), *Cohesion Policy and European Integration: Building Multi-Level Governance*, Oxford: Oxford University Press.

Marks, Gary, Hooghe, Liesbet and Blank, Kermit (1996). 'European Integration from the 1980s: State-Centric *v.* Multi-level Governance', *Journal of Common Market Studies*, vol. 34, no. 3, 341–78.

Marsh, David and Rhodes, R. A. W. (eds) (1992). *Implementing Thatcherite Policies, Audit of an Era*, Buckingham: Open University Press.

Masicotte, Marie-Josée (1999). 'Review Essay: Global Governance and the Global Political Economy: Three Texts in Search of a Synthesis', *Global Governance*, vol. 5, no. 1, 127–48.

Mathews, Jessica T. (1997). 'Power Shift', *Foreign Affairs*, vol. 76, no. 1, 50–66.

Mayntz, Renate (1993). 'Governing Failures and the Problem of Governability', in Jan Kooiman (ed.).

Mearsheimer, John J. (1995). 'A Realist Reply', *International Security*, vol. 20, no. 1, 82–93.

Migdal, Joel S. (1988). *Strong Societies and Weak States. State–Society Relations and State Capabilities in the Third World*, Princeton: Princeton University Press.

Mkandawire, Thandika and Olukoshi, Adebayo (eds) (1995). *Between Liberalisation and Oppression. The Politics of Structural Adjustment in Africa*, Dakar: Codesria Book Series.

Mkandawire, Thandika and Soludo, Charles C. (1999). *Our Continent, Our Future*, Codesria, Trenton/Asmara: Africa World Press, Inc.

Moore, Barrington, Jr (1967). *Social Origins of Dictatorship and Democracy*, London: Penguin Books.

Moore, Mick (1993), 'Declining to Learn from the East? The World bank on Governance and Development', *IDS-Bulletin*, vol. 24, no. 1, 39–51.

Moore, Mick (1995). 'Promoting Good Government by Supporting Institutional Development?', *IDS-Bulletin*, vol. 26, no. 2, 89–97.

Moore, Mick (1997). 'Death without Taxes: Democracy, State Capacity and Aid Dependence in the Fourth World', in Gordon White and Mark Robinson (eds), *Towards a Democratic Developmental State*, Oxford: Oxford University Press.

Moravcsik, Andrew (1993). 'Preferences and Power in the European Community: A Liberal Intergovernmentalist Approach', *Journal of Common Market Studies*, vol. 31, no. 4, 473–524.

Mozaffar, Shaheen and Schedler, Andreas (2002). 'The Comparative Study of Electoral Governance-Introduction', *International Political Science Review*, vol. 23, no. 1, 5–29.

Nanetti, Rafaella Y. (1996). 'EU Cohesion Policy and Territorial Restructuring in the Member States', in Liesbet Hooghe (ed.), *Cohesion Policy and European Integration: Building Multi-Level Governance*, Oxford: Oxford University Press.

Ndulu, Benno and van de Walle, Nicolas (1996). 'The Politics of Economic Renewal in Africa', in Benno Ndulu and Nicolas van de Walle (eds), *Agenda for Africa's Economic Renewal*, Oxford: Transaction Publishers.

Nelson, Joan M. (1994). *Intricate Links: Democratization and Market Reforms in Latin America and Eastern Europe*, Oxford: Transaction Publishers.

Niskanen, William A. Jr (1994). *Bureaucracy and Public Economics*, Cheltenham: Edward Elgar Publishing.

Nørgaard, Ole (2001). 'Democracy, Democratization and Institutional Theory', DEMSTAR Research Report, no. 4, Department of Political Science, University of Aarhus.

North, Douglas C. (1990). *Institutions, Institutional Change and Economic Performance*, Cambridge: Cambridge University Press.

Nsibambi, Apolo (ed.) (1998). *Decentralization and Civil Society in Uganda. The Quest for Good Governance*, Kampala: Fountain Publishers.

Nunnenkamp, Peter (1995). 'What Donors Mean by Good Governance. Heroic Ends, Limited Means, and Traditional Dilemmas of Development Cooperation', *IDS-Bulletin*, vol. 26, no. 2, 9–16.

Nye, Joseph S. (2001). 'Globalization's Democratic Deficit: How to make International Institutions More Accountable', *Foreign Affairs*, New York, vol. 80, no. 4, 2–6.

O'Byrne, Darren J. (2003). *Human Rights. An Introduction*, London: Prentice-Hall.

O'Donnel, Guillermo and Schmitter, Phillippe C. (1986). *Transitions from Authoritarian Rule. Tentative Conclusions about Uncertain Democracies*, Baltimore: Johns Hopkins University Press.

Olesen, Thomas (2002a). 'Fra Seattle til New York: Globalisering og antiglobalisering í lyset af 11. september', in Mehdi Mozaffari (ed), *11. September: Internationale Konsekvenser og Perspektiver*, Århus: Systime.

Olesen, Thomas (2002b). *Long Distance Zapatismo. Globalization and the Construction of Solidarity*, forthcoming, London: Zed Books.

Olowu, Bamidele (1999). 'Redesigning African Civil Service Reforms', *The Journal of Modern African Studies*, vol. 37, no. 1, 1–25.

Olsen, Johan P. (1978). *Politisk Organisering*, Bergen: Universitetsforlaget.

Onis, Ziya (1991). 'The Logic of the Developmental State', *Comparative Politics*, vol. 24, no. 1, 109–26.

Ostrom, Elinor (1990). *Governing the Commons: The Evolution of Institutions for Collective Action*, Cambridge: Cambridge University Press.

Ostrom, Elinor (1991). 'Rational Choice Theory and Institutional Analysis: Toward Complementarity', *American Political Science Review*, vol. 85, no. 1, 237–43.

Ottaway, Marina (2001). 'Corporatism Goes Global: International Organizations, Nongovernmental Organization Networks, and Transnational Business', *Global Governance*, vol. 7, no. 3. 265–93.

Pallesen, Thomas (1997). *Health Care Reforms in Britain and Denmark: The Politics of Economic Success and Failure*, Århus: Politica.

Peters, Guy B. (1999). *Institutional Theory in Political Science. The 'New Institutionalism'*, London and New York: Pinter Publishers.

Peters Guy B. (2000). 'Governance and Comparative Politics', in Jon Pierre (ed.).

Peters, Guy and Wright, Vincent (1996). 'Public Policy and Administration, Old and New', in Robert E. Goodin and Hans-Dieter Klingemann (eds), *A New Handbook of Political Science*, Oxford: Oxford University Press.

Pierre, Jon (ed.) (2000). *Debating Governance. Authority, Steering, and Democracy*, Oxford: Oxford University Press.

Pierre, Jon and Peters, Guy (2000): *Governance, Politics and the State*, New York: St Martins Press.

Pierre, Jon and Stoker, Gerry (2000). 'Towards Multi-level Governance', in Patrick Dunleavy et al. (eds), *Developments in British Politics*, London: Macmillan.

Plattner, Marc F. (2002). 'Globalization and Self-Government', *Journal of Democracy*, vol. 13, no. 3, 54–67.

Polanyi, Karl (1957). *The Great Transformation. The Political and Economic Origins of Our Time*, Boston, MA: Beacon Press.

Przeworski, Adam (1991). *Democracy and the Market*, Cambridge: Cambridge University Press.

Putnam, Robert D. (1994). *Making Democracy Work; Civic Traditions in Modern Italy*, Princeton: Princeton University Press.

Rakner, Lise (1998). 'Reform as a Matter of Political Survival: Political and Economic Liberalization in Zambia 1991–1996', unpublished Ph.D. dissertation, Christian Michelsen Institute, Bergen. June.

Rasmussen, Erik (1971). *Komparativ Politik 1*, Copenhagen: Gyldendal.

Reid, Barbara (1999). 'Reframing the Delivery of Local Housing Services: Networks and the New Competition', in Gerry Stoker (ed.).

Remmer, Karen L. (1997). 'Theoretical Decay and Theoretical Development. The Resurgence of Institutional Analysis', *World Politics*, vol. 50, no. 1, 34–61.

Republic of Uganda (1994). *Civil Service Reform: Context Vision, Objectives, Strategy and Plan*, Ministry of Public Service, Kampala.

Rhodes, R. A. W. (1996). 'The New Governance: Governing without Government', *Political Studies*, XLIV, 652–67.

Rhodes, R. A. W. (1997a). *Understanding Governance. Policy Networks, Governance, Reflexivity and Accountability*, Buckingham: Open University Press.

Rhodes, R. A. W. (1997b). 'Coherence, Capacity and the Hollow Crown', in Weller et al. (eds).

Rhodes, R. A. W. (1999). 'Foreword', in Gerry Stoker (ed.).

Rhodes, R. A. W. (2000). 'Governance and Public Administration', in Jon Pierre (ed.).

Rhodes, R. A. W., Bache, Ian and George, Stephen (1996). 'Policy Networks and Policy-Making in the European Union: A Critical Appraisal', in Liesbet Hooghe (ed.), *Cohesion Policy and European Integration: Building Multi-Level Governance*, Oxford: Oxford University Press.

Ricci, David M. (1971). *Community Power and Democratic Theory: The Logic of Political Analysis*, New York: Random House.

Rokkan, Stein (1981). 'The Growth and Structuring of Mass Politics', in Erik Allardt (ed.), *Nordic Democracy*, Copenhagen: Det Danske Selskab.

Roodman, David Malin (1999). 'Building a Sustainable Society', in World Watch Institute, *State of the World*, New York: W.W. Norton & Company.

Root, Hilton L. (1996). *Small Countries, Big Lessons. Governance and the Rise of East Asia*, Asian Development Bank and Oxford: Oxford University Press.

Rosamund, Ben (1999). *Theories of European Integration*, London: Macmillan.

Rosenau, James N. (1992). 'Governance, Order, and Change in

World Politics', in James N. Rosenau and Ernst-Otto Czempiel (eds), *Governance without Government: Order and Change in World Politics*, Cambridge: Cambridge University Press.

Rosenau, James N. (1995) 'Governance in the Twenty-First Century', *Global Governance*, vol. 1, no. 1, 13–43.

Rosenau, James N. (2000). 'Change, Complexity and Governance in a Globalizing Space', in Jon Pierre (ed.).

Rosenau, James N. and Wang, Hongying (2001). 'Transparency International and Corruption as an Issue of Global Governance', *Global Governance*, vol. 7, no. 1, 25–50.

Rothstein, Bo (1996). 'Political Institutions: An Overview', in Robert E. Goodin and Hans-Dieter Klingemann (eds), *A New Handbook of Political Science*, Oxford: Oxford University Press.

Rueschemeyer, Dietrich and Evans, Peter B. (1985). 'The State and Economic Transformation: Toward an Analysis of the Conditions Underlying Effective Intervention', in Evans, Rueschemeyer and Skocpol (eds).

Rueschemeyer, Dietrich, Stephens, Evelyne Huber and Stephens, John D. (1992). *Capitalist Development and Democracy*, Cambridge: Polity.

Rustow, Dankwart (1970). 'Transitions to Democracy: Toward a Dynamic Model', *Comparative Politics*, vol. 2, no. 3, 337–65.

Rutherford, Kenneth R. (2000). 'The Evolving Arms Control Agenda. Implications of the Role of NGO's in Banning Anti-personnel Landmines', *World Politics*, vol. 53, no. 1, 74–114.

Sandholtz, Wayne (1993). 'Choosing Union: Monetary Politics and Maastricht', *International Organization*, vol. 47, no. 1, 1–40.

Saward, Michael (1997). 'In Search of the Hollow Crown', in Weller, et al. (eds).

Sbragia, Alberta (2000). 'The European Union as Coxswain: Governance by Steering', in Jon Pierre (ed.).

Scharpf, Fritz (1988). 'The Joint-Decision Trap: Lessons from German Federalism and European Integration', *Public Administration*, vol. 66, no. 3, 239–78.

Scharpf, Fritz W. (1994). 'Games Real Actors could Play: Positive and Negative Coordination in Embedded Negotiations', *Journal of Theoretical Politics*, vol. 6, no. 1, 27–53.

Scharpf, Fritz W. (1996). 'Negative and Positive Integration in the Political Economy of European Welfare States', in Gary Marks et al. (eds), *Governance in the European Union*, London: Sage Publications.

Scharpf, Fritz W. (1997a). 'Introduction: The Problem Solving Capacity of Multi-level Governance', *Journal of European Public Policy*, vol. 4, no. 4, 520–38.

Scharpf, Fritz W. (1997b). *Games Real Actors Play. Actor-Centered*

Institutionalism in Policy Research, Boulder, CO: Westview Press.

Schmitter, Philipe C. (1974). 'Still the Century of Corporatism?', *Review of Politics*, vol. 36, no. 2, 85–131.

Schmitter, Philipe C. (1996). 'Imagining the Future of the Europe-Polity with the Help of New Concepts', in Gary Marks et al. (eds), *Governance in the European Union*, London: Sage Publications.

Scott, John (2001). *Power*, Cambridge: Polity.

Senghaas, Dieter (1982). *The European Experience. A Historical Critique of Development Theory*, Leamington Spa: Berg Publishers.

Slaughter, Anne-Marie (1997). 'The Real New World Order', *Foreign Affairs*, vol. 76, no. 5, 183–97.

Sørensen, Eva (2002). *Politikerne og netværksdemokratiet: fra suverøn politiker til meta-guvernør*, Copenhagen: Jurist- og Økonomforbundets Forlag.

Sørensen, Eva and Torfing, Jacob (1999). 'Vi trækker på samme hammel! – en diskursiv magtanalyse af kulturhussagen i Skanderborg', in Anders Berg-Sørensen (ed.), *Politologi i Praksis*, Roskilde: Roskilde Universitetsforlag.

Sørensen, Eva and Torfing, Jacob (2000). 'Fusioneringspolitik, demokrati og politisk handlekraft', in Henrik P. Bang et al. (eds), *Demokrati fra neden: Case studier fra en dansk kommune*, Copenhagen: Jurist- og Økonomforbundets Forlag.

Sørensen, Georg (1991). *Democracy, Dictatorship, and Development. Economic Development in Selected Regimes of the Third World*, London: Macmillan.

Sørensen, Georg (1993a). *Democracy and Democratization: Processes and Prospects in a Changing World*, Boulder, CO: Westview Press.

Sørensen, Georg (ed.) (1993b). *Political Conditionality*, London: Frank Cass.

Sørensen, Georg (2001). *Changes in Statehood. The Transformation of International Relations*, Basingstoke: Palgrave.

Sørensen, Georg (2002). 'Fra 9.11. til 11.9. – Forandring og nye trusler', in Mehdi Mozaffari (ed.), *11. September: Internationale Konsekvenser og Perspektiver*, Århus: Systime.

Stallings, Barbara (1992). 'International Influence on Economic Policy: Debt, Stabilization, and Structural Reform', in Haggard and Kaufman (eds).

Steinmo, Sven (1993). *Taxation and Democracy. Swedish, British and American Approaches to Financing the Modern State*, New Haven: Yale University Press.

Stepan, Alfred and Skach, Cindy (1993). 'Constitutional Frameworks and Democratic Consolidation. Parliamentarism versus Presidentialism', *World Politics*, vol. 46, no. 1, 1–22.

Stiglitz, Joseph E. (2000). 'Introduction', Christopher L. Gilbert and David Vines (eds), *The World Bank. Structure and Policies*, Cambridge: Cambridge University Press.

Stiglitz, Joseph E. (2001). 'The Role of International Financial Institutions in the Current Global Economy', in Chang (ed.).

Stoker, Gerry (1998). 'Governance as Theory: Five Propositions', *Governance–International Social Science Journal*, March, 155, 17–29.

Stoker, Gerry (ed.) (1999). *The New Management of British Local Level Governance*, Basingstoke: Palgrave Macmillan.

Stoker, Gerry (ed.) (2000). *The New Politics of British Local Level Governance*, London: Macmillan.

Stoker, Gerry (2003). 'Pursuing Public Value through Networks of Deliberation and Delivery: Can an Emerging Management Paradigm meet the Challenge of Efficiency and Democracy?', paper presented at the Conference on Democratic Network Governance, Helsingore, 21–3 May.

Strange, Susan (1983). 'Cave! Hic Dragons: A Critique of Regime Analysis', in Krasner (ed.).

Strange, Susan (1996). *The Retreat of the State. The Diffusion of Power in the World Economy*, Cambridge: Cambridge University Press.

Suksi, Markku (2002). 'Good Governance in the Electoral Process', in Hans-Otto Sano and Gudmundur Alfredson (eds), *Human Rights and Good Governance: Building Bridges*, The Hague: Martinus Nijhoff Publishers.

Tendler, Judith (1997). *Good Government in the Tropics*, Baltimore and London: The Johns Hopkins University Press.

Therborn, Goran (1983). 'The Rule of Capital and the Rise of Democracy', in David Held et al. (eds), *States and Societies*, Oxford: Martin Robertson.

Therkildsen, Ole (2000). 'Efficiency, Accountability and Implementation: Public Sector Reform in East and Southern Africa', paper published in UNRISD Discussion Paper Series on 'Decentralization and Public Sector Reform'.

Tilly, Charles (1990). *Coercion, Capital and European States, AD 990–1992*, Oxford: Blackwell Publishers.

Tranholm-Mikkelsen, Jeppe (1991). 'Neo-Functionalism: Obstinate or Obsolete? A Reappraisal in the Light of the New Dynamism of the EC', *Millenium: Journal of International Studies*, vol. 20, no. 1, 1–22.

Tripp, Aili Mari (2000). *Women and Politics in Uganda*, Oxford: James Currey.

Tucker, Robert W. et al. (2002). 'One Year On: Power, Purpose and Strategy in American Foreign Policy', *The National Interest*, issue 69, Fall, 5–34.

Turner, Mark and Hulme, David (1997). *Governance, Administration and Development, Making the State Work*, London: Macmillan.

UNDP (1997). 'Reconceptualizing Governance for Sustainable Human Development: Discussion Paper 2'.

van der Hoeven, Rolph (2001). 'Assessing Aid and Global Governance', *The Journal of Development Studies*, vol. 37, no. 6, 109–18.

van de Walle, Nicolas (2001). *African Economies and the Politics of Permanent Crisis, 1979–1999*, Cambridge: Cambridge University Press.

Vanhanen, Tatu (1990). *The Process of Democratization: A Comparative Study of 147 States, 1980–1988*, New York: Crane Russak.

Vanhanen, Tatu (1997). *Prospects of Democracy: A Study of 172 Countries*, London: Routledge.

Villadsen, Søren (ed.) (1999). *Good Governance and Decentralization. Public Sector Reforms in Developing Countries*, Taastrup: Nordic Consulting Group.

Viotti, Paul R. and Kauppi, Mark V. (1987). *International Relations Theory: Realism, Pluralism, Globalism*, New York: Macmillan.

Wade, Robert (1990). *Governing the Market: Economic Theory and the Role of Government in East Asian Industrialization*, Princeton: Princeton University Press.

Wade, Robert (1993). 'Managing Trade: Taiwan and South Korea as Challenges to Economics and Political Science', *Comparative Politics*, vol. 25, no. 2, 147–67.

Wade, Robert (1996). 'East Asia and the Neo-Liberal World', *New Left Review*, 217, May/June, 3–36.

Wade, Robert (2001). 'Showdown at the World Bank', *New Left Review*, 7, 124–37.

Wallace, Helen and Wallace, William (2000) (eds). *Policy-Making in the European Union*, 4th edn, Oxford: Oxford University Press.

Wallace, William (1999). 'The Sharing of Sovereignty: The European Paradox', *Political Studies*, XLVII, 503–21.

Waltz, Kenneth N. (1979). *Theory of International Politics*, New York: McGraw-Hill, Inc.

Waltz, Kenneth N. (1999). 'Globalization and Governance', *PS, Political Science & Politics*, vol. 32, no. 4: 693–700.

Weber, Max (1978). *Economy and Society. An Outline of Interpretive Sociology*, edited by Guenther Roth and Claus Wittich, Berkeley, CA: University of California Press.

Weingast, Barry (1997). 'The Political Foundations of Democracy and the Rule of Law', *American Political Science Review*, vol. 91, no. 2, 245–63.

Weiss, Linda (1998). *The Myth of the Powerless State. Governing the Economy in a Global Era*, Cambridge: Polity.

Weiss, Linda (1999a). 'Beyond Globalization', *New Left Review*, 238, 126–40.

Weiss, Linda (1999b). 'Globalization and National Governance: Autonomy or Interdependence', *Review of International Studies*, vol. 25, no. 5, 59–88.

Weiss, Linda (2002). 'Introduction: Bringing Domestic Institutions Back In', in Linda Weiss (ed.), *States in a Global Economy: Bringing Domestic Institutions Back In*, Cambridge: Cambridge University.

Weiss, Linda and Hobson, John M. (1995). *States and Economic Development. A Comparative Historical Analysis*, Cambridge: Polity.

Weller, Patrick et al. (eds) (1997). *The Hollow Crown: Countervailing Trends in Core Executives*, London: Macmillan.

Wheeler, Nicholas J. and Dunne, Timothy (1996). 'Hedley Bull's Pluralism of the Intellect and Solidarism of the Will', *International Affairs*, vol. 72, no. 1, 91–107.

White, Gordon (1996). 'Civil Society, Democratization and Development', in Robin Luckham and Gordon White (eds), *Democratization in the South. The Jagged Wave*, Manchester: Manchester University Press.

Whitehead, Laurence (1996). 'Three International Dimensions of Democratization', in Laurence Whitehead (ed.), *The International Dimensions of Democratizations. Europe and the Americas*, Oxford: Oxford University Press.

Wilson, James Q. (1989). *Bureaucracy: What Government Agencies do and Why They do it*, New York: Basic Books.

Wistow, Gerald (1992). 'The National Health Service', in Marsh and Rhodes (eds).

Wolfe, Joel (1991). 'State Power and Ideology in Britain: Mrs Thatcher's Privatization Programme', *Political Studies*, XXXIX, 237–52.

Woo, Jung-en (1991). *Race to the Swift. State and Finance in Korean Industrialization*, New York: Columbia University Press.

Woods, Ngaire (1999). 'Good Governance in International Organizations', *Global Governance*, vol. 5, no. 1, 39–60.

Woods, Ngaire (2000). 'The Challenges of Multilateralism and Governance', in Christopher L. Gilbert and David Vines (eds), *The World Bank. Structure and Policies*, Cambridge: Cambridge University Press.

Woods, Ngaire and Narlikar, Amrita (2001). 'Governance and the

Limits of Accountability: The WTO, the IMF, and the World Bank', *International Social Science Journal*, vol. 53, no. 170, December, 569–82.

World Bank (1989). *Sub-Saharan Africa: From Crisis to Sustainable Growth*, Washington DC.

World Bank (1992). *Governance and Development*, Washington DC.

World Bank (1993). *The East Asian Miracle*, Washington DC.

World Bank (1994). *Governance: The Bank's Experience*, Washington DC.

World Bank (1997). *The State in a Changing World*, World Development Report, Washington DC.

World Bank (1998a). *Development and Human Rights: The Role of the World Bank*, Washington DC.

World Bank (1998b). *Assessing Aid: What Works, What Doesn't, and Why*, Washington DC.

World Bank (2000a). *Attacking Poverty*. World Development Report, Washington DC.

World Bank (2000b). *Can Africa Claim the 21st Century?*, Washington DC.

World Bank (2003). *Sustainable Development in a Dynamic World*, World Development Report. Washington DC.

Yeates, Nicola (2001). *Globalization and Social Policy*, London: Sage Publications.

Zartman, I. William (ed.) (1995). *Collapsed States. The Disintegration and Restoration of Political Order*, Boulder, CO: Lynne Rienner.

Index